Saffron & Sunshine

Saffron & Sunshine

TAPAS, MEZZE AND ANTIPASTI

ELISABETH LUARD

BANTAM PRESS

LONDON · NEW YORK · TORONTO · SYDNEY · AUCKLAND

For my granddaughters,
Jessie and Bonnie, whose companionship
I hope for in years to come.

TRANSWORLD PUBLISHERS
61–63 Uxbridge Road, London W5 5SA
a division of The Random House Group Ltd

RANDOM HOUSE AUSTRALIA (PTY) LTD
20 Alfred Street, Milsons Point, Sydney
New South Wales 2061, Australia

RANDOM HOUSE NEW ZEALAND
18 Poland Road, Glenfield, Auckland 10, New Zealand

RANDOM HOUSE SOUTH AFRICA (PTY) LTD
Endulini, 5a Jubilee Road, Parktown 2193, South Africa

Published 2000 by Bantam Press
a division of Transworld Publishers

Copyright © Elisabeth Luard 2000
Line drawings © Elisabeth Luard 2000
Photography © Jeremy Hopley 2000
Home economist: Meg Jansz

A catalogue record for this book is available from the British Library.
ISBN 0593 043030

Typeset in Gill Sans by Falcon Oast Graphic Art

Printed in Great Britain
by
Butler & Tanner

1 3 5 7 9 10 8 6 4 2

Contents

Acknowledgements

Acknowledgements are due to all those who have kept company with me in bars and markets over the years, and without whose knowledge, enthusiasm and willingness to answer damn-fool questions I would never have been able to complete this book. Among friends who have tolerated my inability to keep my fork out of their plateful: Abner Stein, Venetia Parkes, Edie Coulson, Bruce Donn, Vicky Cervera, Priscilla White, Jennifer Skiff, Jon Sainken, Carmelo Musca, Anissa Helou. Thanks, too, to my husband Nicholas for understanding when dinner was not only late but also a bit on the wild side; to my children and chief tasters – Caspar, Francesca, Poppy and Honey – for telling me exactly what tasted good and what might be done if it didn't.

I also owe an unrepayable debt of gratitude to Dun Gifford and Sara Baer-Sinnott of Oldways Preservation Trust of Boston, Massachusetts, whose passion for the culinary traditions of the Mediterranean and ability to inspire as well as educate allowed me to explore territory previously unknown to me, giving access to people and places I would not otherwise have reached. Among companions and guides on these voyages: Nancy Harmon Jenkins, Aglaia Kremezi, Paula Wolfert, Peggy Knickerbocker, Ari Weinzweig, Michael Bateman, Corby Kummer, Claudia Roden, Anna Del Conte, Diana Farr Louis, Joe Simone, Carole Field, Lynne Rossetto Kasper, Jeffrey Steingarten, Diane Kochilas.

My thanks, too, to Sally Gaminara at Transworld for guiding the manuscript through to publication; for unfailing support in the early stages, Broo Doherty; for the proofreading against what must have been a particularly demanding manuscript, Elizabeth Dobson and Sarah Scott; for her work as designer – the ultimate responsibility – Julia Lloyd. But above all – for the courtesy and blunt good sense with which all problems were tackled, as well as unstinting generosity with her editorial skills – Katrina Whone.

Introduction

Tapas, mezze, antipasti, hors d'oeuvre – whatever name you care to call that cheerful collection of little dishes set out on the table for sharing – are a party in the making, a reminder of the days when we all ate out of the same pot. As a way of eating it's convivial, gregarious, leisurely, but above all libertarian. No Mediterranean housewife would dream of dictating how much and in what combination her guests should eat. In Arab lands in particular the idea of piling food on your own plate – the notion of a person taking more than can be consumed at one mouthful – is alien, even ill-mannered.

The dishes that make up such a meal can be as varied as your imagination and your purse will allow. Mediterranean cooks have always been willing to accommodate new ideas, to try out imported ingredients and, in modern times, to adapt recipes to new labour-saving devices – though even now they take pleasure in the sensuality of stretching a dough, the scent of herbs pounded by hand, the perfume that rises from a home-made broth. Such cooking might take longer than something scooped up from the cook-chill cabinet, but it is a confirmation of skills which, though they may receive no direct financial reward, can be admired and valued.

My own generation – those of us who grew up in the post-war years – has long since replaced the daily trip to market with the weekly supermarket shop, the pestle and mortar with the food processor, the wood-burning stove with the microwave, but there are signs of a new appreciation of traditional ways – not only in the commercial but in the domestic kitchen.

Only last year, while participating in a documentary on the foodways of rural Crete, three generations of women – grandmother, mother, daughter – volunteered to demonstrate the preparation of a particular dish of snails, a task requiring a considerable amount of local knowledge of where and when to gather the molluscs, the choice of the correct wild herbs to flavour the cooking broth, an understanding of the salting, scrubbing and simmering that complete the recipe. Such things might be considered entirely irrelevant to modern life. While the mother – the middle generation – clearly did not approve of the grandmother's labour-intensive preparations and the general mess and clutter that marred the perfection of her fitted kitchen, the daughter – a young woman of the same age and similar education to that of my own children – admired and was willing to learn from her grandmother.

After the work was done and we had settled down to enjoy the feast, the young woman pointed out that – as the technological age advances and the workplace shifts from factory to home – we will all have more leisure, and she at least was delighted to employ it in producing the kind of dishes her grandmother understood so well. What was once necessity reappears as lifestyle.

Traditional cookery – limited by availability of raw materials, seasonality and geography – can never be exactly reproduced elsewhere. Nor should it be. The contents of the storecupboard, the quality of the fresh ingredients, the nature of the heat source, the humour of the cook – all these things are as variable as the weather. The skill to add a little of this and a pinch of that, and if you haven't got one thing to substitute or do without – such knowledge can only be passed down through many lifetimes, and it is this which gave such delight to the young woman eager to learn from her grandmother.

Few of us have a Cretan granny to teach us how to live. And even if we had there's a matter of temperament. Those who live in an easy land live easily. Perhaps for those for whom glut is a seasonal expectation rather than hard won against all odds there is less urgency to stock the storecupboard, to hoard and defend. Northerners had good reason to barricade their larders: refilling them could not simply be left to the turning year. This is not to say that the Mediterranean daily dinner is easily earned. There has been famine, plague and war – enough to trigger the mass emigrations that took so many to the New World. It is simply that, with a following wind and left to her own devices, nature provides. The cradle of western civilization was rocked by a gentle hand. Warm earth, fertile seas, the presence of the olive and the vine, these things were, remain, conducive to the provision of plenty. With plenty comes leisure. With leisure, an appetite for music and dance. No one makes merry on an empty stomach.

Northerners, those for whom the battle has always been for survival, demand discipline at table, as in all things: courses served in strict rotation, dictating quantity and composition by plating up in advance. No Mediterranean bon-viveur would tolerate such overbearing bossiness, however carefully composed. Mediterranean meals, in contrast, have little formal structure – basically, it's each man for himself, dip-in-the-dish and eat-what-you-please. No one gives a fig for art on a plate. Few would thank you for playing around with their raspberry coulis. Mezze, *tapas* and the like are simply a formalization of this casual way of eating. If there are any rules it is perhaps that with communal eating each dish contains one person's portion to share between four. Only on feast days is anything larger presented and even then it's likely to be deconstructed before it takes its place on the table. This proportion holds good however many diners there are.

At the practical level, there's much to recommend the arrangement. It's amiable: the freedom to choose allows those with particular requirements – vegetarians, slimmers, allergy-dieters, plain old don't-like-it-what-is-it? – to decide what they want to eat without having to explain themselves either to the cook or their companions. There's freedom, too, within the dish itself. Sauces are served separately from the foods they complement. Meat and fish, grilled or frittered, is served with quartered lemons – rarely does the marination include the sharpness of lemon juice, unless as a preservative. Salads come with the makings of the dressing – vinegar and olive oil, with particular attention to quality in the latter. Quality is much appreciated in Mediterranean lands. The poorest Andalusian peasant will save up for the best *jamón serrano* – however little he can afford – to celebrate the Christmas feast. Quality is more easily seen when the cooking is of the simplest, or even non-existent. The perfection of a tomato ripened in the sun, the exquisiteness of an oyster, the delicacy of an apricot – such things need no embellishment.

It's flexible: you can add or subtract dishes as you please – as with Chinese meals, allow one whole plateful per person and one extra for the hungry.

It's frugal: a single chicken can feed eight or ten people if it's presented not as the main attraction but as one of several dishes each of which is a star in its own right.

It's good housekeeping, too: leftovers take on new life when dished up with fresh companions.

But above all, it's friendly – a way of declaring a common interest. Prosperity – the kind that emptied the villages of the Mediterranean and sent so many to seek fortune elsewhere – has brought privacy. Perhaps because so few of us now live communal lives, we have come to appreciate the conviviality of eating together as, say, a group of friends might arrange to share a table in a restaurant after work. Since so many more of us now enjoy cooking as well as eating, dishes traditionally prepared by many hands provide a reason for friends and family to gather and share their skills, if only to peel the garlic or pick through the leaves for a salad. There's also an ancient reason for the symbolism of sharing food from the same dish. Those who eat the same food smell right to each other; it all goes back to the cave. This is the reason why, however sophisticated we may be, we offer refreshment to visitors when they cross our thresholds and are a little uneasy when they refuse even a glass of water. Unwillingness to accept hospitality is a declaration of belonging to a different tribe, almost a sign of hostility. This, too, is the reason why business meetings are so often conducted over a meal – and why the purpose of the meeting is not mentioned until at least one course has been shared.

The balance of the dishes served in such a way, as with any individually plated meal, is crucial. There must be a contrast in texture – a little soft, a little crisp; a contrast in bulk – something fortifying as well as something frivolous; something bland to balance the highly spiced. As you will by now have realized, suitable dishes are by no means confined to a bowl of olives and a handful of salted almonds, although these certainly have their place. With the exception of spoon-soups and porridges, any Mediterranean recipe can be adapted for sharing, just so long as it can be lifted or scooped with one hand and conveyed to the mouth without upsetting the neighbours. Sometimes this takes unusual dexterity: watch a Moroccan handle a couscous, a Neapolitan urchin a handful of macaroni, a Valencian his *paella*, a native of Provence a plateful of shellfish.

In this book I have gathered those recipes – none set in stone, certainly without any attempt to be comprehensive – that have pleased me, which demand neither great culinary skill nor exotic ingredients, unless these are easily substituted. The business of the recipe-collector is to say that this dish was cooked in this way by this person at this time of the year in this place, not to provide the definitive recipe. Rather than define, I hope to illuminate. How can any recipe be definitive when even those of us with access to the astonishing variety on our supermarket shelves never cook the same dish the same way twice? Instead, I have looked for those ways of preparing the limited ingredients shared by good cooks working within a particular tradition – that of the Mediterranean – and by so doing hope to share the pleasure of the young Cretan woman in the skills of her grandmother.

Yet there is far more to culinary habit than simply replacing one recipe with another. There's a matter of attitude. Mediterranean lifestyles are leisurely – even now, although the leisure is usually taken after the workday and at weekends. Home – round the kitchen table or under the arbour in the shade of a vine-covered trellis – is still the place where most choose to take their meals. Restaurants are only for those with nowhere else to go. Social life is conducted in the street, during the evening stroll round the town or village square, with a pause for an informal gathering in a bar or café for a *mezze* or a *tapa*, a market-snack or a sugary treat in the *pâtisserie*.

Saffron and sunshine, if they could be distilled and stored in a bottle, would be the very essence of the Mediterranean kitchen. The first, pound for pound the costliest of spices, is valued for the subtlety of its dusty perfume as much as for the brilliance of the colour – bright as summer sunshine – that it lends to all it touches. Yet the source is a modest little flower that grows wild on Mediterranean hillsides; the value comes from the time it takes to gather the tiny stigmas – three to a bloom – the care with which the crop is laid to dry in the sun, and from the patience that allows the colour and flavour to reach maturity. No more than can be taken up on the point of a knife is enough to scent and gild a sauce, turn a panful of rice into a dish fit for a king. As for the second – well, that's the subtlest ingredient of all. The warmth of the sun is unreproduceable, irreplaceable, longed for in the depths of winter, the only thing which, for all our technology, we cannot buy off the shelf.

If the task of the recipe-writer is to provide the practical – ingredients, implements, method – how to deliver the poetry? How to persuade those with busy modern lives that the pleasure lies in the preparation as much as in the consumption? In the company as much as in the cooking? That contentment, that gentle joy, comes to those who know the value rather than the price? Bread, love and wine, and the leisure to enjoy them – as the Spaniards say when they raise a glass in a toast – these are the true ingredients of the Mediterranean kitchen. Everything else is negotiable.

Take your time. Enjoy the saffron and the sunshine – not so much a recipe, more a way of life.

A brief tour of the Mediterranean

When the world was young, long before the empires of Greece and Rome, of Egypt and Byzantium, the movement of people and animals was dictated by geography. The northern and southern shores of the great inland sea the Romans called Mare Nostrum are separated at either end by narrow channels of water which serve both as a natural barrier and, to those prepared to take ship, a watery highway. To the west the Strait of Gibraltar led to the Atlantic and the riches of the New World; to the east the Bosporus gave access to the Black Sea and the route to the Orient. The Pyrenees and the foothills of the Alps further divide the northern shores. To the east the Fertile Crescent – the Asian shores of Turkey, Syria, Lebanon and Israel – halts at the great desert of the Sinai. The south is made up of the lands of the Mahgreb – Egypt and the lush floodplain of the Nile, the drifting dunes of Libya and Tunisia, the rocky plateaux of Morocco.

Religion, as always, is a factor in domestic habit. While the nations of the European shores share a Christian heritage, with little or no restriction on what might or might not be considered fit for the table, the rules of the Catholic fast prohibited the eating of meat, the use of olive oil and the enjoyment of sweet things not only on Fridays and throughout Lent but for the days that preceded all feast days – at one time more than half the year. In Arab lands, where Christians and Jews share many of the Muslim taboos, Christians could not use butter in Lent, while Jewish dietary laws prohibited the cooking of meat with dairy products at any time – which is not at all convenient since clarified butter is the favourite frying fat of the Middle East. In the olive-tree regions Jews and Christians solved the problem by using olive oil, which gave their food a distinctive flavour. In Egypt the rather more pungent sesame oil – *siraj* – is the cooking fat of choice.

Culinary habit is also shaped by philosophical outlook. While the Arab nations looked east to the ancient civilizations of Persia, India and China for their cultural heritage, the Europeans – long before they accepted the religious commitments of Judaeo-Christianity – hammered out their social philosophy on the twin anvils of Greece and Rome. In the hierarchical world of Ancient Rome the ruling class developed a tradition of high cooking, dependent on display, featuring rare or imported foodstuffs in innovative combinations, a concept that continues to this day in the exotic dishes and flamboyant presentation of modern chefs. But in the Oriental tradition, little difference is made between the dishes eaten by rich and poor; the rich simply ate the best bits, and more of them, an egalitarian turn of mind that has not changed over the centuries. This lack of differentiation is a source of pride on many of the islands and among those communities of the northern shores where Muslim rule shaped the character of the people – although the origins of the philosophy may not necessarily be appreciated.

Political boundaries may be drawn and redrawn, but politics have little to do with the lives of ordinary people. Only a few people have influence on decisions made at the top, but everyone goes to market. Whether down at the port bargaining for the fishermen's catch, when the camel-train came in from the desert, or simply during the ordinary run of daily life, the marketplace is where news is exchanged, ideas passed on, innovations discussed. It was through the spice-merchants of the Ottoman Empire that the seeds of the New World's vegetables were introduced to the people of the Old World. Tomatoes, peppers, maize – ingredients now seen as the defining flavours of the Mediterranean – were all unknown before Isabella of Castile provided a persuasive sailor from Genoa with a trio of fragile ships.

While domestic habit divides – the women of one household will criticize another for using too little meat, rancid oil, too much garlic, too heavy a hand with the spices, propaganda which can be applied to whole communities – a shared culinary vocabulary also unites. Throughout the region, specialities are identified by variations on the same name – *kebab, dolma, böreki, macaroni, pastilla.* Even in Spain, where after the re-conquest of Al-Andaluz anything Muslim was likely to earn the perpetrator a hard time with the Inquisition, Moorish names are still used to describe many popular dishes, including *albondigas* – the Spanish version of the ubiquitous meatball.

Each nation – community, what you will – has earned itself a culinary reputation, some deserved, some entirely arbitrary. The cooks of Catalonia don't rate the Andalusians, for all that the Moors can claim responsibility for the introduction of leaf – puff – pastry, sugar-based sweets and nougats as well as sophisticated spicing. The Turks take a dim view of the Greeks – although the Ottomans were still boiling bison in its jacket at a time when Athenians were sipping fine wines while discussing Sophocles. Among Arab nations, the Lebanese have a reputation for excellence – perhaps because as the heartland of the Fertile Crescent so many cooks stirred the broth – while Moroccan palace cooking is the Mahgreb's equivalent of French *haute-cuisine*.

When King Idriss I of Baghdad planted the flag of Islam on the shores of the Mediterranean eight centuries after the birth of Christ, the multi-racial peoples of North Africa were obliged to change their habits. These days they are known collectively as Arabs, although their roots go far deeper. The Phoenicians and Romans spent their wealth here, rested up their garrisons, took wives and sweethearts from among the Berbers who in their turn inter-married with the Bedouin – warriors, merchants, traders in oriental spices, carpets, silks – who wandered with their camel-trains through the deserts of Arabia before settling in the green lands of Lebanon and Syria. This multi-racial gang headed across the Pillars of Hercules, upwards through the Iberian peninsula as far as southern France, until they drew back to the southern provinces of Spain to pitch their tents and build their palaces in the fertile land they named Al-Andaluz, the gateway to paradise.

The grain food of the eastern Mediterranean – the lands settled by the nomadic Bedouin – is burghul, cracked wheat, pre-soaked for ease of cooking. *Kibbeh* (raw meat pounded with burghul) and *tabbouleh* (parsley salad) are both prepared with burghul. The grain food of the eastern Mediterranean – the Mahgreb, the land settled by the Berbers, farmers and sedentary pastoralists – is couscous, the hard kernel of the wheat, pre-cooked and rolled in flour, then steamed over a savoury stew. Although there are no hard and fast rules, a Moroccan couscous usually includes saffron; the Algerians thicken the broth with tomato; the Tunisians spice with ginger and mix the juices with harissa, a fiery sauce of pounded chillis. Couscous – as any practical cook might observe – is something of a missing link, being no more or less than a primitive pasta, diminutive but mirroring in its method of manufacture *trahana*, the finger-rolled dough-scraps of the Turks, which are also found among the Greeks, which in turn merge into the pinch-finger *gnocchis* of Italy, which arrive in Catalonia as *fideos*, the little thread-noodles which are cooked like the *paellas* of the Levante, whose antecedents can be seen in the *andrajos* – dried disks of dough broken into pasta-like shards – of Andalusia.

There are many such circular dances. It is impossible to tell where one begins and the other ends. How, for instance, to tell a Greek from a Turk, the Ottoman from the Hellene? As a general rule, Greek cooks use herbs where Turks use spices, and while the Greek cook is conservative her Turkish equivalent is more likely to pick up tips from the neighbours. The Ottomans, whose empire once stretched from the walls of Vienna to the mountains of the Mahgreb, prided themselves on a sophisticated palate. Their cooks introduced the housewives of eastern Europe to the joys of filo pastry, taught the rest of us how to fry the meat before cooking up a stew, and generally did what they could to improve the standards of catering wherever they settled.

Even more impossible to categorize is the cookery of the islands, stepping stones in the silver sea, unless to observe that island peoples follow their own star, retaining a strong sense of identity which makes them fit subjects for anthropologists. The islands provided the safe harbours in which fishermen and merchant men, pirates too, could take shelter against the winter storms. For all her benevolence in summer, the Mediterranean is by no means kindly in winter. The wrecks that litter her bed provide ample proof of her indifference to the fragile vessels that navigate her – and this, too, has bred a robust and hardy tribe to brave the terrors of the ocean and seek fortune elsewhere.

While the Christian peoples of the Mediterranean are wine-drinkers – vintners and fermenters of the grape – in the Muslim world liquor is forbidden by the Prophet, although even devout followers will tell you that Muhammad changed his mind in the course of his life. Later pronouncements – perhaps because of the association of liquor with gambling, possibly to make a sharper distinction between the Muslim Faithful and the Infidel Christian – prohibited wine-drinking as the work of Satan. Very sensible. When people are drunk they forget to pray and are less inclined to obey the rules. Somewhat mysteriously, *raki* or *arrak* – aniseed-flavoured spirit – is condoned by all but the strictest of Muslims, at least among the male population, since women are not expected to take alcohol at all. Exactly the same reason is often given for the anomaly as is applied to infidelity – you're not supposed to but you do it anyway.

Throughout the region, the traditions that distinguish the home kitchen, traditional guardian of regional habit, survived as long as women kept control of their domestic environment. At the rural level, all food had to be husbanded and harvested. In the urban areas, it was the women who selected the primary materials and prepared them for the table. The changes in lifestyle brought by modern work habits have not been slow to take effect on the northern shores of the region. In Arab lands, respect for tradition leads to a gentler pace of change – nevertheless, change is inevitable. Many of the great dishes that distinguish the Middle Eastern culinary tradition are labour-intensive: the poundings and grindings, wrappings and shapings that go to make Lebanese *kibbeh* or the Turkish *dolma* spring from the kind of inter-generational social gatherings that are becoming increasingly rare.

Throughout the region, fast-food outlets compete with the sellers of street food, supermarkets supplant the daily market. Many modern Arab women go out to work as freely as their Christian sisters – and this, for better or worse, is reflected in domestic habit. Nevertheless, regional differences matter less than underlying philosophy. Although changes in work-patterns have meant that all members of a household no longer meet at table every day, the people of the lands of the Mediterranean retain a strong sense of place, an emotional attachment not only to people but to the soil from which they spring – a sharing of common cause, of which their behaviour at table serves as a daily reminder.

Practical Notes and Glossary

Using This Book

First things first. Decide what you want to cook before you decide how to cook it. Pick your central ingredient – a fine chicken, eggs, fresh fish, particularly perfect vegetables, whatever appeals to you in the marketplace – and build the rest of the meal around it. Each recipe in this book is marked according to its importance – but this is only a guide. Meals can be made up entirely of subsidiary dishes, particularly if you provide a plate of charcuterie or cheese. The idea is that all the usual elements of a plated meal are present, but each element is presented separately. My suggested combinations of dishes at the end of each recipe should point you in the right direction, but use your own instinctive knowledge of the balance of a meal to compose your own combinations.

This balance of flavours, textures, etc, is more important than maintaining regional integrity. The same recipes – though claimed as place-specific with the proprietory fierceness of those well used to begging, borrowing and stealing from the neighbours – pop up in various guises, under different names, from north to south, east to west. If, for instance, your central recipe is a beautiful bread of your own baking, concentrate on dips and dishes with plenty of sauce; if the main attraction is poultry, choose a supporting cast of vegetable dishes and salads; but if seafood has caught your fancy, serve a feast of fish: something soupy – shellfish, perhaps; something crisp and frittered; something luxurious – scarlet prawns still juicy from the grill, a bubbling dish of oven-baked crab.

I'm sure you get the picture. The guiding principle throughout is enjoyment, both for the cook and the guests.

The Recipes

Each recipe – with the exception of those included in the first and last chapters, respectively appetizers and desserts – has been numbered from I to 3 to give a rough guide of its importance on your table. A dish with protein – chicken, fish, meat, cheese or eggs – will normally form the centrepiece of your meal, around which you will choose your supporting dishes. Treat these numbers as a guide only – nothing is set in stone.

(1) Primary dishes: important dishes, the leaders of the pack, those that feature a high proportion of protein – meat, chicken, fish, eggs, cheese. Although given pride of place, quality counts for more than quantity, so if you have a dozen people to feed and only one chicken, chop the joints smaller.

(2) Secondary dishes: complementary dishes, the supporting cast, the chorus – mainly based on vegetables, although if particularly fine (the first asparagus, a generous haul of wild fungi) these can be elevated to a starring role. Also included in the group are the lighter fish and meat dishes.

(3) Bulk: something solid and inexpensive based on grain-foods, bread, pasta. This is the element most easily expanded to accommodate any number of guests.

Quantities

Appetites are always hard to gauge. Most of the recipes are designed to be shared among 4–6 – but this can be expanded or contracted by providing more or fewer subsidiary dishes, extra grain food, salads (keep these simple – tomatoes with basil, peppers in oil, greens with herbs).

To serve 2: allow one primary dish plus one secondary; or two secondary and one for bulk.

To serve 4: allow one primary, two or three secondary, one for bulk.

To serve 6: allow one primary, four secondary and one for bulk; or two primary, three secondary, one for bulk.

As a rough rule of thumb, allow one dish per person plus one extra, much as when ordering in a Chinese restaurant. Within these general guidelines, for up to six people one good primary dish is really all you need (if you are feeding more than six, add another primary dish).

Utensils and Heat Source

The Mediterranean cook traditionally relies on a limited number of cooking implements: boiling pot, frying pan, earthenware dishes and casseroles in which food could be sent to the baker to be finished in the residual heat of the bread oven. In the days when the Mediterranean culinary habit was formed, few households had domestic ovens, and those who baked their own bread did so only once a week, limiting the opportunity to bake cakes or pastries, or finish dishes in the oven. For everyday cooking, the heat source was either a bed of charcoal or the direct heat of the fire – thus the dependence on top-heat for frying and boiling. Where northern traditional cooks might set a dish to cook overnight in a slow oven, the Mediterranean cook would be unwilling to add to the heat of the kitchen – even taking advantage of the warmth of the sun to soften tomatoes for a sauce or pickle fish in lemon juice (Spain's *seviche*), or brine-conserve vegetables (the Middle East's *torshi*). Traditional equipment – knives, the pestle and mortar, the wood-fired oven – makes demands on the modern home cook which for practical reasons cannot always be met. Modern Mediterranean housewives use modern machinery – the food processor, liquidizer, electric whisk, freezer – to lighten the load. With few exceptions, for example the pesto recipe, and mayonnaise, there's no reason not to follow suit.

Glossary of Ingredients

Vegetables. As the direct result of a relationship between seed, soil, water and sunshine, vegetables reflect the conditions under which they're grown. Onions, carrots, potatoes, all the winter roots and gourds and members of the cabbage family grow well in a cold climate, so there's never a reason to buy imported. The reverse is true of tomatoes, peppers, artichokes, aubergines and all the other vegetables that taste so much sweeter for the warmth of the sun. These, inevitably, are available in far greater variety in Mediterranean markets, making the exact reproduction of recipes of less importance than achieving a dish that tastes good. For instance, watery tomatoes must be cooked for longer to achieve the desirable richness, sugar added for sweetness. And Greeks will tell you that elderly aubergines are not worth buying at all. I have tried to take account of expected imperfections in the raw materials, suggesting alternatives and ways of making the best of what's likely to come to hand. Nevertheless, there's no substitute for your own good sense: trust your tastebuds. When choosing Mediterranean vegetables, look at the stalk and calyx as well as the skin, check for browning, reject any that are wrinkled or dried out, or blemished.

Meat and poultry. Whenever possible, choose free-range organic. Not so much of an expense if you are serving it with complementary dishes, since comparatively little is needed; top-of-the-foodchain foods are not required to form the bulk of the meal. Choose small chickens: they have a better flavour, even if the proportion of meat to bone is less satisfactory. Buy wild game whenever you see it: it's lean and well flavoured, and if it proves to be commercially viable our landowners might be encouraged to allow more of it to breed.

Preserved meats. While the prime cuts of a salt-cured wind-dried Mediterranean ham are savoured for their own sake, the bones and trimmings, both fat and lean, are used to flavour other dishes. In recipes that call for a ham bone, the bone from any roast meat makes an acceptable substitute. In recipes that call for diced *serrano* or *prosciutto*, gammon or unsmoked back bacon is a good alternative. Failing these, enrich with extra olive oil and a finishing flavouring of chopped garlic and parsley. Smoked bacon plus a pinch of marjoram and a little paprika can be used to replace *chorizo* or any other Mediterranean storecupboard sausage.

Olive oil. Many rural Mediterranean households still mill and press their own olives for oil, enough to supply their city-dwelling cousins – and these are the oils well worth searching out *in situ*.

Once you have opened a container of olive oil you should reseal it carefully after use, and use up the oil as quickly as possible. Decant oil from large tins into smaller bottles, so that the rest of the oil is not exposed to the air more than necessary. Plastic bottles are suitable only for very short periods of storage; pottery, tin and glass are best, and the storage container should be kept in a cool, dark cupboard.

1. Virgin olive oil is the rip-roaring, untouched raw juice of the olive. It must be below 3 per cent acidity, and chemically untreated. Nevertheless, it can be a blend from different areas, even more than one country. There are subtle shades of virginity within this category rated according to the oil's acidity; oleic acid is determined by the type and quality of the soil, the olive variety, the handling of the olives during harvesting, and the speed with which the fruit is brought to the mill. The highest quality is *extra virgin*, which must be below 1 per cent acidity. *Fine virgin* defines an oil up to 1.5 per cent acidity. The addition of the words *first cold pressing* tell you that the oil is the raw juice of the olive, and that no heat has been used in the extraction. Virgin cold-pressed olive oil is fruity, leafy, peppery – lovely on salads, to brush over food to be grilled, to finish or thicken a sauce. It's less good for frying – quite apart from reversing the trouble taken to ensure that it has not been heated in the first place – because, containing more moisture, it takes longer to reach frying-heat, and the delicious sediment can burn.

2. Olive oil (previously labelled *pure*), must register below the 3.3 per cent acidity level. A blended oil, it can be a mixture of refined (see below) and virgin oils. Oil that is not billed as cold-pressed is usually hot-pressed, a process that uses hot water to make the pulp yield up more oil after the first pressing. The heat inevitably cooks the oil a little, altering the flavour, akin to pasteurization. The difference is noticeable when the oil is used raw, but not when it is used for frying. Olive oil is excellent for frying as its smoke-point is 210°C (the temperature for frying chips is 180°C). The proportion of virgin to refined will be reflected in the price. Find one you like and use it for mayonnaise – the virgins are a little heavy for the purpose.

3. Refined olive oil is oil that has been chemically 'rectified', a treatment undertaken in order to reduce acidity to below the 3.3 per cent level required by law of an oil offered for sale commercially. Such an oil is pale, odourless and flavourless and has to be blended with a virgin oil to give it a bit of character. It was ever thus. It can also have been heat-treated. Heat-treated oils keep better than virgin oils and are good for pickles, flavoured oils (chilli, rosemary, thyme, garlic) and for foods sealed under oil. Palatable but bland.

4. Light olive oil is a relatively new category designed to appeal to the lowest common denominator – our increasingly bland palates. It's a blend of refined and virgin, as above, but it's likely to contain a higher proportion of refined oil. Shame.

Other oils and frying fats. On the southern and eastern shores of the Mediterranean much use is made of nut and seed oils both in cooking and frying. Sesame, poppyseed, walnut, almond and a few mavericks milled from endemic nuts and seeds are traditional, while oils milled from maize, sunflower and pumpkin seeds are post-Columbian. Among the shepherding communities of the Middle East, sheep-tail fat is much appreciated – to each his own.

Clarified butter is the natural cooking fat of Muslim peoples whose origins lie in the desert. Nomadic herdsmen, who were never in one place for long enough to crop and mill raw materials for oil, naturally made use of animal fats. To clarify butter, melt ordinary butter gently in a small pan and pour off the oil, leaving the milky residue behind. If you heat it again for long enough to evaporate all the moisture, it'll keep for a long time without refrigeration – very useful if you're a desert nomad. Cakes and pastries made with clarified butter keep fresh and crisp for longer than those made with ordinary shortenings.

Mediterranean cheeses. There are thousands of shepherd's cheeses throughout the region – each peculiar to a particular area, even a single household. Hand-made and mould-pressed, often bearing the pattern of the container in which they're drained, usually of a size that permits easy transportation, they're eaten at all stages of maturity: fresh, semi-cured, matured. In addition to these larder-stores, there's a range of soft unpressed white-curd cheeses traditionally made with first spring milkings, although now made commercially throughout the year. Cheeses make a valuable contribution to the *mezze* table (see page 37). They are also widely used in Mediterranean cooking as a flavouring, adding both salt and savour.

Soft fresh cheese: curd cheeses, renneted or not, soured or turned with a yoghurt-making bacillus, designed to be eaten fresh, are traditionally made by the housewife herself for use in stuffings for pasta and *böreki*, and sometimes matured with white brandy or *raki* to make a particularly pungent cheese spread – dun-coloured, punchy, absolutely not for wimps. Substitute any fresh white soft cheese – curd or cottage or fromage frais – for the Mediterranean curd cheeses such as *ricotta* or *labna*.

Unmatured pressed-curd cheese: a white curd cheese in the first stage of maturity. Best known is the Greek feta, the Turkish village cheese *beyaz peynir*, the Spanish *queso de Burgos*. Feta is widely available so a substitute is not usually necessary, but crumbly Cheshire would be the nearest approximation. Italian mozzarella, an unusual cheese worked under boiling water to give it enough elasticity to form the characteristic long strings, is traditionally made with buffalo milk and usually eaten fresh (though it can be matured): best substitute in cooking is grated mild Cheddar with a dollop of fresh curd cheese.

Semi-matured pressed-curd cheese: the everyday cheese of the people of the Mediterranean, home made or bought locally in the market, eaten with bread and onion as the field worker's midday break; sometimes rinded, sometimes simply salted or rubbed with spices and/or herbs to form a crust. In cooking, substitute a mild Cheddar or Cheshire. Provençal goat's milk cheeses are miniature rounds of hand-pressed curd – *tommes, crottin* – small enough to eat in a single mouthful, eaten at various stages of maturity, delicious when stored under olive oil with flavouring herbs.

Matured pressed-curd cheese: shepherd's cheeses as above, but left on the shelf for longer and therefore more expensive. A cheese that has had time to develop and mature acquires a denser texture and a more concentrated flavour – virtues that make it much appreciated as an appetizer, particularly with one of the anis-flavoured white spirits – *raki, ouzo,* Pernod. Within the genre, Sicilian and Sardinian pecorino is appreciated for its own sake, although also used as a grating cheese; Spanish manchego, a sheep's milk cheese with a dark rind which keeps the print of the plaited basket in which it's drained, is sometimes matured under oil, when it becomes deliciously pungent; Greek kefalotiri is a hard, strong, salty goat's milk cheese, very good roasted on a dry pan and eaten with a squeeze of lemon, but also used as a seasoning much as one might use salt – sprinkled on salads, on rice, on grilled meats (never on fish), even on chips. The Italian grana – the generic name for granular cheeses such as Parmesan – is appreciated for the grittiness of its texture as well as fragrance and flavour; in cooking it's mostly added to other foods – slivered or grated on pasta or risotto, included in tomato-based sauces, particularly if the dish is *magro* (meatless). Middle Eastern cheeses are mostly of the feta-type, either eaten fresh or salted and matured – with olives and pickled vegetables, the classic accompaniment to *raki.* Any matured pressed-curd cheese can substitute for any other – emigrant Italians, reluctant to pay migratory prices, substitute grating-grana with mature Cheddar left unwrapped in the fridge to harden.

Paprika and pimentón. Peppers ripen naturally from green to red. The shades in between – yellow, orange, brown and black – are the result of selective breeding by modern plantsmen. Botanically, two species can be identified, both naturally hot: the fleshy and mildly fiery *Capsicum annuum*, and the smaller and a great deal more fiery *Capsicum frutescens*. The former has been tamed to produce mild salad peppers, which provide the raw material for the dried peppers much used in Spanish cookery. When milled to a fine powder they become the spice known in Spain as *pimentón* and elsewhere as paprika. Much play is made of the differences between the two, but since Spain imports much of her *pimentón* direct from the mills of Hungary, pioneers in the art of paprika-milling, this is a little hard to credit. The capsicum pepper is remarkably high in vitamin C (weight for weight, higher than an orange), making it a valuable anti-scorbutic in the days when sailors suffered from scurvy.

Chilli. Chillis take the place of imported peppercorns in the storecupboards of the Mediterranean's independent peasantry. Grown in the vegetable patch, picked when red and ripe and dried for storage, they are rarely used fresh. On the eastern and southern shores of the region, green chillis of the milder sort are included in the pickle pot. Dried chillis, as with all other dried peppers, should be deseeded and soaked before use. Dried chillis can be ground to make a fiery spice: chilli powder and cayenne pepper are the same thing, and don't let anyone persuade you otherwise.

Herbs and spices. As a general rule, those who took their culinary lead from the Turks make liberal use of eastern spices: **cumin, cinnamon, nutmeg, cloves, ginger**; those who look to the western tradition use herbs: **oregano, thyme, rosemary, sage, fennel, chive, dill. Peppercorns** are used throughout the region, both white and black – the former is the ripe berry and is hotter, and the latter is the green berry which, when fermented and dried, is more fragrant. Spices are best bought from Middle Eastern stores, where they will be a great deal cheaper and the quality more reliable. When choosing herbs, bear in mind that rosemary, thyme and oregano (wild marjoram) are hard-leaf herbs which lose very little of their volume when they are dried. You'll find the fragrance and flavour of dried Mediterranean herbs far superior to glasshouse-grown specimens, however pretty they may look on the stalk. **Parsley** is used throughout the region, always flat-leaf 'Italian', never the northern curly-leaf, which would be considered far too strong. **Garlic** is used lavishly, both fresh and mature. **Leaf coriander** is used only on the southern – Arab – shores, and on certain of the islands, particularly Cyprus. **Seed coriander** is used on the northern shores, particularly in pickling. **Basil** is used with great enthusiasm in Italy and Provence, but is regarded with indifference in Spain and Greece (unless as a pot of small-leaf kept on the windowsill to discourage flies), and is altogether ignored on the southern shores of the region. **Bayleaves** are used in Turkey to keep marauding insects out of dried figs, but are otherwise appreciated throughout as a pot-herb. Green, unblanched **celery** is also used as a pot-herb and in mixtures of spring leaves. In the eastern and southern areas, from Turkey to the Mahgreb, dried **mint** is often preferred to the fresh leaf as a flavouring: it's considered stronger and more aromatic. Neither dried nor fresh mint appears much on the northern shores, unless on the Greek islands, where it is sometimes included among other fragrant greens. In Spain, **pennyroyal** is used in a broth for cooking the small snails that spend the summer aestivating on thistle skeletons. **Lemons**, both juice and zest, are widely used as a flavouring, as is dried zest of orange, a taste shared by the Greeks and the people of Provence. **Salt-preserved lemons** are used as a flavouring, being gentler and more delicate in flavour than the fresh fruit, throughout the Middle East, but particularly in Morocco. **Mahleb** and **mastic** are the jokers in the pack: the first is the core of the wild cherry-stone, pounded to a paste and used to flavour breads and biscuits; the second is the silvery gum of a certain strain of the wild pistachio found only on the island of Chios, pounded to a powder and used to flavour desserts and ices – its perfume is delicately flowery and resinous. Another oddity – though once so popular on our own islands that Charles Lamb wrote an essay in praise of it – is **salep**, the dried, pounded root of several varieties of ground orchid, which is extremely starchy and remarkably high in protein and is used as a thickening agent in Turkish ice-creams and milk-based drinks.

Saffron is neither a herb nor, strictly speaking, a spice, being the stigmas of a flower, *Crocus sativus,* a pretty little purple-petalled crocus native to the region. When dried – a labour-intensive process – the stigmas resemble tiny crimson threads. Those who measure such things will tell you that the best saffron – first grade from La Mancha, Spain's central plateau – is capable of colouring ten thousand times its own volume, but the amount you need depends on the freshness and the care with which the raw material has been gathered and dried. There is evidence – stone-age middens tell tall tales – that saffron is the oldest flavouring-ingredient known to man. The scent is subtle, elusive – a little of new-mown hay, a little of cinnamon, a hint of jasmine; the flavour, equally elusive, is both bitter and sweet. But saffron is chiefly valued for its colour. The crimson threads, when properly prepared, turn all they touch to gold – not the vulgar yellow of turmeric, nor the ivory yellow delivered by an infusion of marigold petals (which is labelled either Indian or Mexican saffron in Turkish markets) but a delicate yellow, like old gold, the colour of sunshine on sand. To release their power, the tiny threads must be soaked and crushed. This can be done simply by covering the strands with boiling water – the longer you leave them to infuse the stronger the colour: overnight is not too long. Or they can be crisped in a hot pan and crushed before adding to a liquid: heat a clean dry pan to frying temperature, remove it from the heat, sprinkle on the saffron and allow 2 minutes before you crush it. Some people toast before soaking, on the grounds that this develops the flavour. I have no strong opinion on the matter, unless to say that in the particular cor- ner of Andalusia in which I picked up my saffron habits we soaked but never toasted.

Arrak and sherry. Throughout the region the preliminary refreshment, the classic accompaniment to the little nibbles to be found in the first section of this book, is one of the aniseed-flavoured distillations – *arrak* or *raki* in the Middle East, *ouzo* in Greece, Pernod in Provence, *anis* throughout Spain's Levante – always taken with iced water, either to accompany or as a dilutant, when it instantly forms an emulsion, a pretty white cloud. In Andalusia, under Muslim rule for many centuries, the preliminary refreshment is sherry: dry, delicate, straw-pale, nothing like the sticky sweet stuff our grandmothers sipped on the sofa. Choose a fino from the chalky vineyards of Jerez, a manzanilla from the port of Sanlucar with its salty scent of the sea. Dry sherry is always served chilled and never comes without its 'lid', the *tapa* which, in rural areas uncontaminated by tourism, is always offered free.

Sherbets and infusions. In Muslim lands non-alcoholic drinks are taken as refreshment at any time of the day: freshly squeezed fruit juices, nut milks, yoghurt diluted and flavoured, syrup-based sherbets; chocolate flavoured with cinnamon or vanilla; herbal teas and medicinal infusions such as mint, chamomile, lime-blossom; coffee, usually black, very strong and highly sweetened. Recipes for some of these preparations will be found in the last section of the book.

Wine. The practice of the vintner's art is confined to the Christian areas of the region, although even the Prophet permitted wine in Paradise. In Mediterranean lands, wine is always accompanied by food: to consume the one without the other would be, well, like eating bread without salt, fish without lemon. Wine is never set on the table without an accompanying water jug, and – traditionally at least – with little attention paid to anything but palatability. Each wine has its own character, defended to the death by those whose daily pleasure is to drink it, but the notion of château-bottling, the selection of grapes for balance and finish and all the other mysteries of the blender's art, is relatively new to Mediterranean vintners. Fine wines are not necessarily the best things to drink with food, particularly the robust dishes of the Mediterranean. Rough wine – particularly rough red wine – cuts the richness of olive oil, aids digestion and (taken in moderation, of course) is generally considered essential to human happiness and well being. It's not generally a thing to be savoured for its own sake. You'll not find much to sniff and spit in a Mediterranean cellar – *pace* the talented modern winemakers who are producing magnificent wines wherever vines are planted. Sweet wines and wines which have been flavoured and sweet-ened – ladies' treats – are offered at the beginning and, more rarely, the end of a meal. Liqueurs, dry and fiery or sweet and deceptively innocent, are taken at any time of the day or night as a restorative, to soothe the troubled digestion, or simply for the pleasure of it.

Appetizers & nibbles

The dishes in this section are those that need little culinary attention, and as such have earned themselves first place on the table.

The Mediterranean meal is a leisurely affair, informal and amiable. Guests drift to table rather than wasting time in idle talk without sustenance. Only on formal occasions or in very grand households is the northern pattern of hospitality imposed – the pre-dinner drinks, the table settings, the rows of glasses and the massed ranks of cutlery, the expectation that plates and eating instruments will be changed between courses. Northern disciplines do not speak well to the Mediterranean soul.

Instead, on informal occasions with family and friends, as soon as the guests have a glass in their hand and the host has poured the welcoming glass of wine – or *ouzo*, Pernod, *anis*, *raki*, with water to dilute, naturally – there must be plates on the table, and without delay. First to arrive, since quickest to hand, are the storecupboard staples: olives, nuts, cheese. You rarely find cheese served at the end of a Mediterranean meal – its place is as an appetizer.

Preserved meats – lean and tender, none of your fatty slabs of lard – show particular honour to a guest. In the days when every household kept a pig, the annual slaughter provided all the preserved meats needed for the year. The fat was kept for everyday fuel food, more valuable if less esteemed than the lean, which explains why guests are treated to the hams and slicing sausages of which the region has an astonishing variety. Preserved fish such as sardines, anchovies, tuna – either air-dried or conserved under oil and sold by weight from the barrel – make easy, cheap appetizers. The aristocrats, very expensive and absolutely addictive, are *bottargo,* salt-cured grey mullet roe (known in Greece as *tarama*); and Spain's salt-dried tuna (both flesh and roe – the belly-cut being the most esteemed); slice very thin and dress with olive oil and lemon.

More modest – cheap and cheerful, a sideline of the olive-merchant – are salt-pickled vegetables: baby cucumbers, peppers, chillis, roots – carrot, beet-root, turnip. Variety is the spice of life.

All about the olive

The olive tree thrives on the shores of the Mediterranean. It provides, in the form of fruit and oil, the true flavour of the region. No terrace is without its olive grove, no village shop without its barrel of pickled olives, no market which lacks its olive merchant. Even today, no rural household with access to its own olive trees would neglect the annual task of refilling the olive crock.

Those who harvest their own trees for their own use make no difference between table olives and oil olives, unless it is to crop early if the fruit is to be pickled green, or choose the most perfect fruit for the table before sending the rest to the mill. As with juice oranges and eating oranges, it's simply a matter of the most suitable fruit for the job.

Olives ripen from green through violet to black, the stage at which they can be pressed for oil (though some North African varieties are pressed green). The hotter the climate and the nearer to sea level, the earlier the harvest. July is the earliest I have ever seen olives picked for oil (green olives for pickling might be gathered even earlier), while February is the latest. Olives can be prepared for the table at any stage of ripeness – hence the variations in colour.

Straight from the tree, the fruit is mouth-puckeringly bitter and must be treated in some way to leach the bitterness as well as for conservation – soaked in many changes of water, salted or unsalted, with or without wood ash (lye), with or without flavouring aromatics.

Black olives – the ripe fruits – need less attention than unripe green olives. Large black olives such as the big, meaty Greek Kalamata are simply brined and stored under oil. Black olives are also left to wrinkle on the tree like raisins on the vine, a process which concentrates and sweetens the flesh. In mountainous areas such as that of Nyons in Upper Provence the fruits are picked after the first frost and need only be rolled in salt for conservation. In Spain, table olives are traditionally picked while still green and unripe: look out for the tiny golden manzanilla and the big fat queen olive known as the sevil-lano, but avoid the black, which are simply green olives that have been subjected to a process of oxidization, a bit of chemical trickery; best of all are the home-pickled olives, *aceitunas aliñadas,* flavoured with garlic and wild fennel. In North Africa the half-ripe violet is the olive of choice.

Pickled olives

A passable imitation of Spanish home-cured olives can be made by marinating commercially prepared olives for a week or two in an aromatic bath. Green olives are suitable for a brine-based marinade, while black olives are much improved by a flavoured oil.

Green olives with garlic and lemon

Serves 6–8

500g / 1lb green olives
3–4 cloves garlic, with skin, roughly chopped
1 lemon (1 slice, the rest chopped)
1 teaspoon dried thyme
1 teaspoon coriander seeds
1 stick dried fennel (broken into short lengths)
2–3 tablespoons wine vinegar

Pack the olives, garlic and chopped lemon in a well scrubbed jar with the aromatics, vinegar and enough boiled, cooled water to cover. Top with the lemon slice to keep the olives submerged. Lid tightly and leave in the fridge for at least a week to take the flavours. Keeps well in the fridge.

Black olives with chilli

Serves 6–8

500g / 1lb ready-pickled black olives
3–4 dried red chillis, deseeded and crumbled
1 teaspoon cumin seeds, lightly roasted in a dry pan
1 teaspoon coriander seeds, as above
2–3 cloves garlic, skinned and roughly chopped
2–3 tablespoons wine vinegar
150ml / ¼ pint olive oil

Combine all the ingredients and pack in a well scrubbed jar. Set aside for a few days for the flavours to blend. Keeps well in the fridge.

▶ *Tabbouleh (page 84)*

Black and green olive pastes

The Provençal tapenade is a surprisingly new introduction to the Mediterranean repertoire of dips and scoopable purées, a restaurant invention that takes its name from the capers – tapeno in the patois – which perfume the mix. Nevertheless, the idea of pitting and pounding olives to make a savoury paste to eat with bread is nothing new – it is the sophisticated blending with other storecupboard ingredients that makes the difference. Green olives pounded with fresh coriander is a Cypriot speciality but now pops up in Provence as an alternative to the black tapenade. Serve both at the same time for a pretty contrast of colour and flavour.

Serves 6–8

Black tapenade

250g / 8oz black olives, pitted
and chopped
50g / 2oz capers, drained
50g / 2oz tinned anchovy fillets, drained
50g / 2oz tinned tuna, drained

I teaspoon freshly ground black pepper
I teaspoon finely chopped thyme
about 150ml / ¼ pint olive oil
I tablespoon *pastis* or *eau de vie*

Pound all the solid ingredients together to a fine paste in a mortar and then beat in enough olive oil to moisten the mixture to a scoopable purée, finishing with the *pastis*. If the oil pools, a little boiling water will fix it. Or conserve your strength and put the whole lot in the food processor. Pot and lid tightly. Keeps pretty much indefinitely in the fridge.

Green tapenade

350g / 12oz green olives, pitted
and chopped
2 cloves garlic, skinned and chopped
a large handful of coriander,
roughly chopped

3–4 fronds fennel or dill
150ml / ¼ pint olive oil
6 tablespoons wine vinegar
I tablespoon *raki, ouzo* or Pernod
½ teaspoon freshly ground black pepper

Either pound the solid ingredients in a mortar with a pestle, adding the liquids in a steady stream, or put all the ingredients in the food processor and process to a paste. Taste for flavour – you're unlikely to need more salt.

◀ *Grilled asparagus with green herb dressing (page 86); Mallorcan spinach pizza (page 56)*

Torshi
Salt-pickled vegetables

You'll find these throughout the region under different names, variously brined and spiced. This recipe is for the Middle Eastern torshi, but you can vary the spices as you please. Everything goes into the pickle-pot in any combination; particularly pretty is a pairing of turnips and beetroot – both turn pink. The vegetables should retain a crisp bite, and are often eaten on their own as a salad meal with bread.

Makes 4kg / 8lb pickles

For the pickling brine
about 1.5 litres / 3 pints water
about 600ml / 1 pint good red wine vinegar
at least 100g / 4oz sea salt – add more if you use more water

Vegetables
3–4kg / 6–8lb mixed vegetables: carrots, cauliflower, baby turnips, small pickling cucumbers, red, yellow and green peppers, green beans

To flavour
1 tablespoon coriander seeds
3–4 heads garlic, cloves skinned
1 teaspoon dried chillis – about a dozen

Mix the pickling brine ingredients together in a large saucepan. Sterilize your pickling jars – scrub, rinse thoroughly with boiling water and set in a low oven to dry.

Peel and/or hull the vegetables and chop them into bite-sized pieces. Pack the pieces neatly into the jars.

Heat the brine ingredients until boiling. Pour over the vegetables and prod the pieces well with a skewer to shake off the air bubbles that might make the pickle go bad. (Air is the arch-enemy of pickles and preserves.)

Seal the jars down tightly and store in a cool dark larder. Ready to eat in six weeks, but will keep until next year's crop comes along.

Salt-preserved meats

I have direct experience of the mighty Iberico pig, raw material for Spain's favourite *tapa*, *jamón serrano*. Twenty years ago, when I lived with my young family in a remote valley in Andalusia, most households kept a pig to eat up the household scraps. Slaughter was in the autumn, and if the pig owner lived, as we did, in a damp and humid climate by the sea, the meat and lard was prepared in the usual way – as *chorizos*, *morcillas*, bacon and lard – but the hams were sent up to a cousin or friend in a mountain village, where the air was cold and dry. From this habit developed a commercial ham-curing industry, with certain villages achieving particular fame – in Andalusia, Jabugo in the province of Huelva and Trevelez in the province of Granada. Each year, just in time for Christmas, in my kitchen as in those of my neighbours, a pair of hams complete with trotters hung from the rafters along with a string of peppers and a plait of garlic.

The hams of the native Iberico breed – forest foragers, mean and lean, descendants of an ancient race – go to make the prized *pata negra* – black-foot hams. A forest pig is no snout-in-the-trough domestic porker but a muscular beast, protective of its young, with a most discerning palate and a taste for roots and tubers. The only way you can herd a forest pig is to catch the piglets, stuff them in the donkey basket, and hope the sow will follow you home. Hams from such a pig take longer to cure than those from domestic beasts and lose more of their weight than those from coralled creatures, and are consequently much more expensive. They have very little exterior fat, but the meat – of a deep velvety wine-red, almost black – has a rich marbling of creamy fat which melts in the mouth like butter.

The disappearance of forageable forests and the replacement of the donkey with more convenient means of transport have left the Iberico pig vulnerable to the men from the ministry. New regulations require its keepers to confine it to the sty and no pig accustomed to fending for itself takes kindly to coralling. It has now been successfully cross-bred with domestic beasts, and this is probably the only way the admirable creature will survive. Cheaper hams are made with tame beasts of the bacon breed – Landrace, Duroc, Large White – an altogether flabbier slice.

Sausages of the Mediterranean

Sausages to be eaten raw – spiced, salted and dried, sometimes (as with the Spanish *chorizo*) lightly smoked – are always to hand in the well stocked Mediterranean larder. There are so many varieties that it would take another book of equal length to do them justice. And even so, there would certainly be omissions.

Among slicing sausages the best known and most widely available are Italian *salami*, flavoured with garlic, chilli, paprika, fennel seeds, wine. The Provençal equivalent is the *saucisson sec*, a portmanteau name for a thousand delicious all-meat sausages, sometimes cured in a jacket of herbs, rarely smoked, usually encouraged to grow a protective coat of white mould. Spain's *chorizo*, an equally high-class skinful, is flavoured with garlic, oregano, chilli, red wine, sometimes coriander and cumin, but always plenty of *pimentôn* (otherwise known as paprika). Unlike its equivalents in other regions, *chorizo* is also eaten fresh – most exquisite when grilled until the fat spits, and split and smacked on bread. *Sobresada*, a speciality of Spain's Catalan-speaking Levante region, is a variation on the same theme, skinless *chorizo* pounded with pure lard – addictive spread on bread and grilled. Travellers to Morocco will recognize the same ancestry in *merguez*, the fiery little harissa-spiced grilling sausage popular throughout the Mahgreb.

In the same group – sliceable sausages to be eaten raw – but confined to the northern shores of the Mediterranean where religious taboos do not forbid the culinary use of blood, you'll find highly spiced black puddings, among them the Spanish *morcilla*, the French *boudin*, Italy's *buddino*. All can also be sliced and fried and make a delicious little appetizer, particularly with pickled vegetables.

Also worthy of note are two Italian preserved-pork products, *pancetta* and *lardo*: the first is belly pork, the cut that makes streaky bacon, rolled and salted; the second is fat, pure and simple, the thick layer that protects the back fillet; both are salted, crusted with herbs and dried as for *prosciutto*. To eat raw, slice thinly and eat with thick slices of bread and a sprinkle of salt and pepper: very delicious.

Nuts and seeds

The Mediterranean is particularly blessed with tree nuts: almonds, walnuts, pistachios and hazelnuts. The first three are eaten both green and mature. The green stage occurs briefly in the early summer, when the fruit first forms and is still tender; maturity comes in the autumn, when the nuts are ripe. The almond is considered superior to the walnut for the whiteness of its flesh and its flowery fragrance: much of the crop goes to the confectioners. Ground and infused in water, the almond makes a refreshing milky drink, popular wherever wine is forbidden. The pistachio, with its pale green flesh and delicate flavour, is prized even more highly than the almond as a stuffing for honey-drenched pastries and as a salted table nut to accompany the evening glass of *raki*. Pinenuts – the resinous little kernels of the iron-hard seeds of the stone pine which thrives on the Mediterranean littoral – are the poor man's pistachio. They are free for the gathering but expensive to buy, since each iron-hard shell must be cracked with a hammer and the tiny kernel winkled out by hand.

Nuts for storage are usually heat treated – kiln-dried – to prevent them doing as nature intended and pushing up little green shoots. The process is gentle enough not to affect the flavour. Roasting at a higher heat for a longer period produces a deliciously caramelized flavour and crisp texture.

Seeds, the cheapest nuts on the block, are known in Italy as *passatempo*, time-passers, since they take so long to shell. The seeds of the sunflower (which is mostly grown for oil), pumpkin (also milled for oil), melon and marrow seeds are all edible and good. Harvested when perfectly ripe (if necessary, separated from the pulp and dried) these, too, are much improved by roasting.

To roast nuts of all kinds: shell, spread on a baking tray and toast in a moderate oven for 30–40 minutes, until golden brown. Rub in a towel to loosen the skins and shake in a sieve to lose the debris. Salt and leave to cool before storing. In the uplands of northern Italy, they roast their Christmas hazelnuts in the shell – a delicious surprise. To roast seeds allow 20–30 minutes – crack to check, since the husk won't change colour much. With practice, you can become as adept as a Mediterranean urchin at cracking the shells between your teeth and rejecting all but the sweet little nut within.

Devilled almonds

Almonds are everyone's favourite nibble. Throughout the region, but particularly in those lands such as Andalusia where the almond tree thrives, toasted almonds are set on the table with the glass of wine or raki or whatever is the chosen refreshment as automatically as the bowl of olives. A member of the plum family, almonds have stocked the Mediterranean larder since prehistoric times. Native to the more southerly shores, they feature in the inventories of the Palace of Knossos at Crete, were nibbled at the banquets of Babylon, savoured at the court of Charlemagne. The Moors planted almond trees from the Jordan valley in the shady gardens of Granada's Alhambra – but by the time the New World had added the chillis to spice up the mix, the sons of the Mahgreb had withdrawn to the shores of Africa, abandoning for ever the gardens they called the ante-room to paradise. It was the impetuous Isabel of Castile, rather than her careful consort Ferdinand of Aragon, who sold her jewels to fund the voyage of a crazy Genoese adventurer with his talk of a new spice route to the east.

Makes 500g / 1lb

500g / 1lb blanched almonds
1 tablespoon olive oil
1 teaspoon salt
1 tablespoon *pimentón* (paprika)
1 teaspoon ground coriander
1 teaspoon ground cumin
½ teaspoon ground chilli (more if you like it hot)

Preheat the oven to 180°C/350°F/gas 4.

Spread the almonds on an oiled baking tray, trickle with the oil and shake the tin to coat the nuts, add salt, and roast gently for 15–20 minutes until just golden – shake regularly to avoid sticking, and don't let them brown. A perfectly toasted almond squeaks when you bite it. Or halve the heat and double the time – temperature is less important than a watchful eye. Sprinkle with the spices, shake to coat and return to the oven for a moment to set the flavours. Leave to cool before storing in an airtight container.

Roasted chickpeas

Call these the poor man's salted almond. Crisp, nutty and cheap, roasted chickpeas have long been appreciated by Mediterranean children. There's evidence that they were the favourite nibble in pre-Neolithic Sicily: the ancient Egyptians cultivated acres of them. Chickpea plants trailed their delicate leaves over Nebuchadnezzar's hanging gardens at Babylon. Although not usually eaten fresh, there's a short period in mid-summer when they can be eaten green and raw: the flavour is much like fresh peas, but the juices are sufficiently acid to stain your fingers black. In Andalusia, when we grew a crop every year for the storecupboard, my neighbours taught me to add the pinched-out shoots to the beanpot. At feria-time the village baker would put a tray of chickpeas to roast in his cooling bread oven as a special treat for the pupils at the little school my own children attended. The lessons were somewhat unusual. Pupils were taught practical skills such as how to set home-made traps in the bean-patch; once the rabbit was in the bag, they received instruction in the proper way of curing the skin and sewing it up into a waistcoat. Peter Rabbit wouldn't have stood a chance.

Makes about 500g / 1lb

500g / 1lb chickpeas, soaked in cold water overnight
olive oil for greasing
salt (optional)

Preheat the oven to 150°C/300°F/gas 2.

Drain the chickpeas thoroughly and dry them in a cloth. Spread in a single layer on a lightly oiled baking sheet, and set them to roast in a low oven until dry, crisp and golden – about an hour, depending on the age of the original material. Shake regularly to avoid sticking. Or dry-fry the drained chickpeas over the lowest possible heat – be careful, they jump like popcorn. Delicious eaten warm, salted or not, as you please. To store, cool (don't salt) and pack in a jar with a well fitting lid – all the same, the fresher the better.

Hummus bi tahini

The staple of the Middle Eastern mezze table, often served in combination with an aubergine dip, the two purées swirled in concentric circles on the same plate, so that both can be scooped up simultaneously. If you haven't the time or inclination to cook your own chickpeas – they freeze at any stage, ready-soaked or fully cooked – tinned is fine.

Serves 4–6

250g / 8oz chickpeas, soaked overnight in cold water
3 cloves garlic, roughly chopped
3 tablespoons tahini
juice of 1 lemon
1 tablespoon ground cumin
salt and freshly ground black pepper

Drain the chickpeas and put them in a roomy saucepan with plenty of cold water. Don't add salt. Bring to the boil, turn down the heat to simmer, cover loosely and maintain the gentle simmer for the whole length of the cooking time, 1–3 hours, depending on the length of the soaking and the age of the chickpeas. If you need to add more water, make sure it's boiling. When the chickpeas are perfectly soft, drain well, reserving a cupful of the cooking liquor and a few whole chickpeas for decoration.

Tip the cooked, cooled chickpeas with enough liquor to moisten into a blender or food processor (for this preparation above all others, using a processor is unquestionably easier than the traditional pestle and mortar). Add the garlic, tahini, lemon juice, cumin, salt and pepper. Liquidize thoroughly until you have a thick purée – you may need a little more liquid to dilute or a handful of breadcrumbs to thicken. Taste and add whatever is needed in the way of extra seasoning. Decorate with the reserved chickpeas.

Yoghurt and soft cheese

Yoghurt is simply a natural way of extending the shelf life of milk, a perishable protein source, under circumstances in which refrigeration was not an option.

All you need to make your own yoghurt is around 600ml / 1 pint fresh milk warmed to finger-heat, a tablespoonful of yoghurt from an earlier batch (or buy a carton of live yoghurt to start you off), and enough warmth to ensure that it doesn't catch cold, a bit like nursing a sourdough starter. 43°C is the commercially recommended temperature. Your yoghurt will be ready to eat in 6–8 hours. To make a thick strained yoghurt, leave to drip in a clean cloth for a few hours. To carry the process a stage further, beat with a little salt – a scant teaspoonful per pint – and leave to drain overnight. The following morning you will have a relatively small amount of pure white curd cheese and a lot of whey. Roll the curd into little balls and sprinkle with salt. That's all. Serve as a *mezze* (see page 37). Or use in any recipe that calls for curd cheese.

To store, dry the little balls on a clean cloth in a cool larder for two days – roll them around every now and again – and then pack them into a large glass jar (sterilized either in the oven or by scalding with boiling water). Pour in enough olive oil to submerge the balls completely, poking them down to loosen any air bubbles. Seal tightly and keep the jar in the fridge.

Tsatsiki

Sharp-flavoured and refreshing, somewhere between a salad and a dip, this is one of the trio likely to appear on the table in every Greek café as soon as you settle down for an ouzo. The others are taramosalata and melitzanosalata – respectively, purée of salted fish roe and aubergine (pages 190 and 105). In Greece you can buy a particularly thick, drained, sheep's milk yoghurt prepared specially for the making of tsatsiki. Alternatively, leave ordinary yoghurt to drain overnight in a cloth pinned onto the legs of an upturned stool, or in a jelly bag. The thicker the yoghurt and the drier the cucumber, the better the result. Those dainty souls who find raw garlic a little overpowering can replace the pungent bulb with finely chopped spring onion and a handful of shredded mint.

Serves 4–6

1 large tub (about 500g / 15oz) thick, strained yoghurt
1 small cucumber, or ½ large, peeled or not as you please, finely grated
2–3 cloves garlic, finely chopped or grated

Beat the yoghurt in a bowl to liquidize it. Tip the grated cucumber into a colander or sieve and leave to drain for 10 minutes or so. Don't salt it unless you want to speed up the draining process, in which case you will have to rinse it thoroughly before you add it to the yoghurt – salt hardens the casein and makes the yoghurt lumpy. Stir all three ingredients together to blend.

Cheese

The cheeses of the Mediterranean fall into three main groups: fresh white soft-curd cheeses; storable hard cut-curd cheeses (not unlike a dried version of our Cheddar), uncut curd cheeses which melt into long strings (as in mozzarella). The milk animal can be sheep, goat, cow or buffalo – I have news of camel but no direct experience. As far as I can ascertain – cheesemakers being a passionate bunch – all types of cheese can be made with all types of milk. All types too can be served as an appetizer.

For the simplest of *mezze*, serve fresh white curd cheeses with bread, sprinkled with fresh herbs, garlic, paprika, cumin, chilli, pickles, fresh walnuts – whatever pleases you – and trickle with a little olive oil. To serve fresh white pressed-curd cheeses such as feta: slice thickly, trickle with olive oil and sprinkle with oregano and black pepper or *kirmizi biber* – particularly pungent Turkish chilli flakes. To serve semi-mature pressed-curd cheeses (Spanish manchego, Greek kefalotiri, all the storecupboard cheeses of the milder sort): remove the rind, slice or cut in bite-sized cubes, and serve with olives, spring onions, pickled vegetables, radishes. Provençal small goat's cheeses make an excellent appetizer: if fresh, serve with radishes and rough salt; if semi-mature, slice in half horizontally, slip on a round of toasted bread, bubble briefly under the grill and pop on a salad of mustardy leaves; if mature, save for dessert. To serve mature cheeses such as Italian pecorino or grana (including Parmesan): shave thin slivers onto sliced tomatoes or a warm salad of haricot or butterbeans – or any bland salad leaves or vegetables that would benefit from its salty pungency.

Cheese biscuits

A Greek version of a universal recipe – koulourakia me kefalotire. There are plenty of others, but the Greek butter-biscuit is particularly light, rich and fragrant. The aniseeds aid digestion, and the ouzo evaporates as the biscuits bake, ensuring a deliciously crisp crumb. Instead of the butter the shortening can be olive oil (if virgin, heat and allow to cool before using), or fresh pork lard (which is preferred in Spain). Possible additions – toppings, mixings – are sesame seeds, pistachios, pinekernels, paprika. The stronger the cheese, the tastier the biscuits. Double the pleasure with a fresh curd cheese mashed with a little oil for scooping. Reheat to serve: happiness is a warm biscuit.

Makes about 18

250g / 8oz clarified butter, softened
250g / 8oz grated kefalotiri (or any hard cheese, including Cheddar)
250g / 8oz plain flour
1 teaspoon salt
about 2 tablespoons *ouzo* or *raki* or *pastis*
extra flour for dusting
1 teaspoon aniseeds

Beat the butter with the cheese until light and creamy. Work to a soft dough with the flour sieved with the salt, and a little ouzo – enough to make a soft dough. Form into a ball, cover with clingfilm, and leave in a cool place to rest for 30 minutes.

Preheat the oven to 190°C/375°F/gas 5.

On a well floured board, roll the dough lightly into a sausage about 5cm / 2 in in diameter. Cover with clingfilm (at this point you can freeze conveniently ready for slicing) and leave to firm again for 10 minutes or so. Cut on the diagonal into bite-sized disks about as thick as a pound coin. Transfer to a baking tray (no need to grease), sprinkle the tops with aniseed – just a few per biscuit, patted lightly into the surface.

Bake for 12–14 minutes, until pale gold – don't let them brown. Allow to cool a little and transfer carefully to a wire tray. At this point they're soft: don't worry – they'll crisp as they cool. If they're not crisp enough, or you store them carelessly and they go stale, slip them back into the oven to gild a little more. Best when freshly baked, though they keep well in a perfectly airtight tin.

Dipping sauces

Mediterranean man cannot live by bread alone – he needs a trickle of oil and a rub of garlic. There are literally hundreds of recipes for these little preparations throughout the region, some sophisticated, some minimalist, depending on the skill and inclination of the cook. When oil meets yolk under the right conditions the two join together to form an emulsion. Miraculous. But the trick won't work at all unless both ingredients are at the same temperature when you begin.

All recipes serve 4–6

Mayonnaise

2 egg yolks
1 teaspoon mustard (optional, but it helps the emulsion)
about 600ml / ¾ pint olive oil
about 1 teaspoon wine vinegar or lemon juice
about 1 teaspoon salt

In a bowl, whisk the yolks with the optional mustard until they are thoroughly blended. Gradually whisk in the oil drop by drop until you see the emulsion forming, then use a wooden spoon to beat in a steady stream until the sauce is as thick as soft butter, a golden mass that holds its shape on the spoon. The amount of oil the emulsion accepts depends on the size of the yolks, the warmth of the day, the mood of the cook. If, in spite of your tranquillity of mind and the perfection of your ingredients, the stuff does divide into its parts, keep calm, work a little boiling water into one corner until a new emulsion forms, and then draw in the rest. If this doesn't work, start again with another yolk, adding the split mixture as if it were oil. Salt to taste.

If you are not serving the mayonnaise immediately, set it with a splash of boiling water. Store leftovers in the fridge – mayo is vulnerable to bugs. Don't stir, or, sure as eggs is eggs, it'll split. Life's like that. If it does, let it come to room temperature before working it into a new yolk.

The basic emulsion can be diluted and sharpened and flavoured in any way you please. For a *sauce verte* as a dip for raw vegetables combine with chopped herbs – tarragon, parsley, chervil, chives; for a modern *aïoli*, combine with crushed garlic (exquisite with plain-boiled winter vegetables); for a poor-man's *sauce tartar* stir in chopped dill, capers, gherkins, pickled onion; for a *sauce marie rose* for shrimps, stir in a little tomato paste.

Allioli

100g / 4oz whole blanched almonds, roughly chopped
3–4 cloves garlic, crushed
1 tablespoon rough salt
2–3 tablespoons lemon juice or wine vinegar
about 150ml / ¼ pint extra-virgin olive oil

The emulsion can be based on garlic alone, as it was prepared in the days of innocence, of troubadours and maidens as beautiful as they were chaste – before some bright spark, seeking the easy way out, mixed in an egg yolk and transformed it into the modern garlic mayonnaise.

In a mortar pound to a paste the almonds, garlic and salt, moistened with a little of the lemon juice or vinegar – or whizz up in the liquidizer. With a wooden spoon, work in the oil gradually in a thin stream until you have a thick, emulsified sauce. Don't expect it to hold its shape on the spoon or thicken like a mayonnaise. Serve without delay and without refrigeration – the emulsion is fragile. To bring it back if it splits, whisk in a splash of boiling water, working from one corner and drawing in the rest as soon as the emulsion re-forms. If all else fails, work it with a tablespoon of fresh white breadcrumbs or warm mashed potato.

Delicious with raw or plain-cooked vegetables (try it in winter with chunks of pumpkin, sweet potato, quince), with artichokes, hardboiled eggs, raw apples, raw cardoon. Excellent as a dipping sauce for fish, particularly prawns or anything in batter.

Skordalia

1 whole garlic bulb (10–12 cloves), skinned
1 teaspoon salt
about 300ml / ½ pint olive oil
4 tablespoons wine vinegar
1 large potato, boiled in its jacket, skinned while still hot

Pound the garlic cloves with the salt – the Greeks use a special pestle and mortar, but a food processor is less hard on the muscles. Gradually trickle in the oil, adding the vinegar as you go, as if making a mayonnaise, beating vigorously until you have a thick emulsion. Mash the hot potato and beat in the garlicky sauce, a little at a time. The higher the proportion of potato to oil, the thicker the purée, the easier it is to scoop, and the less delicate it is – but I expect you can work all that out for yourself.

The classic Greek accompaniment for savoury fritters, particularly salt cod and deep-fried aubergines, and also, curiously, beetroot salad – roots and leaves, otherwise plain and unadorned. It can be made with oil and garlic alone, with or without the addition of breadcrumbs and/or nuts (pinekernels, pistachios, almonds, walnuts, hazelnuts). Potato, being a post-Columbian import, is the newest of all – and this is the version I give here. Though potato is frowned upon by purists – I've heard it described as a Cypriot habit – it's remarkably good. Choose a mealy potato, a masher, and pick fresh young garlic (you can remove the green shoots from older cloves but the flesh will still be bitter if used raw). Lemon juice can be used instead of vinegar. Possible additions are finely chopped parsley, leaf coriander, chilli, spring onion, cumin, paprika – do as you wish. Mediterranean cooks aren't afraid to innovate.

Bagna Cauda

300ml / ½ pint red wine
8 cloves garlic, skinned and slivered
8–10 salted anchovy fillets
150ml / ¼ pint extra-virgin olive oil
50g / 2oz butter, cut into small pieces

Bring the wine to the boil in a small saucepan – not necessarily the one in which you mean to bring the sauce to table – and bubble up for a few minutes to evaporate the alcohol. Add the garlic, anchovy fillets and the oil, bring back to the boil and stir in the butter.

Turn down the heat and let it all simmer away gently for about 40 minutes, until the anchovies have completely melted and amalgamated with the oil to make a smooth, unctuous and perfectly emulsified sauce – you can help the process along by beating with a wooden spoon. Prepare the sauce in advance if you like and reheat it before bringing it to the table.

Serve with raw vegetables for dipping: carrot, celery, cardoon, baby arti-chokes, red peppers (don't bother with the green – they're unripe fruit and thoroughly indigestible); plain-boiled potatoes; red peppers gently fried in oil – the sweet flesh is remarkably good with the salty dip; unsalted bread, as they bake it in the north of Italy.

To serve, set the pan over some kind of heat source – you can purchase special little earthenware pots with a space beneath for a nightlight – and keep the sauce bubbling while everyone dips in their vegetables.

Pesto genovese

4 handfuls fresh basil (measured as below)
2 cloves garlic, roughly chopped
I teaspoon coarse salt
2 tablespoons pinekernels, toasted
2 heaped tablespoons freshly grated Parmesan
2 tablespoons freshly grated pecorino
about 100ml / 4fl oz extra-virgin olive oil

A handful of basil is as many stalks as will comfortably fit into the circle of your index finger and thumb – apologies for the inexactness! According to my informant, a Genoese granny who has been making pesto since she was knee high to a green Ligurian grasshopper, no other measurement is possible.

For the silkiest of sauces, use a pestle and mortar – it's a revelation. Strip the basil leaves from their stalks. Pound the garlic with the salt to make a soft mush. Work in the leaves one by one with a circular motion, always in the same direction, until all is reduced to a smooth paste. Work in the pinekernels and the cheeses, pounding until the sauce is perfectly smooth. With a wooden spoon, gradually work in as much olive oil as the emulsion will accept.

Salsa romesco

3 large ripe tomatoes, skinned, deseeded and chopped
3 cloves garlic, roughly chopped
I tablespoon toasted hazelnuts
2 red peppers, roasted, deseeded and skinned
2–3 dried chillis, deseeded (or I teaspoon cayenne or ground chilli)
100ml / 4fl oz olive oil
2 tablespoons red wine vinegar
I teaspoon salt and a pinch sugar

The Catalans use dried *romesco* peppers – sweet and a little hot – soaked until soft, then scraped from the skin, but I have given a more easily available alternative.

Drop all the ingredients in the liquidizer and process to a purée. Taste and adjust the seasoning – more sugar? Goes with anything and everything with which you might like to serve a mayonnaise.

Tahiniyeh

200g / 7oz tahini
juice of 2 lemons
about 300ml / ½ pint milk or water
2–3 cloves garlic, crushed with a little salt
salt to taste
about 2 heaped tablespoons fresh breadcrumbs
1 teaspoon ground cumin
1 teaspoon chilli or cayenne or freshly ground white pepper

Optional to finish
finely chopped parsley, spring onion, coriander

Tahini – sesame-seed paste – provides both the thickening and the oily element.

Fork up the tahini in a bowl with the lemon juice until smooth. Whisk or beat in enough milk or water to make a thin cream. Stir in the crushed garlic and enough breadcrumbs to make a scoopable purée. Taste and season with a little more salt, cumin and your choice of pepper. To make a speckled sauce, stir in the greens; to keep it simple, leave them out. Easy.

Breads & wrappers

Home-baked bread – a loaf finished with a topping of herbs, a sprinkle of cheese, shiny black olives, a trickle of oil – should be the first and last resort of the lazy cook. Bake a loaf and you scarcely need to cook anything else. Add a plate of charcuterie, a salad, a piece of cheese – and the meal is done.

Wheat and water are the breadmaker's only essentials, making the quality of both of paramount importance. In the old days, when rural households did their own baking, water was needed in abundance, not simply for mixing but to turn the wheel for the milling of the grain. The quality of the wheat is dictated by soil and climate as well as selective breeding. Bread-making flour is milled from strong, hard grains which yield a sturdy elastic crumb – soft cake flours can never make good bread.

If the bread is to be leavened, there must be yeast – the tiny fungoid organisms that feed on the sugar in fruit, milk products, grain-mash, whatever comes to hand. Wild yeasts can bounce up all over the place. Given time and warmth, a bit of wet dough will attract the necessary and ferment naturally, producing a starter-dough that can carry on from batch to batch for years, even centuries, given a following wind. The secret of leavening was known to the Ancient Egyptians, innovative farmers who evolved a strain of wheat which could be husked without preliminary parching, a process which destroys the raw gluten on which yeast feeds. Since the fungi thrive wherever beer or wine is made, the Christians took over where the Muslims fell behind. The most sophisticated leavened breads are those of the northern shores of the Mediterranean. In Arab lands, although unleavened breads have evolved to include yeast, they retain their primary function as a wrapper and scooper – a vehicle for other foods.

All traditional breads, leavened or unleavened, can be eaten soft and fresh, or stored for later. Stale bread becomes perfectly palatable when toasted: recipes include Italy's *crostini*, the Catalan *pa amb tomaquèt*. Hard bread requires pre-soaking to become palatable, leading to bread-porridges such as the Italian *panzanella* and a lasagne in which slices of bread replace the pasta; the Lebanese *fattoush*; Andalusia's sturdy peasant *gazpacho* (in its rural incarnation a thick garlicky bread-porridge), the Provençal *pan bagnat*. All are dishes delicious enough in their own right to have survived long after the need has gone.

Pan candeal
Andalusian sourdough bread

3

Pan candeal – *Spanish country bread – weighs heavy in the hand, has a dense, cream-coloured, speckled crumb and a deep brown crust. Neither wholemeal nor, strictly speaking, white bread, I have never found anything like it anywhere else in the region. You'll still occasionally find it baked in the old way in country districts, using dough from the day before as a leavening, shaped by hand. If your starter refuses to bubble, start again with water in which you have soaked a handful of chickpeas for long enough for the soaking liquid to fizz – about 24 hours in a warm place. Fermented fruit juice will serve the same purpose.*

Makes two 1kg / 2lb loaves

2kg / 4lb strong white bread flour
1 heaped tablespoon salt
warm water

In a warm bowl, work 100g / 4oz of the flour with 100ml / 4fl oz warm water to make a thick cream. Cover and set aside in a warm place for 24 hours. Work another 100g / 4oz flour and 100ml / 4fl oz of warm water into this mixture and set aside in a warm place for another 24 hours to bubble and ferment. This is your starter dough – the stuff that lightens the bread.

Weigh out 200g / 8oz of the starter dough (freeze the extra – it'll revive with warm water) and work with 750g / 1½lb flour and enough warm water – about 600ml / 1 pint – to make a soft, very wet dough. Cover and leave overnight in a warm place.

The next day, knead in another 750g / 1½lb flour, the salt and about 350ml / 12fl oz warm water. Knead the dough vigorously on a floured surface – push and twist with the crook of your fingers and the heel of your hand – until it is elastic and smooth. Cover and set aside for an hour or two until it has doubled in bulk, when it should be spongy enough to bounce back when you prod it.

Tip the dough out again onto the floured surface and knuckle it vigorously to distribute the air bubbles. Divide it in two, knead each piece into a ball and flatten it into a thick fat cake about the size of a dinnerplate. Flip one half over the other to make a fat semicircular bolster. Give the ends a little twist, like knotting a hankie. Transfer to a baking tray dusted with flour and prick the top in a few places. Cover with a clean cloth and set in a warm place to allow it to recover its volume – 30–40 minutes.

Preheat the oven to maximum – 250°C/475°F/gas 9.

Slip the tray gently into the oven – the loaves deflate easily at this vulnerable moment. Bake for 15 minutes, after which you can do what you like – they won't feel a thing. Turn the oven down to 180°C/350°F/gas 4 and bake for another 40–45 minutes, until the loaves are nicely browned and sound hollow when you tap the base.

Ciabatta

Italian slipper bread

3 | *Ciabatta is a modern invention – Italy's answer to the Middle Eastern* pitta. *It's an ordinary yeast-raised bread dough, flattened like a* ciapatta *– a slipper – and is easy enough to prepare. The cornmeal or semolina gives a rustic texture and colour to the crumb.*

Makes 4 breads

600g / 1lb strong white bread flour
1 tablespoon fine-ground cornmeal (polenta) or semolina
1 teaspoon salt
1 tablespoon olive oil
25g / 1oz fresh yeast (12g / ½oz dried)
about 300ml / ½ pint warm water
extra olive oil and flour and semolina for dusting

Sieve the flour into a warm bowl, stir in the cornmeal and salt and crumble in the yeast much as if you were making pastry. (If you are using dried yeast, follow the instructions on the packet.) Make a well in the middle and pour in the oil and three-quarters of the water.

Using the hook of your hand or the dough-hook on the food processor, work the warm liquid into the dry ingredients, adding as much of the extra water as you need to make a soft, sticky dough, as wet as you can handle. Knead the dough well for about 10 minutes – push and tug – to stretch the gluten, form it into a ball and dust it with flour. Set it to rise under a damp cloth or clingfilm in a warm place for a couple of hours until it has more than doubled in bulk – the aim is a well risen dough with nice big bubbles to make a crisp, light bread.

Preheat the oven to 200°C/400°F/gas 6.

Dust your hands and the table with flour. Scoop out the bubbly dough and knock it down roughly with your fists to distribute the air. Cut it into quarters and work each piece into a ball. Flatten each ball into a *pitta* shape, about 8cm / 3in long by 4–5cm / 1½–2in broad, transfer to semolina-dusted baking sheets, poke the surface in two or three places with your fingers, and trickle the dents with a little oil. Leave to rise in a warm kitchen for 10–15 minutes.

Bake for 18–25 minutes in the preheated oven, until well risen and beautifully brown. Transfer to a wire rack. Eat warm and fresh – extras can be frozen.

> **Good with** . . . any and all salads; *prosciutto* and *salami*; cheese; grilled meats; fish – absolutely everything and anything. Or simply rub the hot crumb with a little garlic, trickle with extra-virgin olive oil and take pleasure in simplicity.

Focaccia

Ligurian sage and onion bread

3

Liguria's version of the Neapolitan pizza, sold hot from the oven to schoolchildren and office workers who form queues outside the specialist bakeries at midday. Sage and onion is a distinctively Ligurian flavouring – although you'll also find toppings of tomato and rosemary. In the seaside town of Recco they make an unleavened focaccia with an oil-rich pasta dough spun on the back of hands to produce fine disks – a process much like filo-making – which are sandwiched together in pairs with dollops of stracchino, a slithery curd cheese not unlike very soft mozzarella.

Serves 4 hungry Ligurians

750g / 1½lb strong white bread flour (00 – double-zero – for preference)
2 tablespoons semolina (not necessary if you use double-zero)
1 teaspoon salt
25g / 1oz fresh yeast (12g / ½oz dried)
100ml / 4fl oz extra-virgin olive oil
about 450ml / ¾ pint warm water
6 sage leaves, chopped
extra flour and semolina for dusting

To finish
1 small onion, very finely sliced vertically
1 tablespoon black olives and small sprigs of sage – top leaves only
a little olive oil and coarse salt

Sieve the flour into a warm bowl with the semolina, salt and crumbled yeast. (If you are using dried yeast, follow the instructions on the packet.) Work in the oil and warm water, gradually drawing enough of the liquid into the flour until you have a smooth, very soft dough-ball. Cover and set in a warm place for an hour or so, until it is light and spongy and has doubled in volume.

Knead the dough on a floured surface with the chopped sage, working thoroughly to distribute the air bubbles. Cut it in half, work each piece into a ball, and press flat. Transfer to a couple of lightly oiled, semolina-dusted baking sheets and pat out to the thickness of your little finger. Dust lightly with semolina, cover loosely with a cloth and leave to rise again for an hour.

Preheat the oven to 230°C/450°F/gas 8.

Sprinkle the risen dough with sliced onion and olives, punch the surface with stiff fingers to make dimples, trickle a little oil into the dips, shove in a few sage tops, scatter with coarse salt and sprinkle lightly with warm water from your fingertips. Bake for 20–25 minutes until puffed and golden.

Good with . . . stuffed squid with fennel (page 179); clams in tomato sauce (page 186).

Pide

Turkish pitta breads

3 *Although Middle Eastern breads appear to differ little one from another – variations are most obvious in shape, thickness, whether griddle- or oven-baked – the texture and flavour of the basic dough depends on the quality and milling methods of the local flour, the taste of the water, the purity and texture of the salt. The pouch in these pittas is produced by allowing a rest period for the dough to puff, and baking in the hottest part of the oven.*

Makes about a dozen

600g / 1lb strong white bread flour
½ teaspoon salt
15g / ½oz fresh yeast (7g / ¼oz dried)
about 300ml / ½ pint warm water
a pinch of sugar

2 tablespoons yoghurt
extra flour for dusting
a little oil for greasing
1 tablespoon nigella or sesame seeds
   for dusting (optional)

Sift the flour with the salt into a warm bowl. Dissolve the yeast in a splash of the warm water and add a pinch of sugar to start it working. (If you are using dried, follow the instructions on the packet.) As soon as it bubbles up, make a well in the centre of the flour and pour in the yeasty water and the yoghurt. Mix well by hand, working in enough of the remaining water to make a soft, sticky dough. Knead the dough on a floured surface until it is quite smooth and elastic – this will take at least 20 minutes. Form the dough into a ball and slick it with oil (pour a little into your hand and swipe it over the dough). Cover with a clean cloth and leave to rise for an hour or two in a warm place, until it has doubled in size.

Preheat the oven to maximum temperature – 250°C/475°F/gas 9.

Punch the dough down with your knuckles and knead it for a few more minutes. Take lumps of dough the size of a medium potato and flatten them on a floured board with your hand – they should be about 0.5cm / ¼in thick. Cover again and leave to rise for another 20 minutes.

Brush a couple of baking sheets with oil and slip them in the oven. When the sheets are smoking hot, smack on the *pittas*, sprinkle with the optional seeds, and dampen them with a sprinkle of cold water from your fingertips to stop them browning. Bake for 6–12 minutes – you can tell when they're done by the rich earthy aroma that replaces the scent of yeast. Transfer to a rack to cool and wrap in a cloth to keep soft. The *pitta* should be soft and white with a pouch inside just made for stuffing.

Good with . . . *tsatsiki* (page 36); *hummus* (page 34); any of the bean purées. Also as a container for any foods that need wrappers – kebabs, grilled meats, fish.

Fougasse aux lardons
Provençal pork-crackling bread

3

A slipper-shaped bread enriched with pork cracklings, perfect with the classic cold hors d'oeuvre of hardboiled eggs (mashed with anchovies), carrot salad dressed with nut oil and toasted sesame seeds, grated celeriac in a mustardy mayonnaise, tinned sardines.

Makes 2 breads to serve 6–8

1kg / 2lb strong white bread flour
1 tablespoon semolina
25g / 1oz fresh yeast (12g / ½oz dried)
about 600ml / 1 pint warm water
50g / 2oz crisp pork-skin cracklings, broken into small pieces
semolina for dusting

Grease two large baking sheets and dust with semolina.

Sift the flour into a large warm bowl and stir in the tablespoon of semolina.

Mix the yeast with 150ml / ¼ pint of the warm water, and sprinkle in 4 heaped tablespoons of the flour – enough to work into a dough-ball with the yeast and water. (If you are using dried yeast follow the instructions on the packet.) Cut a deep cross in the ball and put it in a bowl with the rest of the warm water. Leave it until it swells and bobs to the surface – this will take about 5 minutes.

Make a well in the flour and drop in the dough-ball. Work all well together, adding enough of the warm water to give you a soft, sticky dough. Work in the cracklings. Cut the dough in half and knead each piece into a ball. Flatten the balls lightly with your hand and transfer them to the prepared baking sheets. Pat the balls out evenly with your hand to make slipper shapes about 38cm / 15in long, pulling the dough to stretch. Set to rise for 40–60 minutes in a warm place under a clean cloth or clingfilm, well away from any draught. (Yeast-doughs can catch cold and collapse – a problem if you're giving them only one chance to rise.)

Preheat the oven to 150°C/300°F/gas 2 and set a roasting pan of *boiling* water on the base.

Cut diagonal slashes in the breads, as if marking the veins on a leaf. Leave to rise again for another 10 minutes before transferring to the oven. Bake for 10 minutes, then raise the oven temperature to 200°C/400°F/gas 6. Bake for another 20 minutes or so, until the loaves are well risen, with a crisp brown crust. Transfer to a wire rack to cool.

Good with . . . baked aubergines with anchovies (page 109); Provençal tomatoes (page 123); *ratatouille* (page 125); mushroom *tian* (see page 154).

Piadine con basilico e pinoli
Italian flat-bread with basil and pinekernels

3 *A simple, modern Italian picnic bread for scooping, based on a plain scone dough flavoured with the classic pesto combination, patted out and dry-fried – not unlike a sophisticated wheat-flour tortilla.*

Makes about a dozen

600g / 1lb strong white bread flour
1 teaspoon salt
1 teaspoon bicarbonate of soda
1 tablespoon toasted pinekernels
1 tablespoon chopped basil
300ml / ½ pint milk (soured, preferably)
1 tablespoon olive oil

To finish
olive oil for shallow-frying

Sieve the flour into a warm bowl with the salt and bicarbonate of soda. Toss with the nuts and the basil and make a dip in the centre. Pour in the milk and knead lightly into a smooth, soft dough-ball. Cover with clingfilm and let it rest for half an hour to swell the grain – although if you're in a hurry the dough can be used immediately.

Break off little lumps of dough the size of a small fig, and roll or pat out thinly with floured hands on a floured surface to make flat pancakes no larger than your frying pan.

Heat the pan and add a little oil. When just smoking, drop in the first pancake and cook until it is lightly blistered, turning once. The more oil you use, the crisper will be the pancakes. Transfer to a clean cloth and wrap to keep warm – the pancakes will soften in the cloth. Continue until all are cooked.

Good with . . . anything scoopable, particularly crisp chopped salads – tomato with fennel, cucumber with pitted black olives, roasted red peppers with garlic, mild onion with Cos lettuce, rocket and lamb's lettuce.

Pissaladière aux poireaux
Provençal leek and cheese tart

 Neither a pizza nor a quiche but something in between – an open-topped tart based on a lemon-scented bread dough with a creamy leek filling.

Serves 4–6

For the dough
150g / 6oz strong white bread flour
1 teaspoon dried yeast
½ teaspoon salt
1 teaspoon very finely grated lemon zest
1 egg
2 tablespoons warm water
3 tablespoons olive oil
50g / 2oz hard cheese (Cantal, Gruyère or mature Cheddar), grated

For the filling
3 medium leeks (white part only), thinly sliced
1–2 tablespoons olive oil
2–3 cloves garlic, finely chopped
8–10 black olives, pitted and chopped
1 tablespoon chopped parsley and a little chopped thyme
3 eggs
300ml / ½ pint *crème fraîche* (soured cream)
salt and freshly ground black pepper

First make the pastry. Sift the dry ingredients (including the lemon zest) into a warm bowl and make a well in the middle. Crack in the egg, add the water and the oil and work all together into a soft, smooth dough-ball – you may need a little more water. Set it to rise under a damp cloth in a warm place until it has doubled in bulk – about an hour. Oil a 23cm / 9in flan tin and roll out the dough to fit – it should be thin on the base, thicker on the sides, and rise about a finger's width above the tin's edge. Sprinkle with the grated cheese.

Preheat the oven to 190°C/375°F/gas 5.

Meanwhile, make the filling. Fry the leeks gently in the oil until they soften. Add the garlic, olives, parsley and thyme, cover loosely and leave to cook gently for 5–6 minutes. Remove from the heat and leave to cool before mixing with the eggs forked up with the cream. Season and pour into the tart base. Bake for 40–45 minutes, until the filling is golden but still a little wobbly in the centre. Serve warm.

Good with . . . something crisp in the way of raw vegetables; a tapenade (page 27).

Gözleme
Turkish flatbreads stuffed with greens

3

Unleavened bread, thin and soft, baked over a charcoal fire – this is the kind of food that would have been familiar to our cavemen ancestors. The cooking instrument is a dome-shaped iron griddle whose curve is just right to take the variable heat of a campfire. Turkish rural housewives bake it at home, but you'll also find it cooked to order in the marketplace. Unlike most market snacks, gözleme are usually prepared by women – matrons and grannies making a little pin-money – who sit crosslegged in front of the cooking-fires, broomhandle rolling-pin at the ready.

Serves 4

100g / 4oz strong white bread flour
½ teaspoon salt
1 tablespoon olive oil or melted butter
about 5 tablespoons warm water
extra olive oil or butter to grease the pan

For the filling
4–5 spring onions, trimmed and finely chopped
1–2 cloves garlic, finely chopped
a big handful (about 50g / 2oz) rocket or spinach, shredded
½ teaspoon Turkish mild chilli flakes (*kirmizi biber*) or fresh red chilli, deseeded and
    finely chopped
100g / 4oz feta, crumbled (or cottage cheese)

Sieve the flour and salt into a bowl. Work in the oil and water until you have a nice smooth dough. Knead it a little more. Divide it into four and work each piece into a ball. Cover with a cloth and leave to rest for 20 minutes or so.

On a floured surface, using a well floured rolling-pin (a broomhandle is the preferred instrument in Turkey), roll out each piece into a very thin disk 12–15cm / 5–6in in diameter.

Heat and lightly grease a heavy frying pan or griddle and slap on one of the disks. Use your fingers to move it around so that it blisters and browns. Brush the top with more oil or butter and flip it over.

While the underside is cooking sprinkle the cooked side with a quarter of the filling ingredients. When the underside is done, lift the *gözleme* onto a piece of greaseproof paper and roll it up into a cone. Continue with the other three, and eat hot, straight from the griddle.

> **Good with . . .** stuffed mussels (page 182); meat or fish kebabs.

Pizza napolitana

The most famous of fast-food, an invention credited to the bakers of Naples. At its most basic, this is bread dough topped with a few slices of tomato and mozzarella, trickled with olive oil, perfumed with oregano. Nothing to it, so long as the tomatoes are perfectly ripe, the mozzarella made with buffalo milk, the oil the pure fresh juice of the olive and the oregano wild-gathered from sunny Mediterranean hillsides.

Serves 4

For the dough
500g / 1lb strong white bread flour
½ teaspoon salt
300ml / ½ pint warm water
25g / 1oz fresh yeast (12g / ½oz dried)
2 tablespoons olive oil
extra flour for dusting

For the topping
500g / 1lb ripe plum tomatoes, sliced
125g / 4oz mozzarella, drained and sliced
1 teaspoon dried oregano
2–3 tablespoons olive oil

First make the dough. Sieve the flour into a warm mixing bowl with the salt and make a well in the centre. Dissolve the yeast in a cupful of the warm water and pour it into the well in the flour. (If you are using dried yeast follow the instructions on the packet.) Work this into the flour along with the oil and enough warm water to make a soft, slightly sticky dough. Knead on a lightly floured surface for 10 minutes, until you have a smooth, soft ball. The wetter you can handle the dough the lighter will be the bread: keep flour on the side and dust your hands frequently to avoid sticking. Drop the dough in an oiled bowl, brush with a little more oil and cover tightly with clingfilm. Leave in a warm place to double its bulk – about an hour.

Preheat the oven to maximum – 250°C/475°F/gas 9 – allow plenty of time to get it really hot.

Divide the dough into four pieces, knead each into a ball and pat it out by hand until it is as thin as cardboard. Transfer to a baking sheet dusted lightly with flour. Top each pizza with sliced tomatoes, a few rounds of mozzarella and a sprinkle of oregano. Trickle with oil and bake for 10–15 minutes, until the dough is nicely blistered and the cheese all buttery and bubbling.

Eat fresh from the oven, as they do in Naples, without knife or fork. Close your eyes, take a deep breath, smell the sunshine.

Good with . . . *salami, prosciutto.*

Coca de verdura
Mallorcan spinach pizza

Traditionalists will tell you that a proper coca is simply a flour-and-water dough allowed to ferment in the sun, trickled with oil and baked in the embers of a shepherd's campfire. The traditional fuel being sheep or goat's droppings, you may expect to find little bits of charcoal stuck to the bottom. Serves you right for going native.

Serves 2–4

For the dough
100g / 4oz strong white bread flour
½ teaspoon salt
15g / ½oz fresh yeast (7g / ¼oz dried)
about 4 tablespoons warm water
2 tablespoons melted lard (Spanish lard is very pure and clean) or olive oil

For the topping
a handful of spinach, rinsed, dried and shredded
salt
2 mild onions, thinly sliced
1 tablespoon pinekernels
1 clove garlic, finely chopped
a few slices *chorizo*, or *longaniza* (or any other spicy *salame*)
1 tablespoon chopped marjoram
2–3 tablespoons olive oil

Sieve the flour with the salt into a warm bowl. Dissolve the yeast in the warm water and leave for a few minutes in a warm place until frothy. (If you are using dried yeast follow the instructions on the packet.) Make a well in the flour and pour in the yeast mixture and the lard or oil. Knead well until the dough forms a ball which leaves the sides of the bowl clean – you may need more flour. Drop the dough back in the bowl, cover with a damp cloth or clingfilm and leave in a warm place until the dough has doubled in size – an hour or so, depending on the weather.

Preheat the oven to 240°C/450°F/gas 8.

Knead the dough vigorously to distribute the air bubbles, cut in half and pat each piece out to a diameter of 35cm/14in. Transfer to oiled and flour-dusted baking sheets, spread with the shredded spinach, salt lightly, top with onion, pinekernels, chopped garlic, sausage and marjoram, and trickle with olive oil. Bake for about 20–30 minutes, until the crust is puffy and blistered at the edges.

Good with . . . grilled asparagus (page 86); slivers of salty goat's cheese dressed with oil and paprika.

Pan bagnat
Provençal tomato bread

2

A modest pleasure but good: the Provençal field-worker's piece-for-the-pocket, as taken by harvesters into the olive groves for the midday break. Should you happen to find yourself in southern France you'll see that the bakeries sell special round rolls of the right size for the purpose. The filling is often the leftovers from the Salade niçoise. The late-lamented M. F. K. Fisher, grande dame of America's romantic food writers, described her daughter's music teacher as having completed the recipe by placing her pan bagnat *beneath the cushion on her music stool and sitting on it throughout the lesson.*

Serves 1

half-*baguette* or *ciabatta* (day-old)
garlic clove, halved
olive oil
wine vinegar
tomato, thickly sliced
Cos lettuce leaves, roughly shredded
cucumber, sliced (skinned or not, as you please)
mild onion, finely sliced
anchovy fillets
tinned tuna, drained
capers, drained
black olives, pitted

Split the bread lengthwise, scoop out most of the crumb and rub the rough surface with the garlic clove. Sprinkle with olive oil and a few drops of vinegar, and lay slices of tomato on both sides. Layer in the remaining ingredients, seasoning as you go. Basically, this is a Salade niçoise shoved into a roll. Close it up, squash it down firmly with your hand, and wrap neatly in greaseproof or waxed paper. Weight it down for an hour or two under a plate topped by a heavy object. For absolute authenticity, take it with you and either sit on it or shove it under a stone until it's deliciously squidgy and well marinated.

Good with . . . a well matured *crottin*, the deliciously piquant little hand-made goat's cheeses on sale in every Provençal market; a thick slice of *jambon de Bayonne* or a few slivers of *saucisson sec*.

Fattoush

Lebanese toasted bread and herb salad

For reasons that will be obvious to anyone who has ever lived in isolated places where grain-food is the staple, man cannot live by stale bread alone. If your guests are unused to the notion of a soaked-bread salad, set out all the ingredients separately and encourage everyone to choose and dress their own.

Serves 4

2 *pitta* breads (or Lebanese *khoubiz*)
I small crisp lettuce, coarsely shredded
a large handful of soft salad leaves (purslane, lamb's lettuce, baby spinach)
I green pepper, deseeded and diced
I small cucumber, diced (peeled or not, as you please)
a large handful of mint, leaves only, chopped
a large handful of flat-leaf parsley, chopped
a small bunch of spring onions, trimmed and chopped

To dress
I–2 cloves garlic
I teaspoon coarse salt
2–3 lemons, juice and finely grated zest
150ml / ¼ pint olive oil

Split and toast the bread until the crumb is crisp and brown. Tear or chop into small pieces.

Combine with the salad ingredients in a bowl and leave for 10 minutes or so to soften and to allow the flavours to marry.

Crush the garlic with the salt, and fork in the remaining dressing ingredients. Toss the salad with the dressing. Serve at room temperature, in individual bowls.

> **Good with . . .** kebabs – *souvlakia* (page 230); grilled lamb; *köfte* (page 234).

▶ *Serbian salad (page 102)*

Crostini

Italian savoury toasts

Although they started life as a simple antipasto *– a little more sophisticated than bread and oil, not as much trouble as a purpose-made dish – crostini are now very much part of the fast-food culture. Since office-workers no longer return home for the midday meal, lunch-counters serving what are basically open sandwiches offer an even quicker alternative to the pizza parlour.*

Fresh, toasted, fried or oven-baked bread can be used as the base. Whenever you have leftover bread – ciabatta, baguette, good white bread of any kind – slice and toast it in a low oven until well gilded, crisp and dry. Transfer to a baking rack to cool and store in an airtight tin until needed. The toppings are as variable as sandwich fillings – although rather more artistry can go into the presentation.

Quick crostini toppings

A paste made of anchovies, capers and black olives.

A sliver of *prosciutto* on a slice of ripe tomato.

Chopped hardboiled eggs pounded to a paste with salted anchovies, olive oil and pepper.

Tinned tuna (choose high-quality, preserved in olive oil) and finely chopped spring onion.

Finely sliced *prosciutto* or *salame* with a curl of fresh butter on top.

Slivers of *bottarga* or any other salted fish roe on finely sliced mild onion, olive oil to finish.

Sicilian *caponata*.

Porcini in umido (page 150).

Chicken livers sautéed with garlic and parsley.

Sliced tomato and slivers of Parmesan.

Freshly made pesto (page 42).

Olive oil and shavings of white truffle.

Slices of mozzarella and tomato with olive oil and basil leaves.

Wild mushrooms sautéed in olive oil with finely chopped garlic and parsley.

Simplest of all – a rub of garlic and a trickle of fresh, peppery olive oil.

◀ *Greek beetroot salad (page 130)*

Pa amb tomaquèt

Catalan bread and tomato

2

A quick snack to be taken at any time of the day or night, but particularly breakfast – call it the first tapa of the day. Thick slices of dense-crumbed sourdough bread, pan candeal (see page 47), are popped on a little metal toasting plate with a grid, which sits directly over a flame. The bread is singed – lightly caramelized – rather than toasted. The surface is then rubbed with garlic, trickled with oil and finished with a rub of cut tomato. Success depends on a very precise choice of ingredients: dense-crumbed bread baked in a wood-oven, the freshest garlic, the ripest tomato, the greenest and pepperiest of olive oils. The Catalans grow special rubbing-tomatoes with very soft but not watery flesh.

Serves 4

4 thick slices any dense-crumbed country bread – *pan candeal*
1 clove garlic
2 tablespoons olive oil
2 large ripe beef tomatoes

Preheat the oven to 240°C/450°F/gas 8.

If you're using *ciabatta*, halve it lengthwise and cut in two again to give you four slabs. Set the *ciabatta* or bread slices on a baking sheet, rub the cut surface of the bread with garlic and trickle with oil.

Halve the tomatoes horizontally and set them on the baking sheet with the bread, cut side down. Roast in the hot oven for 20 minutes or so, until the bread is toasted and the tomatoes soft.

Skin and deseed the tomatoes, mash the pulp a little, and spread on the toasted bread.

> **Good with** ... any of Catalonia's vast repertoire of *embutidos* – preserved pork products – particularly *jamón serrano*, *chorizo*, *butifarra*, *longaniza*, *morcilla* (a delicious paprika-and-marjoram-flavoured black pudding).

Lasagne di magro
Italian vegetable bread pudding

A meatless lasagne made with bread rather than pasta, a homely recipe from a chef who cooks in one of the great restaurants in Milan – he says it was the first dish he ever cooked for his mum.

Serves 4

8 slices yesterday's bread, buttered, cut into fingers
4 tablespoons olive oil
1 medium onion, finely chopped
2 cloves garlic, finely chopped
1 large carrot, diced small
1 red pepper, deseeded and finely diced
1 aubergine, finely diced
2 medium courgettes, finely diced
1 teaspoon dried mixed herbs
salt and freshly ground black pepper
2 tablespoons chopped almonds or walnuts
3 eggs
450ml / ¾ pint milk
a pinch of grated nutmeg
3–4 tablespoons grated hard cheese

Preheat the oven to 180°C/350°F/gas 4.

Heat the oil in a frying pan and add the vegetables in the order given, frying a little between each addition. Season with herbs, salt and pepper. Cover loosely and leave the vegetables to cook gently together until perfectly tender – 5–10 minutes.

Beat the eggs into the milk and season with salt, pepper and a little nutmeg.

Arrange a third of the bread, buttered side down, in a shallow ovenproof dish, preferably oblong or square. Pour in a third of the milk-and-egg, sprinkle with a little cheese, then spread on half the vegetable mixture and half the nuts. Repeat. Top with a final layer of bread, custard and cheese.

Slip the dish into the oven and bake for 30–35 minutes, until golden and bubbling. Leave to cool a little and set. Cut into squares to serve, like a bread pudding.

Good with . . . a crisp fennel salad – so good for the digestion.

Paximadia salata

Cretan bread salad

2

Not so much a recipe as a practical solution to the problem of making hard-tack good to eat. The daily bread of rural Crete is the local version of paximadia, *twice-baked barley bread, hard as iron and almost impossible to eat unless you soak it first – preferably, you will be told, in spring water from the mountain streams that make the island one of the most fertile in the Mediterranean. The Cretans use a vast array of edible wild greens in the salad bowl, the most palatable and prolific of which are encouraged as a catch-crop under the olive trees. Nowadays, with the population shifting to the towns and the tourist enclaves on the coast, those who have not forgotten the old ways can command a fair price for their gatherings. In Heraklion market in April I counted more than a dozen wild-gathered leaves, among them borage, poppy, dandelion, silene, corncockle, purslane and the little green bulbs and feathery fronds of wild fennel. Apart from their value as food, all have medicinal properties known to the gatherers and valued by their customers.*

Serves 4

4 wholegrain rolls, the sturdier the better
2 ripe beef tomatoes
olive oil for dressing
4 handfuls spring salad leaves – rocket, spinach, mustard-greens, baby beet,
   watercress, lamb's lettuce, celery leaves
4 tablespoons black Greek olives, pitted and chopped
4 tablespoons crumbled feta
fresh oregano or marjoram leaves
coarse salt
quartered lemons to serve

Split the rolls – tear, don't cut – and set them to bake in a medium oven (180°C/350°F/gas 4) until they are perfectly brown and crisp. In a dry climate they'll keep like this for years. No need to store them in an airtight box: a cotton bag hung in an airy place is quite sufficient.

Halve the tomatoes horizontally, scoop out the pips and, holding the skin side firmly in one hand, grate the flesh. Set the rolls, torn side up, on individual plates or shallow bowls. Sprinkle each portion with a little olive oil and enough water to soften, top with a spoonful of grated tomato, pile on a few leaves, and finish with chopped olives, crumbled feta and a sprinkle of oregano or marjoram. Finish with more olive oil and a sprinkle of salt. Serve with quartered lemons for squeezing.

Good with . . . plain grilled fish or octopus dressed with oil and vinegar.

Eggs & dairy

This section deals with the use of eggs and cheese in cooking. For notes on individual cheeses and the making of mayonnaise, the Mediterranean substitute for butter – call it the original olive-oil spread – see pages 16–18 and 39.

The Mediterranean housewife is not profligate with her protein. The products of the barnyard – eggs and dairy preparations (fresh milk rarely, cream for a treat, cheese daily, eggs in season) – were, still are, the mainstay of the rural diet. No one kills a productive animal until it's outlived its usefulness.

In the days before we all had fridges, there was a need to conserve seasonal glut. The Mediterranean winter is short – spring comes early and autumn late, so that fresh foods are rarely off the menu for long. Nevertheless, particularly in the rural areas the prudent housewife stocked her storecupboard against the inevitable shortages brought by the turning year. The cheese made in the spring and summer when the milk animals can be put out to pasture is easily stored for winter. The egg poses different problems: the only way to preserve it for any length of time is by boiling it until the white and yolk have hardened completely, a technique practised by Mediterranean Catholics during Lent, when, for religious reasons, eggs could not be eaten. Or, as in Egypt, for long enough for the yolk to become soft again – a conservation technique that mirrors that of the Orient.

Since one of the main virtues of the egg is that it cooks quickly and can easily be converted into something delicious by the addition of small amounts of other ingredients – spring shoots, scraps of ham, leftover cheese – recipes are both simple and universal. From east to west, north to south, you'll find the same combinations with minor variations. Eggs boiled in their shells and eaten with an oil-based sauce; eggs scrambled in the pan with or without the addition of a little ham, a slice of sausage, flavouring herbs; egg-pancakes such as the Spanish *tortilla*, Italian *frittata*, the Egyptian *eggah* are made more solid with the addition of potato or some other fortifying ingredient.

Cheese is almost equally versatile, though much is consumed without further attention. A wedge of cheese and a bowl of olives is the first thing the housewife sets on the table, and is the simplest – also, when home-produced, the cheapest – of all the little dishes of the Mediterranean. A sliver of salty goat's cheese, a scraping of pecorino, a slice of kefalotiri is the perfect companion to a glass of wine or a sip of *ouzo*. And if the cheese is judged too bland it will come with a dish of pickles, a salty sprinkle of capers. If too strong – and there are some that are very pungent indeed – it can be mashed with a little fresh curd, or dressed with olive oil, or spread on a thick slab of unsalted bread.

At the end of winter, when the cheese is hard and dry, the application of heat – as with the north Italian *frico*, the Greek *saganiki* – provides a way of softening or crisping to make it palatable.

Laban bi sikkar
Middle Eastern yoghurt drink

2

A non-alcoholic thirst-quencher – a refreshing drink of yoghurt, flavoured or not as you please, diluted with iced water. You need natural yoghurt, the kind that looks a little grainy on the surface rather than perfectly smooth – smoothness is a sign of the presence of stabilizers or thickeners, which behave unpredictably when diluted or whisked. Strained sheep's-milk yoghurts will need more dilution – allow one part yoghurt to one part water. For a sweet version, stir in a little sugar and perhaps a drop or two of vanilla extract. For a summer refresher, combine with fresh fruit pulped in the liquidizer. For a Turkish version, add a splash of rosewater – just enough to perfume.

Serves 4–6

I large tub (500g / IIb) natural yoghurt
about 300ml / ½ pint cold water
a little salt or sugar, depending on your taste

Optional to finish
fresh mint leaves
a little ground cumin, coriander seed, ginger, nutmeg or cinnamon
a splash of rosewater (Turkish-style)

Or combine with
300ml / ½ pint freshly pulped fruit – strawberry, banana, custard apple, mango, papaya, pineapple, avocado

Tip the yoghurt into a jug, whisk until lump-free, then add the water gradually until you have a smooth milk – you'll need more or less water according to the thickness of the yoghurt. Or process everything in the liquidizer.

Add salt or sugar to taste (if you add the salt before you dilute the yoghurt, the casein in the yoghurt will coagulate). On a hot day, stir in a little finely chopped mint just before serving, saving a few leaves for decoration. On a cool day, finish with a sprinkle of spice. For a special occasion, whisk with your chosen fruit pulp. To serve, pour over ice cubes in tall glasses, with a mint leaf apiece.

Combine with . . . any *mezze* when *raki* is not appropriate or unlikely to be appreciated. Fruit *labans* are perfect with the honey-drenched fritters and nut-stuffed, syrup-soaked pastries so beloved by the sweet-toothed Middle Easterners. When accompanying sweet things – either as a snack or as the conclusion to a meal – offer as a trio with iced water and tiny cups of sweetened Turkish coffee.

Tommes à l'huile
Provençal goat's cheeses in olive oil

2

Tommes, little round white-curd cheeses about the size of a baby's fist, are sold in every Mediterranean market, usually by the maker, and can be found in delicatessens, Middle Eastern shops and our own farmers' markets. When fresh, they're bland: the marination not only preserves but enriches and flavours.

Serves 6–8

6–8 fresh *tommes* or small fresh white curd cheeses, about 50g / 2oz each (see page 35)
approx I litre / 2 pints olive oil
I heaped teaspoon dried savory
I teaspoon dried thyme
I teaspoon dried tarragon
½ teaspoon juniper berries
I sprig rosemary

Drop the savory and thyme into a large jar (sterilized by scalding with boiling water or in a low oven). Lay in the cheeses, sprinkling in the tarragon and juniper berries as you go. Drop the rosemary twig on top. Pour in the oil to cover – the cheeses must be completely submerged. Cover tightly and store in a cool place. Serve with a few drops of the marinating oil. The cheeses can be replaced with new ones as you empty the jar.

Göreme

Turkish cheese dip

2

A salty cheese dip whose origins escape me. All I know is that the first time I tasted it was in Tangier in the high old days of smugglers and their molls, a speciality of a little café on the waterfront owned by a Turkish sailor who had served as a chef on Aristotle Onassis's yacht. His employer had been very fond of it – which was enough to recommend it to his customers. You need a well-matured cheese that has been cheddared and well salted – that is, the curds have been cut so that the finished cheese is crumbly. Salting hardens the casein in the milk, making the texture much firmer.

Serves 6–8

300g / 10oz thick yoghurt
300g / 10oz feta or any other salty white cheese, crumbled
2 cloves garlic, crushed
1 teaspoon ground cumin
1 teaspoon ground cardamom seeds
½ teaspoon cayenne pepper or chilli powder

To finish
1 teaspoon paprika mixed with 1 tablespoon olive oil
black olives

Push all the ingredients through a sieve and beat until smooth, or drop in the food processor and process to a purée. Taste and add salt if necessary.

Swirl onto a plate, decorate prettily with the paprika oil, and finish with a few whole black olives. Provide *pitta* or any other flat-bread for scooping, naturally.

Good with . . . something crisp and well spiced, such as Moroccan cigars (page 248); Turkish triangles with spinach (page 96), *brik à l'oeuf* (page 75).

Frico

Italian fried cheese

There are a thousand ways of making use of dried-up ends of cheese – mostly involving the grill. This is how they do it in Carnia, a Celtic stronghold in the mountainous region at the head of the Adriatic, where much use is made of the griddle and the porridge pot (in which the New World cornmeal replaces the Old World's oats).

Serves 4–6

First method
500g / 1lb hard cheese – pecorino, provolone, Cheddar

Grate the cheese the day before you mean to use it, toss it to incorporate as much air as possible and leave uncovered overnight to dry.

Heat a griddle or heavy iron pan (or non-stick frying pan – let's not go overboard on the authenticity) and sprinkle with grated cheese. Not too much, just enough to cover the base. Squish it down with a fork as it melts and crisps. When you have a nice brown lacy pancake (don't turn it), remove and serve immediately.

For a more elegant finish, flick the pancake directly from the hot pan onto a small upturned bowl or cup: it will harden into a little container for a dollop of soft polenta.

Second method
500g / 1lb hard cheese – pecorino, provolone, Cheddar
olive oil for deep-frying

Grate the cheese and dry overnight as in the first method. Heat the oil in a roomy fryer. When a faint blue haze rises, sprinkle in a handful of the grated cheese. Swirl it quickly with a fork until it melts into strings and remove as soon as it crisps and gilds. Don't take your eye off it for a second – the gap between brown and burnt is very short.

> **Good with . . .** pickled vegetables (pickled turnips is what you'd get in Carnia); grilled or soft polenta; any grilled meats and vegetables.

Pohovan kaçkavalj

Croatian breaded cheese

2

All cheese-making communities have melted cheese dishes – rarebits, fondues and the like – a method of using up storecupboard cheese at the end of winter. In the Balkans, a plain fondue – melted cheese softened with butter or cream, sometimes combined with little cubes of crisp-fried bacon – is served in individual earthenware bowls rather than in a single pot, and eaten with a spoon. The most common Balkan cheeses – sir, sirene – are white cut-curd (cheddared) cheeses similar to the Greek feta, which crumble easily and are more suitable for eating raw. For this dish you need a cooked cheese that keeps its shape when melted: locally, this would be Kashkaval, a matured pressed cheese.

Serves 6–8

500g / 1lb hard cheese (Kashkaval, Gruyère, Cheddar), rind removed
2–3 tablespoons flour
1 teaspoon paprika
2–3 eggs
very fine breadcrumbs (fresh or dried)
olive oil or clarified butter (see page 16) for deep-frying

Slice the cheese quite thickly. Mix the flour and the paprika on a shallow plate. Fork up the eggs in a dish. Spread the breadcrumbs on another plate.

Rinse the cheese quickly in cold water, dust it through the flour, dip it in the egg and press it firmly into the breadcrumbs, making sure all sides are well coated. Leave to rest for 10 minutes, to dry the coating a little.

Heat the oil or butter in a deep pan until the surface shimmers and a faint blue haze rises. It must be good and hot to seal the outside of the cheese before the interior melts. Slip in the breaded cheese. Remove with a slotted spoon as soon as the outside crisps and browns. Drain on kitchen paper. Serve straight from the pan – nothing is more indigestible than cold cooked cheese.

Combine with . . . pickled cucumbers; a chopped salad – Serbian salad (page 102); grilled peppers finished with a little chilli.

Buñuelitos de queso

Andalusian cheese fritters

2

Although Andalusia produces no great cheeses, there's an ancient tradition of homemade goat's cheese turned with the curd from the stomach of a newborn kid. The curd is salted and drained in handmade baskets made of plaited esparto grass, a dwarf palm with long tough fibres used for matting and donkey baskets. The cheeses, which take the pattern of each individual maker, are wheel-shaped for ease of storage – not too big, not too small, about the size of a campesino's sombrero. This is what to do with the scraps left over at the end of winter.

Serves 4–6

3 eggs
3 tablespoons milk
175g / 6oz grated hard cheese (manchego, Cheddar, Gruyère)
3 tablespoons flour
1 tablespoon grated or very finely chopped onion
1 tablespoon chopped parsley
1 teaspoon paprika
salt and freshly ground black pepper
olive oil for frying

Whisk the eggs and milk together. Stir in the cheese. Work in the flour, beating to avoid lumps. Add the onion, parsley and paprika. Season with salt and pepper.

Heat two-fingers' depth of oil in a frying pan. When lightly hazed with blue, drop in teaspoonfuls of the mixture – not too many or the oil temperature will drop too steeply. Fry them until crisp and golden brown, turning once, and transfer briefly to kitchen paper to drain. Serve straight from the stove.

> **Good with . . .** *salsa romesco* (page 42) for dipping; finely sliced *jamón serrano* and *chorizo*; mushrooms with garlic and parsley (page 152).

Fonduta coi tartufi bianchi

Italian fondue with white truffles

The fondue of northern Italy is an exquisite emulsion of egg yolks, creamy milk and melted cheese. At the right time of year, in the right place — specifically, in and around the Piedmontese town of Alba at the beginning of winter — the dish is finished with fine shavings of tartufo bianco, the precious white truffle. The flavour of this smooth-skinned tuber with its pale creamy flesh — young garlic and well-aged Parmesan — provides the perfect counterpoint. But if you can't lay your hands on a truffle, no matter. A fonduta is still a fine thing.

Serves 4–6

350g / 12oz fontina (or Gruyère, Emmental, Cantal)
450ml / ¾ pint creamy milk or single cream
6 large egg yolks
salt and white pepper

To finish
1 white truffle of whatever size you can afford (optional)

First, don't hurry: a well made *fonduta* takes over an hour to prepare, very little of which is spent slaving over a hot stove.

Chop the cheese into tiny pieces with a sharp knife or in a food processor – the result is smoother than if you grate it. Warm the milk or cream to blood temperature. Mix the chopped cheese with the warm milk in a bowl set over a saucepanful of boiling water. Cover with a clean cloth and keep the water at the slowest possible simmer for 30 minutes to allow the cheese to melt very gently into the milk, stirring occasionally.

Whisk in the egg yolks. Turn up the heat a little and whisk while the mixture thickens. Be patient. Treat it like a custard rather than scrambled eggs. As soon as it's thick enough to coat the back of a wooden spoon, remove from the heat. If it splits, whisk in a teaspoon of cornflour mixed with a little cold water.

Brush the truffle, carefully removing any sand or grit, and wipe gently – if it is very dirty, rinse it briefly. Pour the *fonduta* over thick slabs of toasted bread and cover with thin curls of raw truffle, using the cucumber slicer on the grater. The Italians have a special instrument for the job – useful if you anticipate many such banquets.

> Good with . . . as an alternative vehicle for the *fonduta*, plain boiled or jacket potatoes; a fennel salad (anything indigestible and cheesy is all the better for a little fennel).

Skaltsouina

Cretan cheese pies

 These little pies can be sweet or savoury, fried or baked. For the sweet version, fill them with soft curd cheese mixed with sugar and nuts and spiced with cinnamon.

Serves 4–6

For the pastry
250g / 8oz plain flour
a pinch of salt
1 tablespoon olive oil
4 tablespoons water

For the filling
150g / 5oz feta, crumbled
1 medium onion or 4–5 spring onions, very finely chopped
1 beaten egg
2 tablespoons finely chopped mint
1 tablespoon finely chopped parsley
salt and freshly ground black pepper

To finish
olive oil for frying

First make the pastry: sieve the flour with the salt into a bowl. Make a dip in the middle and pour in the oil. Work in enough water to make a soft, pliable dough. Knead until smooth. Cover with a clean cloth or drop into a plastic bag and leave in a cool place to rest for 30 minutes.

Meanwhile, mix together all the filling ingredients.

Roll out the pastry thinly. Using a coffee-saucer as template, cut into rounds (about 7.5cm / 4in). Drop a teaspoon of the filling onto one half of each round, dampen the edges and fold over into half-moon shapes, pressing the edges to seal.

Heat a finger's depth of oil in a frying pan and fry the pasties until golden brown – allow about 2 minutes on each side.

> Combine with . . . *tsatsiki* for dipping (page 36); a Greek garden salad (omit the feta and replace with a few chunks of tinned tuna) (page 83); Spanish peppers in oil (page 121); a bowl of Kalamata olives – juicy and sweet; pickled capers in oil; nicest with Cretan wild greens – *vliki* – dressed with olive oil and lemon juice; a combination of green asparagus, sprouting broccoli, baby green beans is the closest approximation.

Beid hamine

Egyptian preserved eggs

2

The main problem with eggs, now just as in the time of the Pharaohs' chicken hatcheries, is storage. Egg shells are porous and vulnerable to spoilage and, left to their own devices, the contents of an unfertilized egg – or one which has been fertilized, if not kept warm and permitted to hatch into a chick – will rot. However, when boiled in its shell for long enough to sterilize the innards, not only can an egg be preserved almost indefinitely but it won't crack when transported. Nevertheless, hardboiled eggs are somewhat indigestible, lacking the delicious unctuousness of the fresh and softboiled. Those with eggs to spare discovered that during long cooking the yolks first harden and then soften again to a creamy smoothness while the whites caramelize a little. In this recipe the onion skins are used for colour rather than flavour – coffee grounds will serve the same function. On feast days – particularly the Prophet's birthday – they are often coloured red with food dye, as are those with which Orthodox Greeks celebrate the birth of Christ. Red is the colour of good fortune.

To prepare a dozen eggs

12 fresh eggs
a handful of onion skins

To serve
salt, ground cumin, coriander and cinnamon

Fill a large pan with enough cold water to submerge the eggs very generously. Bring the pan gently to a simmer – the water should tremble, no more – add the onion skins, and cover loosely. Leave to cook for about 6 hours – in a very low oven if you prefer.

Serve the eggs peeled or not as you please, with a dipping salt flavoured with ground cumin, coriander and cinnamon.

Good with . . . *fattoush* (page 58), the Lebanese bread salad, or as part of a *mezze* trio of *ful-medames* (page 253) and *hummus bi tahini* (page 34).

Brik à l'oeuf

Tunisian egg borek

This is Tunisia's favourite mezze — a crisp pastry envelope enclosing a runny-yolked egg. It takes a little confidence, but once you've mastered the trick of slipping the parcel filled with raw egg into the hot oil, you'll find the result addictive. The pastry used in Tunisia, as in Morocco, is ouaka, a fine sheet of pastry formed by dabbing a little ball of dough onto a lightly greased domed griddle — more robust than filo, not unlike a very thin pancake. The closest is the Turkish gözleme dough.

Serves 6

1 recipe *gözleme* dough (see page 54), 6 sheets *ouaka* or 12 sheets filo
2–3 spring onions, very finely chopped
1 small tin tuna in oil (80g / 3oz), drained (optional)
2 tablespoons chopped coriander leaves or parsley
2 tablespoons capers
6 small eggs
salt and freshly ground black pepper
oil for deep-frying

To serve
harissa **(see page 232)**

If you are using *gözleme* dough, divide it into six pieces and roll into very fine disks. If you are using *ouaka*, allow one sheet per egg. If you are using filo you'll need double thickness, each piece the size of a large dinner plate.

Drop little piles of the chopped spring onion, coriander or parsley, capers and the optional tuna on one side of each pastry disk. Season with salt and pepper.

Heat about five fingers' depth of oil in a frying pan. When it's good and hot crack an egg on to one of the disks, season, fold up quickly and drop immediately into the hot oil. The egg white will harden and seal the envelope instantly. Fry for 2–3 minutes, turning once. Remove and transfer to kitchen paper to drain. Continue until all are done.

Brik must be eaten as soon as they are ready. Pick them up by the corners and bite into the middle. Watch out for the hot yolk, which will surely run down your chin. A dab of *harissa* adds a little fire.

> **Good with . . .** Moroccan bean purée (page 104); *tabbouleh* (page 84); any of the Middle Eastern salad dips.

Tortilla española
Spanish potato omelette

Cheap and cheerful, the Hispanic world's favourite snack. Include any vegetables that take your fancy – the recipe works as long as the vegetables are chopped evenly and the proportion of solids to eggs remains equal: diced peppers, spinach, peas, beans, mushrooms both wild and cultivated – in Catalonia they cook it with saffron milk-caps, orange-fleshed autumn fungi with a firm, meaty texture. In Granada they have a gypsy version made with sweetbreads, brains and tripe – the variety meats sold by the butchers of any affluent city to their poorer customers.

Serves 4–6

3–4 tablespoons olive oil
1 medium potato per egg, peeled and diced or slivered
4 tablespoons finely chopped onion (mild Spanish onion, for preference)
4 medium eggs
chopped parsley, marjoram, a few scraps of *jamón serrano* (optional)
salt and freshly ground black pepper

In a small frying pan (whatever you would use to cook an individual omelette) heat enough oil to submerge the diced potato. When lightly hazed with blue, drop in the potatoes, fry for a few minutes and add the onion. When the potato is perfectly soft but not browned, remove and drain in a sieve set over a bowl to catch the drippings.

Meanwhile, fork up the eggs lightly in a bowl with the herbs or ham, if that's your choice. Season. Stir in the potato as soon as it has cooled a little. Pour all but a tablespoon of oil out of the pan, and reheat. When good and hot, pour in the egg and potato, prodding it down so the potato is fully submerged in egg. Fry gently – too high a heat will make the *tortilla* leathery. As it cooks, shake to loosen the base and neaten the sides with a spatula to build up a deep straight edge. To speed up the cooking process, cover loosely.

As soon as the egg begins to set, invert a plate over the top, and, with a quick flick of the wrist, flip the whole thing over so the *tortilla* ends up on the plate, cooked side uppermost. Be brave – it's no harder than flipping a pancake. Slip it back in the pan and brown the other side (you may need a little more oil). Don't overcook – the centre should remain juicy. When it feels firm but still squidgy slip it out onto its plate – it'll set a little more as it cools. Pat off excess oil with kitchen paper. Serve at room temperature, cut into wedges or cubes.

Good with . . . peppers in oil (page 121); Andalusian broad beans with ham (page 89).

Eggah-bi-Batinjen

Egyptian aubergine omelettes

Bite-sized patties, a quick treat for unexpected visitors. The eggah *is the Middle Eastern equivalent of the Spanish* tortilla *– you can cook the mixture as a single omelette, dividing it into small squares for serving.*

Serves 4–6

For the omelettes
3 large eggs
2 aubergines, diced and fried until tender
3 tablespoons finely chopped coriander
3 tablespoons finely chopped parsley
1 teaspoon *harissa* (shop-bought, or homemade (page 232) – or use 2–3 dried red
   chillis, soaked, pounded with salt, and 1 garlic clove)
salt and freshly ground black pepper
oil for shallow-frying

For the sauce
2 ripe tomatoes, deseeded and finely chopped
1 medium onion, finely chopped
2 green chillis, deseeded and finely chopped
2 tablespoons chopped coriander
2 tablespoons green or purple olives, pitted and chopped
1 lemon, juice and zest
1 teaspoon sugar
extra chopped coriander and a little oil and paprika, to finish (optional)

Fork up the eggs and stir in the diced, cooked, cooled aubergine. Fold in the herbs and harissa or chilli, and season with salt and pepper.

In a frying pan, heat a finger's depth of oil. Drop in tablespoons of the mixture, patting each dollop roughly into a pancake with the back of the spoon. Fry, turning once, until golden and crisp. Remove and drain on kitchen paper. If you want to get rid of excess oil, transfer the omelettes to a baking tray lined with kitchen paper and reheat in a low oven for about 10 minutes, after which most of the oil will have been exuded into the paper.

Combine the sauce ingredients and serve as a dip – or drop a teaspoonful on top of each omelette and finish with a sprinkle of chopped coriander and a thread of oil worked with a little paprika.

> **Combine with . . .** Cos lettuce leaves and spring onions for wrapping; a little bowl of *harissa* with *aish* or a wholemeal *pitta* (page 50); or any other Arab flat-bread for scooping.

La trouchia
Provençal broad bean omelette

The Provençal omelette is pretty much identical to the Spanish tortilla *and the Italian* frittata *— the egg is used to bind other ingredients, usually vegetables, to make a portable food that can be taken to the fields, something that can be quickly prepared with whatever comes to hand and will satisfy hunger.* La trouchia *is made in the early summer with young broad beans still in the pod, and later in the season with the mature beans podded and slipped out of their skins. In winter, the chard — blea — is used on its own. In times gone by, the people of Marseilles earned themselves the nickname* caga-blea *(I'm sure you can work that out for yourself) because of the amount of greens they ate.*

Serves 4–6

4 eggs
2 tablespoons freshly grated Cantal or any hard cheese
I teaspoon chopped marjoram
2–3 spring onions, finely chopped
salt and freshly ground black pepper
250g / 8oz young broad beans, podded or not as suits the season
250g / 8oz chard or any robust spinachy leaves, shredded
2 tablespoons olive oil

Beat the eggs lightly with the grated cheese, marjoram, spring onions, salt and pepper. Blanch the beans and wilt the shredded greens (pour boiling water over them in a bowl, drain and press the greens dry).

Heat the oil in a medium-sized frying pan that will deliver an omelette at least an inch thick. As soon as it's good and hot, add the beans and greens, wait until the oil sizzles, and then pour in the egg mixture. Stir with a fork to incorporate the first settings of the egg. Then turn the heat down low, cover loosely and leave to cook gently for 6–8 minutes, until the edges are set and the middle is beginning to firm. Slip the omelette out onto a plate, add a little more oil to the pan, and reverse the plate so the omelette lands face down in the pan. Cook it for another 2–3 minutes, until it has browned a little, then reverse the whole thing back onto a plate. Pat off excess oil, leave to cool and serve at room temperature.

Good with . . . *ratatouille* (page 125); a plate of classy charcuterie.

Torta alla ligure

Ligurian vegetable omelette

This is what the Ligurians take to the olive groves when there's work to be done. As with the French quiche or the Spanish omelet, it's variable in composition. By the sea, tiny fish fry – bi[a]nchetti – replace the anchovies. The curd cheese used by the Ligurians to soften the mix is quagliata – soft, pleasantly acidic, with an oddly slithery texture.

Serves 6–8

2 medium potatoes, peeled and chunked
500g / 1lb green beans, topped and tailed
4 tablespoons extra-virgin olive oil
1 smallish onion, finely chopped
2 cloves garlic, finely chopped
1 small tin (50g / 2oz) anchovies, drained
1 small bunch flat-leaf parsley, chopped
100g / 4oz ricotta
2 tablespoons *crème fraîche*, or double cream with a squeeze of lemon
2 tablespoons freshly grated Parmesan
1 tablespoon finely chopped marjoram
4 eggs, lightly forked

To finish
4 tablespoons homemade dried breadcrumbs
olive oil for drizzling

Cook the potatoes in boiling salted water until they are quite tender, drain well, mash roughly with a fork and reserve. Cook the green beans lightly in salted water (they should retain a little bite). Drain thoroughly, chop roughly and reserve.

Preheat the oven to 180°C/350°F/gas 4.

Warm the oil in a frying pan and add the chopped onion and garlic. Fry until soft but not browned, and add the anchovies, squishing with a fork to soften. Add the parsley and let it sizzle for a second. Add the beans and turn them in the aromatic sauce. Tip the mixture into the mashed potatoes in a bowl, and blend thoroughly with the remaining ingredients, using your hands.

Oil a shallow cake tin or earthenware baking dish (about 20cm/8in diameter) and sprinkle with some of the breadcrumbs, shaking out the excess. Turn the vegetable mixture into the tin, smooth the top and sprinkle with the remaining breadcrumbs. Drizzle with a little more olive oil and bake for 40–45 minutes, until just set but still a little trembly in the middle.

Good with . . . *ciabatta* (page 48) and finely sliced *lardo* – cured pork fat.

Duelos y quebrantos

Spanish eggs with ham and chorizo

The name literally means 'wounds and suffering', perhaps because of the pink ham and the scarlet juices from the paprika sausage which 'bleed' into the eggs. A dish claimed by the inhabitants of the high central plateau of La Mancha, where Don Quixote tilted at windmills, but also popular in Andalusia, where the locally cured hams of Trevélez and Jabugo are rated the most exquisite in all Spain. Spaniards, even the poorest, value quality and will buy the best for a celebration, even if it's only the scraps from the bone – useful in dishes such as this, and a little goes a long way. The best serrano ham comes from the half-wild red-bristled pigs which feed on acorns in the cork-oak forests of Andalusia.

Serves 4–6

3–4 tablespoons diced *jamón serrano* or *prosciutto*
a few slices diced *chorizo* (or any other paprika-spiced sausage)
1 tablespoon olive oil
1–2 cloves garlic, skinned and slivered
1 teaspoon *pimentón* (mild paprika)
4 eggs
salt and freshly ground black pepper

To serve
country bread – one with a dense, creamy crumb

Fry the ham and *chorizo* in the oil in a heatproof earthenware casserole or small frying pan, until the meat browns, the fat runs and the *chorizo* crumbles and crisps. Add the garlic slivers and let them take a little colour. Stir in the paprika and remove from the heat.

Meanwhile, lightly fork the eggs with a little salt and pepper.

Add the eggs to the contents of the casserole or pan, return to the heat and stir over the flame until the eggs scramble. As soon as they begin to set, remove from the heat. Serve either in the earthenware casserole in which they were cooked or heaped on pieces of toasted bread – nothing too dainty.

> Good with . . . Andalusian sourdough bread (page 47); Spanish spinach with fried bread (page 94); grilled fungi (page 152); a bowl of olives and maybe a few pickled anchovies (page 161).

Spring greens & shoots

Spring comes early to the shores of the Mediterranean. Soon after the turn of the year the first green shoots appear between the olive trees – catch crops and wild gatherings on which rural households once relied. Every corner of the region has its own ideas on what is and isn't palatable – curiously, ancestral memory seems to play a larger part in the selection process than availability. Until recent times all country dwellers knew exactly what to pick.

When I lived in Andalusia with my growing family it was my children who first showed me where to find the Mediterranean wild garlic, *Allium triquetrum*, to stir into a stew; how to gather wild asparagus from beneath the prickly little bushes which survived even the worst of the forest fires. Later, I learned how to prepare the wild greens of Italy, many of them familiar from my days as a botanical painter: borage, amaranth, the powdery-leaved goosefoot, dandelion – known as *pis-en-lit* in Provence for its diuretic properties; peppery wild rocket, beet tops, turnip greens, gluey little rosettes of lamb's lettuce. More surprising – billed as cooking greens, along with lady's smock and bladder campion – were the base buds of the common poppy, *Papaver rhoeas*. Among spring shoots billed as asparagus were caper and hop shoots, and – oddest of all, encountered in Apulia in recent years – the bean-field *orobanche*, an orchid-like plant which, lacking chlorophyll, draws its sustenance from its host.

Greens, both cultivated and wild – all those spinach-like leaves possessed of varying degrees of tenderness and bitterness, pepperiness and mildness, smoothness and glueyness – are interchangeable. It's the balance that counts. Trust your tastebuds as to what leaf can be substituted for another. Curly-leaf English parsley is stronger and coarser than the Mediterranean flat-leaf Italian parsley, and far too pungent for a *tabbouleh*, so if curly-leaf is all you can find, dilute its strength with an equal volume of shredded baby spinach. In a salad, the bitterness of wild-gathered greens can be reproduced by the inclusion of a little mustard in the dressing. In cooking, a handful of radish or turnip tops adds a touch of the rough to the filling for a quiche, a stuffing for pasta. To replace the flavour of wild garlic, allow last year's garlic bulb to sprout – the little green shoots, so bitter when in their infancy inside the clove, soon achieve a delicate mildness when they reach the light. But above all, experiment. No Mediterranean housewife would dream of obeying any recipe to the letter – the heart rules the head.

Salata horiatiki
Greek garden salad

2

A chunky salad familiar to all tourists, but still very much a part of Greek culture. This is a peasant dish, so make it rough and ready. Possible additional inclusions are hardboiled eggs, salt herrings, salt cod – bakaliaros – blistered on a hot griddle to draw the salt, torn into small pieces. Compare it with a salade niçoise and you will understand exactly how much is shared by the inhabitants of these sunny shores. The Greeks will tell you they taught the fishwives of Marseilles how to prepare a bouillabaisse – but don't mention it down the Canabière.

Serves 4–6

1 slice stale white bread or *pitta*, toasted crisp
juice of 1 lemon
about 6 tablespoons olive oil
1 crisp lettuce (Cos or Webb's Wonder), chunked
3–4 tomatoes, chunked
1 small cucumber, chunked
1 mild onion, slivered
1 tablespoon capers, drained
1 tablespoon large black or purple olives
salt
lemon quarters to serve

Crumble the toasted bread into a bowl, soak it with the lemon juice and fork in enough oil to make a soft, thick dressing. Season.

To serve, mix everything together and provide extra lemon quarters for squeezing.

> Good with ... something fishy such as grilled or slow-simmered octopus (page 176); a dish of stewed cuttlefish or squid (pages 178–81); fish kebabs (page 173); Turkish stuffed mussels (page 182). To satisfy hunger, fat chips fried crisp in olive oil, sprinkled with finely grated salty cheese such as kefalotiri or feta.

Tabbouleh
Lebanese parsley salad

One of the greatest of all green salads, tabbouleh's central ingredient is parsley – flat-leaf for preference, hand-chopped for succulence (food processors play havoc with the juices). The burghul is secondary, although the proportion of grain to green varies from cook to cook. Volume rather than weight is the meaningful measurement. In Israel, couscous sometimes replaces the burghul and young spinach does duty for parsley: unthinkable elsewhere. Perhaps because she is such a young country and her citizens come from a long diaspora, Israel is cheerfully uninhibited about culinary substitutions.

Serves 4–6

250g / 8oz flat-leaf parsley on the stalk, finely chopped
6–8 spring onions, finely chopped
5 tablespoons olive oil
2 tablespoons lemon juice
1 heaped teaspoon salt
½ teaspoon ground allspice
½ teaspoon freshly ground black pepper
50g / 2oz burghul, preferably fine-ground
2–3 tomatoes, skinned, deseeded and diced
50g / 2oz mint leaves

Optional extras
diced cucumber
diced green peppers
pomegranate seeds

In a roomy bowl toss the parsley and spring onions with the olive oil, lemon juice, salt, allspice and pepper. Rinse the burghul in a sieve until the water runs clear and shake well to dry. Combine with the parsley and set the bowl in the fridge for 30 minutes for the grain to drink the juices. Toss with the chopped tomatoes and any optional extras (chop and add the mint when you are ready to serve – if you do this ahead of time it will blacken). Taste and adjust the seasoning.

> Serve with . . . crisp lettuce leaves with which to make little parcels; radishes; black olives and hardboiled eggs. Good served as in every pitstop down the Jordan valley, stuffed in a *pitta* pocket with a piping hot falafel (page 257) and a dollop of *tahini*.

Asparagi al uovo e olio

Asparagus with egg and oil

The asparagus, although much improved by cross-breeding with a New World species, is native to the Mediterranean, so one can safely assume that the Romans ate it, giving the Italians fair claim to having started the whole profitable business of its cultivation. In medieval times the tender shoots were trekked over the Alps to be sold in Vienna and the other markets of the Habsburg empire. The spears remained fresh even after the five-day journey since the snow which still blanketed the mountains in the spring provided a natural fridge throughout the journey. The main source of supply was the asparagus farms of Tavagnacco in Udine, in the north-east corner of Italy. Among the growers size is the most prized attribute. Competitions are held in which priapic silver trophies are awarded to equally priapic spears, each weighing several kilos.

The growers themselves call this deceptively simple recipe – all the ingredients must be of the freshest and most perfect – Asparagus Bismarck, an appropriate commemoration of the Iron Chancellor whose countrymen provided the market for their trade-goods.

Serves 4

1kg / 2lb large, fat white asparagus
4 free-range eggs
4 tablespoons good olive oil
sea salt and pepper

Wash and trim the asparagus, slicing off any dry ends and peeling off tough skin. Bring salted water to the boil in a tall narrow pan that will accommodate the asparagus vertically (for a makeshift asparagus steamer the growers use an empty olive oil can with the top opened up). Or, like me, you can use the horizontal method: lay the spears in a deep roasting tin, cover with boiling water, salt generously, bring to the boil and cook for 6–10 minutes, depending on the thickness of the spears – until the tips are tender but the stalks not yet floppy. Remove immediately, drain and pile on a napkin on a hot plate.

Meanwhile, hardboil the eggs: start at room temperature, bring them to the boil from cold and allow 6 minutes, no more. Serve the warm asparagus with the eggs, with the olive oil and pepper on the side: each person should use a fork to mash his own egg yolk with the oil to make a dipping sauce. Be generous with the salt. Pepper or not, as you please.

> Good with . . . plain-boiled new potatoes to mop up the egg and oil; a *frittata* with wild-gathered spring greens; Italian rice and cheese balls (page 263), fried cheese (page 69).

Asparagos a la parrilla con salsa verde
Grilled asparagus with green herb dressing

2

Grilled asparagus may sound unlikely but it is surprisingly delicious. The flavour comes through clear and clean and the asparagus remains juicy and lightly blistered with caramelized juices. For grilling, you need green asparagus as thick as your thumb. Cultivated asparagus is relatively new in Andalusia: until recent times, obeying that instinct which dictates that shop-bought goods are better than fresh, tinned white asparagus with bottled mayonnaise was considered a greater delicacy, while the wild-gathered spears – Asparagos triguera (wheat-asparagus) – were seen as poor man's food, fit only for inclusion in a tortilla, the daily dinner of the field-worker. In Spain the most usual method of grilling at home is to slap the food directly onto a thick metal plate – plancha – with which Spanish cookers come ready-equipped. Vegetables are not generally considered suitable for the plancha, but exception is made for asparagus, peppers, cultivated mushrooms (champignons de Paris) *and – in Catalonia – an arbitrary selection of wild-gathered fungi, particularly* boletus (cèpe/porcini) *and* lactarius (orange-tears).

Serves 4–6

1kg / 2lb fat green asparagus
150ml / ¼ pint olive oil
1 tablespoon coarse salt
a big handful of soft-leaved herbs – parsley, spring onion, marjoram, tarragon, mint
yolk of 1 hardboiled egg or 1 tablespoon French mustard
2–3 tablespoons wine vinegar or lemon juice

Wash and trim the asparagus, discarding the woody bits and peeling off any hard skin. Brush each spear all over with olive oil, paying particular attention to the tips. Sprinkle the spears with salt crystals.

Preheat the grill – it needs to be good and hot.

Put the rest of the ingredients into the liquidizer and purée them to a thick green sauce. Arrange the asparagus on the grill-pan, tips pointing outwards. Grill until they steam and blister black a little – 4 or 5 minutes in all – turning to cook all sides. That's all. Hand the sauce separately.

> Good with . . . Mallorcan spinach pizza (page 56); *jamón serrano*; finely sliced *chorizo*.

Cassolette d'asperges
Provençal asparagus gratin

Madame Traverse of Ville-sur-Auzon, a little village on the slopes of Mount Ventoux in Haute Provence, specializes in early asparagus, a profitable crop since the first into the marketplace makes the money. The shoots grow with miraculous speed overnight, pushing their way towards the light from their sandy beds. Those for the German market must be pure white, so the shoots must be gathered before dawn, using a special long-handled knife thrust deep into the earthed-up crowns. The French like theirs tipped with purple, so harvesting must be soon after sunrise, when the tips have just emerged into the light. The Anglo-Saxons like them green – the last gathering of the morning. The cassolette is Madame Traverse's way with the broken spears that cannot be sold.

Serves 4–6

1kg / 2lb fresh asparagus (broken spears are fine)
2 tablespoons butter or oil
2 tablespoons flour
600ml / 1 pint chicken stock
2 cloves garlic, finely chopped
2 heaped tablespoons chopped parsley
50g / 2oz finely chopped ham
2 hardboiled eggs, finely chopped
50g / 2oz fresh cream cheese or mascarpone
salt, freshly ground black pepper and nutmeg

To finish
50g / 2oz grated cheese (Cantal, Gruyère, Cheddar)

Preheat the grill or the oven to 200°C/400°F/gas 6.

Wash the asparagus and snap off the tender tips (save the stalks for soup). Cook until just tender in boiling salted water – 5–6 minutes, and don't let them boil too fiercely. Drain thoroughly and lay in a gratin dish.

Meanwhile, melt the butter in a saucepan, stir in the flour and fry until sandy. Whisk in the broth gradually and simmer gently until the sauce thickens. Stir in the remaining ingredients and remove from the heat. Taste and season with salt, pepper and nutmeg. Pour the sauce over the asparagus and sprinkle with grated cheese.

Grill or bake for 10–15 minutes, until brown and bubbling.

> **Combine with . . .** green *tapenade* (page 27); Provençal leek and cheese tart (page 53).

Koukia

Greek broad beans cooked in their pods

2

The flavour of the young pod of the broad bean is rather like okra, and it has a similar gluey texture. Dishes such as this are found throughout the region. Later on in the season the same method can be applied to podded broad beans. In the winter the dish is made with dried beans – fava should be soaked for 48 hours and are best slipped out of their skins (for instructions see page 251). The same method – long, slow stewing until the juices evaporate – can be applied to almost any vegetable: green beans, okra, chard, spinach, chunked pumpkin, artichoke hearts, courgettes, potatoes, peppers, aubergines. If you include chopped tomatoes, whole olives and garlic, you have a Greek plaki.

Serves 4–6

1 kg / 2lb young unpodded broad beans *or* 500g / 1lb shelled broad beans plus 250g / 8oz okra
6 tablespoons olive oil
juice of 1–2 lemons

To finish
1 mild onion, finely chopped
flat-leaf parsley, chopped
fresh fennel or dill fronds, chopped
mint leaves, chopped
salt and freshly ground black pepper

String the beans and chop them into short lengths, pod and all, following the curve of the bean. If you are using older podded beans and okra, top and tail the okra. Warm the oil in a roomy pan or casserole, add the beans (and okra) and let them sizzle for a moment before pouring in just enough water to submerge the pods.

Bubble up, turn down the heat, cover tightly and simmer very gently for 1½ hours, until the beans are mushy, the juices evaporated, and only oil remains. (Take the lid off towards the end of the cooking to assist the evaporation process.) Stir in the lemon juice and one or all of the finishing ingredients and check seasoning. Serve at room temperature – all such dishes, sauced with their own oily juices, are eaten neither hot nor cold but naturally warm, as if left to simmer a little longer in the sun.

> **Good with** . . . *souvlakia* (page 230), of course, what else? Grilled or pan-roasted kefalotiri cheese with quartered lemons; something luxurious in the way of grilled meat (or fish or fowl), marinated with oil and lemon and sprinkled with oregano.

Habas a la rondeña

Andalusian broad beans with ham

2

Although Ronda – the most romantic of Andalusia's mountain citadels – was founded by the Romans, it was the Moorish caliphs who planted and irrigated its fertile vega, the market gardens that still provide the citizens with fresh vegetables all year round. This dish, a simple stew of broad beans flavoured with serrano ham, is made in the winter with dried beans and in the spring with the young beans still in their fur-lined pods. The flavour of the pods is delicate and a little viscous, rather like okra. The jamón serrano which gives the dish its character comes from the hams yielded by the lean, muscular half-wild red-bristled Iberian pigs that forage for cork-oak acorns – bellotas – in the great forest of Almoreima.

Serves 4–6

1 kg / 2lb whole young broad beans, unpodded or 750g / 1½lb podded broad beans
4 tablespoons olive oil
50g / 2oz chopped *jamón serrano* or Parma ham or lean bacon
1 small glass dry sherry
2 cloves garlic, roughly chopped
2 tablespoons chopped flat-leaf parsley
1 tablespoon chopped marjoram or oregano
salt, freshly ground black pepper and a little sugar

To finish
a handful of breadcrumbs
bread cubes, fried crisp in olive oil with garlic and parsley (optional)

Top and tail the pods and chop into short lengths, following the curve of the beans. Put everything into a casserole or heavy pan, adding enough water to just submerge the beans. Bring to the boil and season with salt, pepper and a pinch of sugar to cut the acidity of the wine. Turn down the heat to a steady simmer, cover loosely and cook until the beans are perfectly tender – 40–50 minutes. Add more boiling water if necessary. The pods first turn navy-blue, then cook out to a soft, pale green.

Remove the lid, turn up the heat and bubble to reduce the juices to a rich sauce, then stir in a handful of breadcrumbs to thicken. If you like, finish with a crisp topping of *migas* – bread cubes fried crisp with a little chopped garlic and parsley.

Good with . . . quartered hardboiled eggs; Spanish ham croquettes (page 226).

Judias con almendras
Andalusian green beans with almonds

2

The perfect balance of texture and flavour in a dish from Valencia, where the Moors planted avenues of almond trees and date palms to remind them of home. Spain has a somewhat ambivalent attitude towards the Moorish ascendancy, not surprisingly since their legacy, in Catalonia and on the Balearic islands as well as more obviously in Andalusia, is evident in the architecture, culture and domestic habit of the people. Music, poetry – all bear the stamp of the east. Walk up the narrow streets of any of the white villages that cling to the steep ravines of the Andalusian hinterland, or take a stroll around the ramparts of the fortified castles of frontier towns such as Jeréz or Jimena, and you might think yourself anywhere on the southern shores of the Mediterranean and not in Europe at all.

Serves 4–6

750g / 1½lb green beans, topped and tailed and cut into short lengths
4 tablespoons olive oil
50g / 2oz slivered blanched almonds
1 teaspoon *pimentón* (paprika)
1 teaspoon ground cumin
juice and zest of 1 lemon
coarse salt

Bring a pan of salted water to the boil and throw in the beans. Cook them until tender but still green and firm – 4–6 minutes. Drain and pass them under cold water to halt the cooking process.

Heat the olive oil in a small frying pan and fry the almonds until golden – a few seconds only or you will burn both nuts and oil. Remove from the heat, stir in the paprika and cumin, and tip onto the beans. Season with lemon juice and a little coarse salt.

Good with . . . Andalusian sourdough bread (page 47); a white or red *gazpacho* (pages 100 and 101); something satisfying such as a potato *tortilla* (page 76); something crisp such as ham croquettes (page 226); *patatas bravas* (page 136); Catalan grilled mushrooms with garlic (page 152).

▶ *Andalusian broad beans with ham (page 89); Spanish spiced chicken with peppers (page 203)*

Stufato di broccoli alla pugliese

Apulian broccoli with chilli and garlic

2

The Pugliese love chillis, which take the place of imported peppercorns in a cuisine that is basically cucina povere. *This is not so much poor-cooking as the cooking of the poor – seasonal, using only what can easily be grown or gathered, making the best possible use of a limited larder, a style equally relished by the rich. Apulia is the heel of Italy's boot – a long way from Rome and even further from Milan – its rocky coastline once a haven for Barbary pirates, leaving the inhabitants no choice but to retreat to the mountains and tend their vegetable patches. In Apulia they grow a variety of broccoli that looks like a large green cauliflower, tender and mild-flavoured, ideal for this dish.*

Serves 4–6

750g / 1½lb broccoli – the larger the heads the better
5–6 cloves garlic, whole, with skin
4 tablespoons extra-virgin olive oil
2–3 dried red chillis (more if you like it really hot), deseeded and torn
salt (no pepper)

Divide the broccoli into small florets. Trim the stalks and cut into short lengths. Blanch in salted water for 3 minutes, then drain.

Heat the oil gently with the chillis and the garlic until little bubbles form round the vegetables. Add the broccoli florets and turn briefly in the hot oil, then reduce the heat, season with a little salt, cover tightly and cook gently for 25–30 minutes, stirring occasionally. Serve with or without the garlic. The broccoli will be deliciously mushy and bathed in its own aromatic oil.

> Good with . . . a mozzarella and tomato salad; a bowl of Apulia's huge green olives – as big as damsons – pickled with lye (a process that turns them a vivid emerald); generous slabs of sourdough bread with olive oil for trickling – Apulia is famous for the excellence of its bread and the delicacy of its olive oil, still a well kept secret since until recently most of the oil from its ancient olive groves was shipped north for bottling in Tuscany.

◀ *Provençal baked aubergines with anchovies (page 109)*

Tourta de blea

Provençal chard quiche

You can make this traditional open pie with your usual shortcrust pastry if you prefer, but the oil pastry is unusual and good. The filling can be sweetened with sugar and served as a dessert.

Serves 4–6

For the pastry
250g / 8oz plain flour
½ teaspoon salt
6 tablespoons olive oil

For the filling
4 tablespoons olive oil
2 onions, finely chopped
3 cloves garlic, finely chopped
1 tablespoon raisins
½ teaspoon dried thyme
500g / 1lb chard, stalks and leaves, rinsed and chopped
salt
2 large eggs
2 tablespoons single cream or *crème fraîche*
½ lemon, juice and finely grated zest
freshly ground black pepper
4 tablespoons black olives, pitted and chopped

Sieve the flour and the salt into a bowl and work in the oil and enough warm water to make a smooth dough. Work lightly until it forms a ball that leaves the sides of the mixing bowl clean. Cover with clingfilm and leave to rest in the fridge for 30 minutes.

To make the filling, heat the oil in a roomy saucepan and fry the onions and garlic gently until they soften and gild. Add the raisins and thyme. Drop in the chard, salt lightly, cover and let it all cook down until tender in its own juices and the water that clings to the leaves. Bubble up to evaporate excess liquid. Remove the pan from the heat and leave to cool a little. Fork up the eggs with the cream and stir into the contents of the pan. Season with lemon juice, lemon zest and pepper.

Preheat the oven to 200°C/400°F/gas 6.

Roll out the pastry and line a 30cm/12in tart tin. Prick the base and bake for 10 minutes to set the surface. Spread in the filling and sprinkle with the olives. Lower the heat to 180°C/350°F/gas 4 and bake for 35–40 minutes, until the pastry is crisp and the filling set.

Good with . . . chanterelles with parsley and garlic (page 147); Provençal tomatoes (page 123).

Prasopita

Greek spinach pie

Airy layers of buttery filo enclose a fresh green filling – a spring treat, much appreciated at Easter when it's made with the wild-gathered greens of which Greek foragers can recognize a prodigious number.

Serves 6–8

For the pastry
1 packet filo pastry (about 270g / 9oz)
100g / 4oz clarified butter (see page 16), melted

For the filling
1kg / 2lb leeks, trimmed and finely sliced
2 large handfuls mixed greens (spinach, rocket, dandelion), shredded
1 tablespoon clarified butter (see page 16)
500g / 1lb fresh curd cheese
4 eggs, forked
1 tablespoon chopped dill
salt, freshly ground black pepper, a pinch of grated nutmeg

Preheat the oven to 190°C/375°F/gas 5.

Wash the leeks and greens thoroughly, leaving them quite damp. Cook them gently with the butter in a lidded saucepan, shaking the pan to avoid sticking. As soon as the leeks soften and the leaves wilt, remove from the heat, drain if necessary and leave to cool. Squeeze with your hands to extract any remaining moisture. Mix the greens into the soft cheese, beat in the eggs, add the dill and season with salt, pepper and nutmeg.

Brush a 25cm / 10in pie tin with butter and line with a layer of filo, using two overlapping sheets, leaving a generous edge flopping over the sides. Brush with melted butter and repeat until only one sheet of filo remains. Spread the filling over the pastry, top with the remaining sheet of pastry, and fold over the floppy edges to enclose. Brush with butter and sprinkle with a little cold water from your fingers. Bake for 40–45 minutes, until the pastry is crisp and brown. Serve warm, cut into bite-sized diamonds.

Good with . . . a Greek salad (page 83); a bowl of olives and another of toasted pistachios or almonds or both.

Espinacas con migas
Spanish spinach with fried bread

2

Nothing to it, really – a dish of greens, wild-gathered or cultivated, wilted in their own juices, sharpened with vinegar and topped with a crisp little hat of fried bread. It's no surprise, considering the seven centuries of Moorish presence in Andalusia, that a similar dish is to be found throughout northern Africa, although the topping is more likely to be toasted chopped nuts – almonds, peanuts, sesame seeds. North African spring greens considered suitable include the young leaves of pumpkin and sweet potato as well as wild leaves such as the Egyptian favourite, melokia, *a member of the sticky-juiced Malva family.*

Serves 4–6

750g / 1½lb spinach or any edible greens, rinsed and shredded
salt

To finish
4 tablespoons olive oil
2–3 slices day-old bread, cubed small
1–2 cloves garlic, finely chopped
salt and freshly ground black pepper
1 tablespoon sherry vinegar

Cook the shredded spinach in a tightly lidded pan with a little salt and the water that clings to the leaves, shaking to avoid sticking. This will take no more than 3–4 minutes.

Meanwhile, heat the oil in a small frying pan. When lightly hazed with blue, toss in the bread cubes and fry for a few minutes, turning them in the hot oil. Sprinkle in the garlic and fry until the bread is perfectly crisp and brown. Remove and reserve. As soon as the spinach is cooked, drain well and turn it in the hot frying pan with the remains of the oil. Season with salt and pepper, finish with a sprinkle of vinegar and serve topped with a sprinkling of bread cubes.

> Good with ... Andalusian grilled paprika-crusted pork (page 227); chickpea stew with *chorizo* (page 256); *patatas bravas* (page 136); grilled lamb cutlets – in Spain, small but toothsome. A slice of Valencian madeira cake with a little glass of Malaga moscatel would be an appropriate conclusion.

Gnocchi alla fiorentina
Italian spinach dumplings

These soft little green dumplings dressed with sage-infused melted butter make a delicate antipasto. The secret is to make sure the spinach and the curd cheese are really dry – squeeze out all the moisture before mixing with the rest of the ingredients. If it's still too wet to work, add more breadcrumbs.

Serves 4–6

2 big handfuls spinach, picked over and rinsed
4 tablespoons fresh white breadcrumbs
250g / 8oz ricotta (or any fresh curd cheese)
3 egg yolks
50g / 2oz grated Parmesan
½ teaspoon grated nutmeg
salt and freshly ground black pepper

To finish
2–3 tablespoons flour

To dress
melted butter
2–3 sage leaves, shredded
grated Parmesan

Cook the spinach in a lidded pan in the water that clings to the leaves after washing, salting lightly and shaking it over the heat until the leaves wilt. Drain thoroughly, squeezing out excess water with your hand, and chop finely. Allow to cool.

Work with the remaining ingredients and season generously with nutmeg, salt and pepper. Leave to firm in the fridge for an hour or two – overnight, if convenient.

With lightly floured hands on a flour-dusted board, form teaspoonfuls of the mixture into torpedo shaped croquettes. At this point you can freeze the *gnocchi* for cooking later. Bring a pan of salted water to the boil. Lower in a batch of the *gnocchi* – a few at a time, not enough for the temperature to drop below a simmer. Poach gently until they rise. Remove with a slotted spoon and arrange in a hot, lightly buttered dish. Dress with melted butter warmed with the shredded sage. You can finish it with extra sage leaves dropped into a little very hot oil and fried until just crisp.

Good with . . . Parma ham with *grissini*; young raw vegetables with coarse salt – peas and broad beans in the pod, slivered fennel, tender young artichokes, baby turnips.

Ispanak böreki
Turkish triangles with spinach

2

A sophisticated Ottoman stuffing, creamy, delicately spiced, given a little sweetness with a few sultanas. As everywhere throughout the Middle East, the wrapper is fine sheets of stretched or rolled dough – known as yufka in Turkey. If you would rather bake than fry, brush between the layers of pastry with melted butter and bake in a moderately hot oven – 190°C/375°F/ gas 5 – for 20 minutes, until puffed and golden.

Serves 4–6

1 packet filo pastry (about 270g / 9oz)
350g / 12oz mixed leaves (spinach, chard, rocket), shredded
1 small bunch flat-leaf parsley
100g / 4oz cream cheese (the real stuff – not low-fat)
50g / 2oz grated cheese (feta, Cheddar)
1 tablespoon sultanas, soaked in a little water to plump
1 teaspoon ground cinnamon
½ teaspoon ground nutmeg
salt and freshly ground black pepper
olive oil for shallow-frying

Defrost the filo pastry. Meanwhile, wash the greens, but don't dry them. Put them in a pan with the water that clings to them and shake over a high heat until well wilted – 3–4 minutes. Drain in a sieve, squeezing to remove as much liquid as possible. Squeeze again with your hands as soon as the greens are cool enough to handle. Chop very thoroughly with the parsley. Beat the greens with the two cheeses and the sultanas. Taste and season with cinnamon, nutmeg, salt and pepper.

Cut the filo through its folded or rolled thickness into strips 7cm/3in by 30cm/12in. Work with one strip at a time, keeping the rest clingfilmed (the pastry quickly dries and cracks). Put a teaspoon of the filling on the near corner of a single thickness of filo. Fold it over to make a triangle, fold again to make another triangle, and so on up the strip, always rolling away from you, until you have a well wrapped, leakproof parcel. Seal the last fold with a wet finger. Continue with the remaining pastry strips and filling.

Heat enough oil in a heavy frying pan to submerge the *böreki*. When the oil is lightly hazed with blue, fry a few at a time, turning once, until the pastry is well puffed and golden. Drain on kitchen paper.

Combine with . . . a bowl of yoghurt and mint for dipping; fish kebabs.

Summer vegetables

Vegetables, whether home-grown or bought daily in the marketplace, make up the bulk of the Mediterranean diet. Mediterranean housewives are well versed in their virtues and wouldn't dream of treating them with disrespect. Recipes are simple, cooking is minimal (sometimes just the application of the warmth of the sun), dressings rely heavily on olive oil and herbs, with lemon or vinegar to sharpen, the better to appreciate the sweetness.

Aubergines, peppers, tomatoes, courgettes, artichokes – of these five great sisters of the Mediterranean's summer harvest, only the first and the last are native. Somewhat surprisingly, the other three are New World introductions – welcome, to be sure, but nevertheless of recent enough arrival to be considered a little exotic on the Arab shores of the region, where they took rather longer to become established. Okra, a member of the mallow family, is much to the taste of Arab cooks but on European shores is only popular in Greece and the Balkans.

For this reason, the aubergine purées that are so much enjoyed on the *mezze* table have survived in many different forms throughout the region. Provençal cooks of the old school will often make a *ratatouille* based on aubergine and onion but without peppers or courgettes – including a little tomato, perhaps, but making sure it does not overwhelm the other flavours. As for the chilli, this most addictive of all vegetables – when the capsicums first arrived in Europe all were fiery – was the most immediately appealing to frugal Mediterranean cooks, since it could be planted in the herb patch to replace expensive imported peppercorns.

At the same time, fava (broad) beans were replaced on the northern shores of the Mediterranean by the New World's tribe of haricot, white and butter beans which, like the fava, can be eaten fresh or dried for storage. Broad beans are also eaten while the pods are still soft and furry and have only just begun to show the curve of the bean. The whole bean pod, stringed if necessary, is simply chopped into short lengths and cooked whole, a pleasure all too brief since the pods soon acquire the telltale shine of maturity. When fully developed the beans must be podded and, if tough, slipped out of their skins. Recipes for young broad beans in their pods can be made with mature podded beans: it's simply a matter of adapting the recipe a little – less liquid, a touch more oil.

All about chillis

The mouth says it's fiery, the brain says be careful, the taste buds say it's terrific. The chilli is the vegetable equivalent of the scarlet woman – delicious but dangerous. The attraction lies in the substance that delivers the message: capsaicin, an alkaloid with all the characteristics of poison. The fieriness is concentrated not so much in the seeds themselves but in the white woolly fibres which attach the seeds to the flesh.

The capsicum, the species of which chilli is a member, has a remarkably high sugar content, which is why it roasts so deliciously, caramelizing just before it burns. It's good for you, too – delivering, weight for weight, a higher dose of vitamin C than an orange.

Peppers ripen naturally from green to red – although, being a fruit, if they're picked very unripe they can wither before they turn scarlet. The shades in between – yellow, orange, brown, black – are the result of selective breeding by modern plantsmen. Botanically, two species can be identified, both naturally hot: the fleshy *Capsicum annuum*, and the smaller, fierier, *Capsicum frutescens*. The former has been tamed to produce the mild salad peppers; the latter is mostly responsible for the hot chillis that take the place of imported peppercorns in the storecupboards of the Mediterranean's independent peasantry.

The riper the fruit, the sweeter the flavour. Your tastebuds will tell you how much to use, but test with caution: cut off an end and lick rather than chew since the really hot ones are pretty explosive. Don't rub your eyes when handling, and rinse your fingers in cold water afterwards. Dried chillis should be deseeded and soaked before use. As for the powdered spice, chilli pepper and cayenne are the same thing.

The chilli and its milder brothers are all nightshades, that gastronomically ambivalent botanical family that includes the potato, the aubergine, the tomato, tobacco and – most toxic of plants – the deadly nightshade. Addictive stuff: chemists tell us that the brains of those with a passion for hot curries produce endorphins, exactly the same chemicals manufactured by racing drivers, mountaineers and high-wire artists to cope with danger. The best coolers are drinking-yoghurt or a cordial made with a sweetened, flavoured vinegar. You have been warned.

Ajo blanco
White gazpacho

2 *A sophisticated summer refresher from Granada, an infusion of almond milk heavily impregnated with garlic, which owes its pedigree to the sybaritic Moors. Serve it in small quantities or dilute with iced water: it has a kick like a mule.*

Serves 6–8

1 slice yesterday's bread, crusts removed
50g / 2oz blanched almonds
2 cloves garlic, skinned
1 tablespoon olive oil
about 1 litre / 1½ pints ice-cold water
1 tablespoon white wine vinegar
salt and sugar to season

To finish
A few small white grapes, peeled and pipped

Put the bread, almonds, garlic, oil, and a pint of the water into the blender, and process thoroughly. Add enough of the remaining water to give the consistency of thin milk.

Serve in small tumblers, well chilled. The usual instruction from those who know is to float a couple of grapes on top of each serving. Mine always drop to the bottom – no matter.

Warn participants that this is a high-garlic area.

Good with . . . cracked green olives marinated with fennel and lemon; devilled almonds (page 32); a *paella* made with wild rabbit and snails; grilled meats – spiced kebabs (page 228); carnival hamburgers (page 233); grilled quail; baby artichokes quartered and fried in olive oil.

Gazpacho
Spanish iced tomato soup

2

You wouldn't think this sophisticated iced soup started life as a simple bread porridge, eaten hot in winter and cold in summer – a peasant dish, sturdy and nourishing, a way of making hard bread palatable. In winter the traditional soaking liquid was a ladleful of hot broth, with a little garlic for flavour; in summer, as now, the liquid was simply cold water and a few chopped raw vegetables; for a touch of luxury, a sprinkling of chopped serrano ham, hard-boiled egg, bacalao – salt cod. Its history – although the dish is still to be found in its original form in many households of rural Andalusia – explains its modern incarnation as an iced tomato soup, lightly thickened with bread, with a variety of garnishes.

Serves 4–6

1kg / 2lb ripe tomatoes, skinned and chopped
¼ mild Spanish onion, skinned and chopped
½ cucumber, skinned and chopped
½ red pepper, deseeded and chopped
1–2 slices yesterday's bread, crusts removed, roughly torn
2 tablespoons olive oil
2 tablespoons wine vinegar
1 litre / 1½ pints cold water
salt, freshly ground black pepper, sugar to taste

Put all the ingredients in the liquidizer and process thoroughly. Taste and season – it may need a little more vinegar or sugar. You can dilute it further if you like – deliciously refreshing on a hot day in the Spanish sun.

Serve as cold as possible, but keep it away from the ice-cubes. Hand small bowls of whatever you please in the way of finishing touch – cucumber, tomato, pepper, onion, hardboiled egg, *serrano* ham, croûtons – all diced small.

Good with . . . a *paella* (page 261); something hot and crisp such as salt cod fritters (page 193); Andalusian ham croquettes (page 226); a *tortilla* – most suitably the version prepared in Granada's gypsy quarter, the Sacromonte, which includes sweetbreads and brains and other variety meats I'm far too dainty to mention.

Srpska salata
Serbian salad

2

This is the classic Balkan salad, as recommended by the Serbian salad-seller in the market in Belgrade one sunny autumn day before the troubles. The recipe is distinguished, explained my informant, from a Croatian salad by the presence of nuts – pinekernels or almonds can be substituted for the walnuts, milky and sweet when fresh – and from Macedonian by the absence of olive oil. In Albania, she told me disapprovingly, they don't bother to dress their salads at all. The bread which normally accompanies it is a soft-crumbed yeast-raised flat-bread, pogaça, which, as with the Ligurian focaccia, started life as a hearth-bread, a flattened disk of unleavened dough baked in the embers – soft and palatable when perfectly fresh, hard and fit only for soaking when cooled.

Serves 4–6

2 red peppers, deseeded and diced
2 small or 1 large cucumber, deseeded and diced
4 fine ripe tomatoes, deseeded and diced
1 mild red onion, finely chopped
2–3 tablespoons shelled fresh walnuts, skinned
1 teaspoon salt
juice of 1 lemon
about 6 tablespoons oil (sesame or corn oil)
4 tablespoons chopped flat-leaf parsley
2 tablespoons chopped dill

To serve
soft-crumbed flat-bread (*focaccia, ciabatta,* baps)
finely sliced lemons dressed with sugar

Combine all the ingredients in a large bowl and leave them for an hour or two for the flavours to develop. Serve with bread for dipping and a dish of very thinly sliced lemon, peeled or unpeeled, well sugared.

> Good with . . . Turkish triangles with spinach (page 96), finely sliced *prsiut*, the local *prosciutto*; home-made cracklings, pork skin cubed and fried crisp in fresh lard; slivers of salt-dried fish roe (*tarama* or *bottarga*); squares of cheese wrapped in vine-leaves and grilled until melted; fried cheese (page 69); cubes of feta dressed with a trickle of oil and a pinch of chilli flakes.

Dolmades
Greek stuffed vine-leaves

The definitive mezze: right size, right shape, right flavour. The vine-leaves are collected when young and tender in the early summer and either stored under brine or, in modern times, kept in a sealed jar in the fridge or frozen. Once the jar's been opened, the leaves quickly deteriorate. In Turkey, dolmas are just any old stuffed vegetables. In the Balkans the same treatment is often given to cabbage – fresh in summer, salted in winter (see page 138 for Serbian stuffed cabbage rolls).

Makes 25–30 little rolls

250g / 8oz vine-leaves, fresh, frozen or brine-packed
250g / 8oz round (risotto or 'pudding') rice
6 tablespoons olive oil
2 large shallots or medium onions, finely chopped
2 cloves garlic, finely chopped
25g / 1oz pinekernels, toasted
2 tablespoons chopped dill
2 tablespoons chopped flat-leaf parsley
2 lemons, juice and zest
salt and crushed dried chilli

Rinse the vine-leaves – if brined, simmer for 10 minutes to tenderize. Pick over the rice. In a heavy sauté pan heat a little of the oil and fry the chopped onions and garlic until they soften. Add the rice, pinekernels, herbs and lemon zest and stir over the heat until the grains turn opaque. Add the juice of one lemon and enough water to submerge the rice. Bubble up, season with salt and chilli, and cook for 5 minutes. Turn into a bowl and reserve.

Line the empty pan with a double layer of the more raggedy of the vine-leaves. Stuff the remainder: lay each leaf flat on the table with the stalk end towards you and drop a teaspoonful of the rice onto the broadest part. Using both hands, fold the sides of the leaf over the filling and roll up tightly towards the pointed end to make a little bolster-shaped parcel. As you finish each roll, lay it in the pan with the loose end tucked under. Continue stuffing until all the rice is used up and the pan is full. Sprinkle with the remaining lemon juice and oil and pour in enough hot water to just cover the parcels. Place a heavy plate on top to stop the *dolmades* moving around. Cook on a low heat for 50–60 minutes, until the rice is tender and the juices all absorbed.

Leave overnight to cool. Keeps for a week – longer in the fridge.

> **Good with . . .** Greek stewed lamb (page 240); *köfte* (page 234); Greek vegetable fritters (page 111).

Byessar

Moroccan broad bean purée

2 *A Moroccan salad purée of the same school as hummus. However, as befits the sophisticated French-influenced cuisine of Morocco, this version is flavoured with marjoram and finished with spring onions. Usually made with dried broad beans or split peas, it's particularly good made with mature fresh beans, podded and skinned.*

Serves 4–6

500g / 1lb shelled mature broad beans, skinned
2 cloves garlic, peeled and roughly crushed with the back of a knife
1 teaspoon chopped oregano or marjoram or thyme leaves
1 teaspoon ground cumin
1 teaspoon salt
150ml / ¼ pint virgin olive oil (the greener the better)
freshly ground black pepper

To finish
½ mild onion, slivered or
2–3 spring onions, trimmed and finely chopped

Put the broad beans in a saucepan with enough salted water to cover. Bring to the boil and simmer until tender – about 15 minutes. Drain, reserving a teacupful of the cooking liquid. Transfer the beans and the reserved cooking liquid to the blender and whizz to a purée with the remaining ingredients, adding the oil last, in a thin stream, as if making a mayonnaise. Taste and adjust the seasoning – more salt? Perhaps a little more garlic or lemon juice? Trust your tastebuds. It all depends on the leafiness of the olive oil and the youth of the beans.

To finish, stir in the slivered onion or spring onions. Serve at room temperature. Eat with bread, using the first three fingers of your right hand only and don't tear off more than you can eat at any one time – grabbing a large hunk for yourself is considered bad manners and greedy.

> Good with . . . a little dish of dipping-salt flavoured with cumin and chilli; *ciabatta* – the closest thing to Moroccan *kisrah* – or hot *pitta* for scooping; raw vegetables.

Melintzanosalata
Greek aubergine purée

2

This is one of those ubiquitous little dishes that appear on every mezze table throughout the lands that came under Arab influence, including Catalonia and Andalusia, where it's known as pez-de-tierra – earth-fish, a fast-day dish in the days when the Catholic Church dictated the diet (fasting days were Wednesdays, Fridays and the eve of all feast days, as well as the Easter and Christmas Lent). A scoopable purée, something between a salad and a sauce, always eaten with bread. Very simple to prepare and easy to adapt to regional preferences. The Moroccans like to season it with cumin and coriander, the Greeks sometimes stir in a flavouring of fresh herbs – oregano, marjoram, thyme. On the islands you may find it finished with chopped olives, capers, finely diced tomato. In Macedonia they enliven it with chilli. In Turkish Anatolia they use yoghurt instead of oil to moisten the purée, sweeten it with a little grape or pomegranate syrup – pekmez – and finish it with mint and toasted almonds. Suit yourself.

Serves 6–8

4 large, firm aubergines, hulls left on
4 cloves garlic, crushed with 1 tablespoon coarse salt
200ml / 7fl oz olive oil
about 4 tablespoons lemon juice or wine vinegar
extra olive oil mixed with a little chilli powder and paprika to decorate

Preheat the oven to 180°C/350°F/gas 4.

Arrange the whole aubergines on a baking tray and roast them for 1½–2 hours, until the flesh collapses. This dry-roasting gives them an exquisitely smoky flavour. Skin them as soon as they're cool enough to handle – either split them and scoop the flesh from the skin or hold them under the cold tap, in which case the skin will come off quite easily (squeeze the flesh dry if you do this). Or, if you like your purée speckled, don't bother to skin them – the flavour will be even better.

Mash or whizz the flesh up in the food processor with the garlic-and-salt paste, adding the oil and lemon juice or vinegar until you have a thick, pale purée. Taste and season. If the oil pools, add a handful of breadcrumbs or a spoonful of mashed potato.

Decorate with a swirl of chilli powder and paprika mixed with oil, or ground cinnamon, cardamom or cumin – whatever pleases.

> **Good with . . .** a scooping-bread *pitta* or any of its brethren; beans with *bottarga* (page 259) to make a change from the usual *hummus* (page 34); vegetable fritters – *briami* (page 111).

Mutabbel

Lebanese aubergine purée with sesame

2

This is the Lebanese–Syrian version of the familiar aubergine purée which pops up all over the Mediterranean (you'll also find it billed as baba ganoush*). Tahini – the sesame seed paste that is also used to enrich* hummus, *its natural partner – replaces the olive oil used elsewhere in the region. In Israel you'll very likely find it made with bottled mayonnaise: each to his own. Don't worry if you can't find* tahini; *smooth peanut butter makes a convincing substitute.*

Serves 4–6

3 large aubergines, hulls left on
3–4 cloves garlic, skinned and halved
juice of 2 lemons
4 tablespoons *tahini*
2 tablespoons chopped parsley
salt and crushed dried chilli

To finish (optional)
2 tablespoons olive oil coloured scarlet with a pinch of paprika
1 teaspoon cumin seeds, toasted in a dry pan

Preheat the oven to 180°C/350°F/gas 4. Make two slashes in each aubergine and press a half-clove of garlic into each slit. Bake the aubergines in the oven until soft – this will take about an hour. Take them out and allow to cool. Halve the aubergines and scrape the flesh off the thin skin – if you don't remove the skin the purée will have little black-purple specks throughout what should really be a pale cream. Drop the flesh and garlic in the liquidizer with the lemon juice and *tahini*. Process until smooth. Stir in the chopped parsley, taste and season with salt and chilli. To finish, be artistic with the olive oil and the cumin.

Good with . . . *hummus* (page 34) – the traditional way to serve the two purées is on a large flat plate with the *mutabbel* in the centre and the *hummus* round the outside, like a large pale sunflower. Accompany with *khoubiz*, the Lebanese yeast-raised flat-bread (or any of the Mediterranean flat-breads). To eat, break off a small piece of bread and scoop through both purées simultaneously. Good with *hamine* eggs (page 74) and red peppers in oil (page 121).

Melanzane a mannella

Neapolitan baked aubergines with cheese

Aubergines done the way they like it in Campania, the province that has Naples as its hub. A baked ratatouille *layered with cheese and sharpened with a little vinegar – the essence of a Mediterranean summer.*

Serves 6–8

3–4 fine fat aubergines, sliced
150ml / ¼ pint olive oil
2–3 courgettes, sliced
500g / 1lb ripe tomatoes, skinned and sliced (or tinned plum tomatoes)
a handful of basil, chopped
1 tablespoon balsamic vinegar
1–2 cloves garlic, finely chopped
2–3 tablespoons fresh breadcrumbs
2 mozzarellas (about 125g / 5oz each), drained and sliced
salt and freshly ground black pepper

Put the sliced aubergines in a colander, sprinkle with salt and leave to drain for half an hour. Shake off the salt and pat dry with kitchen paper.

Preheat the oven to 190°C/375°F/gas 5.

Heat half the oil in a frying pan and slip in the aubergine slices, a few at a time. Fry until they soften. Remove to a colander and leave to drain, adding the drainings back to the pan as you go. Fry the courgette slices – adding more oil as you need it – until soft and golden. Remove and reserve. Finally, fry the tomatoes, letting them melt down a little to concentrate the juices.

Layer half the vegetables in a gratin dish and sprinkle with the chopped basil, the vinegar and salt and pepper. Cover with sliced mozzarella and finish with the remaining vegetables. Top with garlic and breadcrumbs. Finish with a trickle of oil and bake for 30–40 minutes, until brown and bubbling. Serve at room temperature, Mediterranean-style.

Good with . . . pan-fried chicken (page 204); deep-fried baby artichokes; *focaccia* (page 49).

Imam bayaldi

Turkish stuffed aubergines

2 *A lovely dish that takes care and patience, this is seductively titled 'the imam swooned with pleasure' — graceful culinary propaganda in the Ottoman mould. The secret of success is to keep all the ingredients distinct: they must be delicately intertwined rather than a mush.*

Serves 6–8

3–4 fine, firm-fleshed aubergines, hulled
1 large onion, finely sliced vertically
3 large tomatoes, skinned and chopped
6 cloves garlic, finely chopped
1 tablespoon finely chopped parsley
1 tablespoon finely chopped dill
1 tablespoon finely chopped basil
1 teaspoon salt
150ml / ¼ pint olive oil
4 tablespoons water
1 teaspoon sugar
quartered lemons to serve

Cut the aubergines in half lengthways. Sprinkle with salt and leave to weep for 5 minutes. Rinse off the salt and place the halves side by side, flesh side up, in a wide, lidded casserole.

Mix the onion, tomatoes, garlic and herbs in a bowl with the teaspoon of salt and a tablespoon of the oil. Carefully pile the mixture on top of each half-aubergine until all the flesh is covered. Mix the rest of the oil with the water and sugar and pour it over and around. Cover the casserole and cook gently for 1–2 hours. Baste occasionally with the liquid, pushing the onion and tomato mixture down into the aubergine halves as they cook. The aubergines should end up soft and flat, sitting in a golden, slightly caramelized pool of oil.

Leave to cool. Spoon the oil over before serving with quartered lemons.

Good with . . . *pitta* bread for mopping (page 50); rice-stuffed mussels (page 182); Turkish minced meat kebabs (page 231).

Aubergines farcies aux anchoies

Provençal baked aubergines with anchovies

 A gorgeously rich dish, full of the scents and flavours of Provence. Choose plump, firm aubergines without blemish or bruise.

Serves 4–6

4 fine fat aubergines, hulled and halved lengthwise
salt
150ml / ¼ pint olive oil
1–2 cloves garlic, chopped
1 medium onion, finely slivered vertically
3–4 large tomatoes, skinned and chopped (or tinned plum tomatoes)
1 tablespoon black olives, pitted and chopped
6–8 anchovy fillets, roughly chopped
1 egg, lightly forked
3–4 tablespoons fresh breadcrumbs
1 tablespoon chopped parsley
1 teaspoon dried thyme
1 teaspoon dried marjoram
freshly ground black pepper

With a sharp knife scoop out the insides of the halved aubergines, leaving a shell about 1cm / ½in thick. Chop and reserve the flesh. Sprinkle the inside of the shells with salt and set in a colander to drain.

Heat half the oil in a frying pan and fry the garlic and onion until soft and lightly gilded. Add the reserved chopped aubergine flesh and fry gently for about 5 minutes, until squishy. Add the tomatoes, the olives and anchovies and bubble up. Turn down the heat and leave the mixture to simmer uncovered for about 10 minutes, mashing with a wooden spoon until it is thick and shiny. Leave to cool a little before mixing in the egg, breadcrumbs and herbs. Taste and season with freshly ground pepper; no salt – the anchovies and olives are quite salty enough.

Preheat the oven to 180°C/350°F/gas 4.

Rinse the salt from the aubergine shells, pat dry and fry in the remaining oil, cut-side down, for about 5 minutes, just enough to soften the flesh. Transfer gently to a sieve set over a bowl, leave to drip for another 5 minutes, then arrange them in a single layer, mouths up, in a gratin dish – they should fit neatly. Divide the stuffing mixture between the shells and trickle with the oily drippings from the bowl. Bake for 45–50 minutes, basting every now and then, until the aubergine shells are tender and the stuffing has a deliciously crisp hat.

> Good with . . . *pain de lapin* (page 199); a plate of sliced *saucisson sec* and *jambon de Bayonne* – the French *prosciutto.*

Papoutsakia
Greek baked aubergines

 A recipe from the Greek island of Ithaca, Ulysses' mythical homeland. For a meatless dish, omit the meat sauce and double the quantity of tomato sauce.

Serves 6–8

6 firm, plump aubergines, hulled and halved lengthwise
olive oil for frying

For the meat sauce
500g / 1lb minced beef or lamb
2 onions and 3–4 cloves garlic, finely chopped
a short stick of cinnamon and a handful of parsley, finely chopped
4 ripe tomatoes, skinned and chopped, plus 1 tablespoon tomato purée
salt and freshly ground black pepper

For the tomato sauce
2–3 tablespoons olive oil
1 onion and 2–3 cloves garlic, finely chopped
600ml / 1 pint concentrated tomato juice or *passata*

For the white sauce
4 tablespoons clarified butter (see page 16) or olive oil
75g / 3oz flour
1 litre (scant 2 pints) full-cream milk
3 eggs, lightly forked
salt, freshly ground black pepper, a pinch of grated nutmeg
50g / 2oz hard cheese (kefalotiri for preference), grated

Make criss-cross cuts in the cut sides of the aubergines. Heat the oil in a large, heavy frying pan and put in the aubergines, face-down, to fry gently until soft (they shrink amazingly). Transfer to a sieve to drain thoroughly.

Meanwhile, attend to the sauces. Put all the meat ingredients in a saucepan, cover and leave to simmer for an hour until the meat is tender. In another pan, simmer the tomato ingredients uncovered for about half an hour, until reduced to a thick jammy sauce. In a third pan (no problem with the washing-up in Greece), make the white sauce: melt the butter, stir in the flour and fry until it goes sandy, whisk in the milk gradually and simmer until the sauce thickens, remove, allow to cool a little, and then whisk in the eggs plus half the grated cheese. Taste and season with salt, pepper and nutmeg.

Preheat the oven to 180°C/350°F/gas 4. Arrange the drained, cooled aubergines in a shallow baking dish. Squish the soft part of the aubergine with a fork, spoon in the meat stuffing, top with the tomato sauce followed by the white sauce and finish with the remaining cheese. Bake in the oven for about 20 minutes, until brown and bubbling.

Good with . . . Greek garden salad (page 83).

Briami tiganiti

Greek vegetable fritters

Mediterranean cooks love to fry, and so do I. Any Greek or Spanish or Italian housewife can flip an airy fritter in two shakes of a donkey's tail. This preference for the frying pan is partly because it's quick, easy and no one wants to slave over a hot stove in the heat of summer; partly because it's an economical use of heat-source in a landscape not overly endowed with wood for fuel; partly because olive is the perfect frying oil – and don't let anyone persuade you otherwise. Non-virgin blended oils are best for the purpose – an oil that has been heat-treated and filtered.

Serves 4–6

olive oil for shallow-frying
1.5kg / 3lb mixed summer vegetables, finely sliced: courgettes (including flowers),
 aubergines, artichoke hearts, onion rings
about 300ml / ½ pint water, milk or beer
250g / 8oz strong bread flour
1 tablespoon semolina
coarse salt

On a deep plate or dish mix the flour with the semolina and a generous amount of salt. Heat the oil in a roomy frying pan until a faint blue haze rises.

Flip the vegetable slices first in the milk or water or beer, and then in the flour mixture. Some people drop them in flour first, water afterwards. Slip the slices in the boiling oil, a few at a time. Fry until crisp and golden. Drain on kitchen paper and eat immediately.

Good with . . . *skordalia* (page 41), the only possible accompaniment.

Carciofi ripieni
Italian stuffed artichokes

The earliest of the Mediterranean's summer vegetables, the artichoke is actually the flower-bud of a large thistle. At the beginning of the season, when the heads are young and tender, the French and Italians like to eat the small varieties raw, dipped in salt or olive oil infused with garlic and anchovies, or, as in Apulia, with olio santo *– olive oil infused with the tiny dried red chillis called* peperoncini.

Serves 4–6

8 prepared artichoke hearts (see below)
a little vinegar or lemon juice
salt

For the stuffing
4 tablespoons fresh breadcrumbs, fried crisp in a little butter or oil
1 small tin (100g / 4oz) tuna, drained and flaked
1–2 anchovy fillets, crushed (or a little anchovy paste)
2 tablespoons chopped parsley
2–3 tablespoons milk or single cream
salt and freshly ground black pepper
2 tablespoons olive oil to trickle

Drop the prepared artichoke hearts in plenty of boiling salted water with a little vinegar or lemon juice, and cook until tender – 20–30 minutes. Drain well and arrange on a lightly oiled baking sheet.

Preheat the oven to 180°C / 350°F / gas 4.

Mix all the stuffing ingredients except the oil together with just enough milk to bind, and spoon a little onto each heart. Trickle with the oil and bake for 10 minutes or so, until the top is nicely crisped. Serve at room temperature.

> Good with . . . hot *ciabatta* (page 48); *foccacia* (page 49) slivered fennel with oil and lemon.

To prepare artichokes: set ready a bowl of cold water with the juice of half a lemon. Trim the artichoke stalks close to the base. Scrape the stalks to remove the hard exterior fibres – the tender centre can be eaten – and drop them into the lemony water so they don't discolour. Snap off the tough outer leaves of the artichoke, then, with a sharp knife, cut off the tops of the remaining leaves to within half an inch of the base, leaving only the tender section close to the heart. Nick out the inner leaves, exposing the hairy choke. Remove the choke with a small sharp spoon and drop the prepared bases into the water. The artichoke hearts are now ready for cooking.

Aginares ke koukia ladera
Cretan artichokes and broad beans stewed in oil

2

Ancient flavours are preserved in this distinctively Cretan dish, which is no doubt not much different from that prepared in the palace kitchens at Knossos. The Cretans will tell you it was they who civilized the Greeks – at table as in all other things. When Theseus met the Minotaur, it was the Greeks who were the barbarians.

Serves 4–6

8 small prepared artichoke hearts (see page 112), quartered
500g / 1lb podded broad beans, skinned if they are old and tough
1 medium potato, diced
a large bunch of spring onions, trimmed and sliced
2–3 young carrots, scraped and sliced
6 tablespoons olive oil
salt and freshly ground black pepper

To finish
juice of half a lemon
a handful of dill, finely chopped
a handful of mint leaves
extra oil
quartered lemons to serve

Arrange all the prepared vegetables in a shallow heatproof casserole and pour in enough water to half submerge them. Add the oil, season, bring to the boil, turn down the heat, cover loosely and simmer gently for 30–40 minutes. Add a little more boiling water if needed to prevent sticking. When the vegetables are perfectly tender, remove the lid and stir in the lemon juice. Bubble up, stir in the chopped dill, remove from the heat and leave to cool. Finish with freshly chopped mint, a little more oil, and serve at room temperature with quartered lemons.

Good with . . . *souvlakia* (page 230); fish kebabs; wilted bitter leaves – chicory, dandelion, radicchio, rocket – dressed with oil and lemon.

Artichauts à la barigoule
Provençal artichokes to taste like truffles

2

Throughout the summer in Provençal markets artichokes are sold with their stalks in great bunches for little more than the price of a cabbage, allowing housewives to be as profligate as they please. For a few extra sous *you can buy the hearts ready-prepared. The aromatic cooking broth is designed to give the artichokes the flavour of the* barigoule, *a pale-fleshed summer truffle.*

Serves 4–6

**8–12 prepared artichoke hearts (see page 112), plus the upper stalks,
    trimmed and scraped**
4 tablespoons olive oil
1 large onion, finely chopped
2–3 cloves garlic, finely chopped
1 carrot, finely chopped
1–2 sticks green celery, trimmed and finely chopped
3 tablespoons black olives, pitted and finely chopped
2 tablespoons chopped *jambon cru* or lean bacon
1 small glass white wine
1–2 sprigs dried or fresh thyme, crumbled or chopped
2 dried or fresh sage leaves, crumbled or chopped
1–2 bayleaves
salt and freshly ground black pepper
a pinch of sugar

To finish
1 tablespoon chopped parsley
2–3 tablespoons fresh breadcrumbs

Quarter the prepared hearts, and chop the stalks into short bean-sized lengths.

Heat the olive oil in a heavy pan or heatproof casserole, add the onion and garlic and fry gently until they take a little colour. Add the carrot, celery, olives, ham or bacon, and fry for a few minutes more. Stir in the artichoke pieces – hearts and stalks – and bubble up. Add the wine and enough water to barely cover and bubble up again. Tuck in the herbs and turn down the heat, season with salt, pepper and a little sugar, cover loosely and leave to simmer for 30–40 minutes, until the artichokes are perfectly tender. Or cover with foil and bake in the oven for 45 minutes at 180°C/350°F/gas 4. By the end, the liquid will have reduced to an aromatic few tablespoonfuls – if there's too much bubble it up fiercely to evaporate the excess. Stir in the parsley and enough fresh breadcrumbs to take up all the juice. Serve at room temperature.

Good with ... *tapenade* (page 27); hardboiled eggs; Provençal pork-crackling bread (page 51).

Alcachofas rellenas granadienses

Andalusian stuffed artichokes

A dish from Granada, last of the great Moorish cities of Al-Andaluz to fall to Catholic Spain. The city's fertile market garden, the vega – still irrigated by the conduits built by her Arab architects – is famous for the splendour of its artichokes. The inclusion of ham makes the dish strictly post-Muslim, an important consideration when the Inquisition was asking personal questions.

Serves 4–6

8 large prepared artichoke hearts (see page 112)
½ lemon for rubbing

For the stuffing
500g / 1lb spinach, rinsed and shredded
100g / 4oz *jamón serrano* (or *prosciutto* or lean bacon), finely chopped
2–3 anchovy fillets, chopped
2–3 tablespoons fresh breadcrumbs
1 egg

For the cooking broth
1 small carrot, finely chopped
1 small onion, finely chopped
1–2 cloves garlic, chopped
3–4 tablespoons olive oil
1 sprig thyme and 1 bayleaf
salt and freshly ground black pepper
1 small glass white wine
1 small glass water

Rub the cut surfaces of the artichoke hearts with lemon to avoid browning.

To make the stuffing, drop the spinach in a pan with the water that clings to the leaves, cover tightly and shake over the heat until the leaves wilt, drain thoroughly, squeezing out excess water, and chop thoroughly. Using your hands, work all the stuffing ingredients together until well blended. Form the mixture into eight little balls and pop them into the artichoke hearts.

Meanwhile, in a roomy pan that will accommodate the artichoke hearts in a single layer, soften the vegetables in the oil with the herbs. Lay the artichoke hearts in the pan, season and fry gently. After 10 minutes add the wine and a glassful of water. Bubble up, turn down the heat and leave to stew gently in this aromatic bath, tightly lidded, for 30–40 minutes, until tender.

Remove the artichokes and arrange on a dish. Bubble up the juices to reduce, and pour over the artichokes.

Good with . . . *feria* hamburgers (page 233) or spiced kebabs (page 228).

Fonds d'artichauts aux petits pois

Provençal artichoke hearts with peas

2   *Choose artichokes as if they were flower-buds, which is indeed what they are. They must look fresh, lively and with no brown patches. Once cooked, they do not keep. Using only the hearts may seem wasteful – all those discarded leaves – but actually you're simply throwing away the inedible.*

Serves 4–6

8–12 prepared artichoke hearts (see page 112)
a squeeze of vinegar or lemon juice
100g / 4oz shelled fresh peas
8 tablespoons olive oil
1 tablespoon French mustard
juice and grated zest of 1 lemon
salt and freshly ground black pepper
2–3 finely chopped spring onions
1 tablespoon finely chopped parsley
1 teaspoon capers
1 hardboiled egg, chopped

Cook the artichoke hearts in plenty of boiling salted water acidulated with the vinegar or lemon juice. They will be tender in 20–30 minutes.

Meanwhile, cook the peas briefly until tender in a little boiling water, and drain.

Make a vinaigrette by whisking the oil with the mustard and lemon juice. Taste and season.

Drain and slice the artichoke hearts and toss with the vinaigrette, lemon zest, peas, spring onions, parsley, capers and hardboiled egg.

Good with . . . oyster mushroom *tian* (page 154); Provençal leek and cheese tart (page 53).

Kolokithakiapita tiganita

Greek courgette fritters

2

For this recipe I am indebted to Lazarus, keeper of the cooking pot at the Restaurant Polyphemus on the island of Ithaca, who had it from his mother-in-law, a native of the island of Kos. In winter he makes it with pumpkin, in autumn with marrows: overgrown courgettes — nobody goes to the trouble of growing separate varieties.

Serves 4–6

500g / 1lb courgettes, hulled and grated
salt
1 onion, grated
2–3 eggs, lightly forked
1 heaped tablespoon chopped mint
2 heaped tablespoons chopped parsley
salt and freshly ground black pepper

To finish
very finely crushed homemade toasted breadcrumbs
(Greeks can buy these from the baker)
olive oil for shallow-frying

Salt the grated courgettes and leave in a colander to juice and drain for 30 minutes. Shake dry, pressing to remove any extra liquid.

Mix the drained courgettes with the rest of the ingredients, season and form into little patties — as round and plump as the mixture will allow. Press lightly into the breadcrumbs, making sure they're well coated.

Heat the oil and fry the patties until the coating is crisply golden, turning them once, very carefully. Remove and drain on kitchen paper. Serve immediately — they won't keep.

Good with . . . *dolmades* (see page 103); octopus with oil and lemon (page 176); beetroot salad with *skordalia* (page 41); salt cod fritters (page 193); a cinnamon-spiced lamb stew (page 240).

Maydanoz böreki
Turkish filo triangles with parsley

2

Böreki, *the most popular Turkish appetizer, are little filo pastry envelopes, usually triangular, filled with a delicate stuffing. The principle can be applied to any vegetable or minced meat or chicken, so ring the changes with whatever comes to hand.*

Serves 4–6

For the stuffing
6 heaped tablespoons chopped parsley
250g / 8oz feta cheese, crumbled
½ onion, grated
I egg, lightly forked
I teaspoon crushed chilli
I teaspoon ground cinnamon
½ teaspoon grated nutmeg
salt and freshly ground white pepper
I packet filo pastry (about 270g / 9oz)
oil for frying

Work all the stuffing ingredients together with your hands until well blended.

To assemble the *böreki*: cut through the folded/rolled thickness of the pastry to produce strips 7cm / 3in wide by the full length of the pastry. Work on one strip at a time and keep the rest of the pastry covered with clingfilm to prevent its drying out. Put a teaspoon of the filling on the near corner of the strip. Fold it over to make a triangle, fold again to make another triangle, and so on up the strip, always rolling away from you, until you have a well wrapped little *börek* covered in 4–5 thicknesses of pastry. Seal the last fold with a wet finger. Continue until all are done – keep them separate or they stick to each other like glue.

Heat enough oil to submerge the little parcels. When lightly hazed with blue – just enough to gild a little square of bread as soon as it hits the oil – fry the *böreki* a few at a time, turning once, until the pastry is well puffed and golden. Drain on kitchen paper. Serve warm.

> **Good with . . .** a bowl of thick yoghurt mixed with finely chopped spring onions for dipping.

Kungulleshka tépjekura

Albanian vegetable marrow in a cream sauce

Albania is the smallest country in the Balkans and the least populated, since much of the interior is inhospitably mountainous and thickly forested. However, the coastal plain – the Albanian Riviera which includes the capital, Tirana – is as fertile as anyone might wish. The climate is much like that of southern Italy and well suited to the cultivation of olives, citrus fruits, figs, wheat, maize, with vegetables grown in water-conserving polytunnels. Albanian culinary habit is basically Ottoman, a relic of the Turkish domination which has survived not only in the religion – most Albanians are Muslim – but in many of her foodways, including the preservation of the raki ritual of which the mezze is an integral part. This might be as simple as a sliver of sheep's cheese, a plateful of hardboiled eggs, a handful of olives – or, as here, something a little more sophisticated to share out of a common dish.

Serves 4–6

1 young marrow – or 3–4 medium courgettes – about 500g / 1lb
1 tablespoon wine vinegar
1 teaspoon salt

For the topping
2 egg yolks
1 tablespoon plain flour
50g / 2oz clarified butter (see page 16), melted
300g / 10oz thick sheep's milk yoghurt (*kos*)
2 tablespoons crumbled strong white cheese (feta comes closest)
1 teaspoon grated nutmeg
salt and freshly ground black pepper

Preheat the oven to 200°C/400°F/gas 6

If you are using a marrow, scoop out the woolly centre with the seeds, peel if the skin looks a little tough, and cut into bite-sized cubes. If you are using courgettes, dice them. Drop the diced vegetable into a panful of boiling water and add the vinegar and the salt. Bring back to the boil and cook for 5–10 minutes, until tender but still quite firm. Drain thoroughly and arrange in a shallow earthenware or gratin dish.

Meanwhile, whisk or liquidize the topping ingredients to make a rich, savoury custard. Pour this over the vegetables in the dish and bake for 20–30 minutes, until the sauce is thick and the top is blistered and bubbling.

> **Good with** . . . crisp-fried bread croûtons; finely sliced *salami*, *torshi* – salt-pickled vegetables (page 28).

Calabazinas valencianas

Valencian stuffed baby marrows with saffron rice

 Choose the little round tender-skinned marrows specially grown for stuffing – or pick well grown, plump courgettes. Lean bacon is an acceptable substitute for serrano *ham; vegetarians might like to use chopped olives. The cooks of Valencia, an elegant, palm-fringed port on Spain's Levante coast, are Spain's acknowledged rice-experts.*

Serves 4–6

6–8 round baby marrows or large courgettes, hulled
4 tablespoons olive oil
I smallish onion, finely chopped
100g / 4oz podded peas
50g / 2oz chopped *serrano* ham or lean bacon
I tablespoon chopped marjoram
I teaspoon dried thyme
6–8 tablespoons leftover rice (*paella* is perfect)
I egg, lightly forked
I lemon, juice and finely grated zest
pinch of saffron threads infused in 150ml / ¼ pint boiling water
salt and freshly ground black pepper

Cut the courgettes or marrows in half (through the equator if round, length-ways if long). If the centres are woolly, use a teaspoon to scoop out and discard the fluff and seeds. Hollow out the shells to the thickness of your little finger, and arrange in an earthenware dish or roasting tin – best if they fit neatly without too many gaps. Dice the scooped-out flesh and reserve.

Heat 2 tablespoons of the oil in a small frying pan. When lightly hazed with blue, add the chopped onion and fry gently until it softens and gilds. Add the reserved chopped marrow, stir over the heat until it softens and collapses, then stir in the peas, ham and herbs. Season, remove from the heat, leave to cool and then mix thoroughly with the rice, the forked-up egg and lemon zest. Add the lemon juice to the saffron water.

Preheat the oven to 180°C/350°F/gas 4.

Stuff the marrow shells with the rice mixture, trickle with the remaining oil and pour the saffron water into the gaps. Cover with foil (shiny side down, so that the heat is reflected onto the food) and bake for 30–40 minutes, until the marrows are perfectly tender. Remove the foil for the final 10 minutes and baste with the saffron-scented juices to crisp and gild the rice a little. Serve at room temperature.

Good with . . . chilled *gazpacho* (page 101), deep-fried anchovy fans (page 163).

Pimientos en aceite
Spanish peppers in oil

2

A very simple preparation, worth making in quantity as it keeps for weeks in the fridge: just pack the peppers in a jar in their own oily juices, top up with more olive oil so that they are submerged, and lid tightly. The extra oil won't go to waste — use it to dress a potato salad, or in a seafood mayonnaise. I don't bother to skin the peppers: I just fish out any little spars that make themselves obvious during the frying. Serve with toasted pan candeal or any dense-crumbed bread. The proper way to toast such bread is on a little grid placed over a naked flame, so that the crumb singes rather than toasts, imparting a wonderful smoky flavour and the lightest possible crisping — perfect for soaking up the oil and as a foil for the sweetness of the vegetable. See page 47 for the recipe and bake your own.

Serves 4–6

3 large red peppers, hulled, halved, deseeded
about 6 tablespoons olive oil
2–3 cloves garlic, skinned and sliced

Slice the peppers vertically into strips. Warm the oil in a small frying pan, add the peppers and fry them gently until they are perfectly soft and the juices have evaporated so that the oil is once again clear. As the oil heats up, the sugar in the peppers will caramelize, which will give the finished dish a lovely roasted flavour. Throw in the garlic at the last minute — it should soften but not brown. Serve the peppers dressed with their own garlic-flavoured oil, with thick slices of sturdy bread to mop up the juices.

Good with . . . potato *tortilla* (page 76); fish brochettes; Andalusian spiced kebabs (page 228); rice or ham *croquetas* (page 226).

Pimientos rellenos
Valencian stuffed peppers

A dish from Alcoy, a hill town in the mountains behind Valencia. The peppers favoured for the recipe are ñoras – the mild-flavoured, sweet-fleshed pimenton pepper, a variety suitable for drying. In autumn you'll see strings of them hanging alongside the skeins of garlic and loops of chorizo which flavour the winter beanpot.

Serves 8

8 large red peppers
about 6 tablespoons olive oil
3 cloves garlic, finely chopped
100g / 4oz *jamón serrano*, **chopped small**
1 tablespoon *pimentón* **or paprika**
a handful of parsley, finely chopped
1kg / 2lb tomatoes, skinned and chopped
a generous knifetip of saffron (about 12 threads), soaked in a little boiling water
500g / 1lb round rice (*paella*, *risotto* **or 'pudding')**
salt and freshly ground black pepper
1 small glass water
a little extra olive oil

Wipe the peppers, cut off a lid round the stalk end, leaving the stalk in place, and empty out the seeds. Arrange the peppers upright, mouths pointing heavenwards, in a shallow ovenproof earthenware casserole or roasting tin, wedged together snug as herrings in a barrel.

Preheat the oven to 190°C/375°F/gas 5.

Heat the oil gently in a roomy frying pan, sprinkle in the garlic and let it soften a little. Add the ham, paprika and parsley and cook for 2–3 minutes, until it smells deliciously fragrant. Add the tomatoes and bubble up, squishing with a wooden spoon. Add the saffron with its soaking water, and stir in the rice. Season. Bubble up again, allow 2 minutes, remove from the heat. Stuff the rice into the peppers – no more than half full as the grains need room to swell. Pop back the lids. Trickle with a little more oil and 1 glassful of water, cover with foil, transfer to the oven and cook for about 1¼ hours. Test by biting a grain of rice: the ones on top will have to be very soft if the middle is to be properly cooked. Serve at room temperature. Memories are made of this.

Combine with . . . Andalusian rabbit with sherry (page 215); braised lamb (page 239); carnival hamburgers (page 233).

▶ *Valencian stuffed baby marrows with saffron rice (page 120)*

Tomates à la provençale

Provençal tomatoes

2

As with all very simple dishes, not so much a recipe as a reaction. In this case, to those wonderfully juicy, solid-fleshed tomatoes of the Mediterranean littoral. Vegetables and fruits that have been permitted to come to sweet maturity in their own time, as nature intended, swelled by the rain and ripened by the sun, need very little culinary attention. These tomatoes achieve their marvellously concentrated sweetness through long gentle frying – how wonderful it is that the judicious application of heat can transform the ordinary into the sublime. The same technique can be applied to baby onions, quartered hearts of fennel (sharpen with a little lemon zest and juice), new potatoes scrubbed and scraped, artichoke hearts, bite-sized chunks of pumpkin. To vegetables not generously endowed with natural juices you may need to add a little liquid – water or white wine – use your own good sense. Whatever your choice, have patience. Good things come to those who wait.

Serves 4–8

8 large perfectly ripe beef tomatoes
3 tablespoons olive oil
2 cloves garlic, skinned
1 teaspoon coarse salt
a handful of parsley, de-stalked

Cut the tomatoes in half and scoop out and discard the seeds. Warm the oil in a wide, shallow pan. Put in the tomatoes, cut side down, in a single layer. Let them fry very gently for 40–45 minutes, shaking the pan from time to time so that the tomatoes do not stick and burn.

Crush the garlic with the salt, and then mince it very finely with the parsley. Turn the tomatoes flesh side up, and sprinkle with this aromatic mixture. Continue to cook very very gently on the other side – another half-hour is certainly not too long.

> Good with . . . *focaccia* with sage (page 49); fat chips thrice-fried in olive oil until really crisp; potatoes with saffron (page 137); any artichoke dish; a *tian* (page 154) or *omelette*.

◄ *Cypriot cinnamon pumpkin pies (page 140)*

Domates gemistes

Greek stuffed tomatoes

For this dish to be as good as it can be, choose large, firm, ripe beef tomatoes and use extra-virgin Greek olive oil. Don't be discouraged by the relative cheapness of Greek olive oil, and the lack of fancy packaging. Kalamata is my own favourite – I buy it by the gallon and use it for everything. The Greeks, after all, invented the stuff. Use this mixture to stuff any vegetable you please.

Serves 4–6

8 large tomatoes
salt and freshly ground black pepper
2 teaspoons sugar
5–6 tablespoons olive oil
2 large onions, finely chopped
2 tablespoons finely chopped mint
2 tablespoons finely chopped parsley (flat-leaf is best)
2 tablespoons toasted pinekernels (or slivered almonds) (optional)
175g / 6oz long-grain rice
1 tablespoon sultanas, soaked in a little water to swell
2 tablespoons tomato paste dissolved in 150ml / ¼ pint water

Preheat the oven to 180°C/350°F/gas 4.

Slice the tops off the tomatoes and reserve. Scoop out the innards carefully with a teaspoon, taking care not to break the skin. Discard the pips and reserve the pulp. Sprinkle the scooped-out shells with salt and sugar and arrange on a roomy baking tray.

Heat 3 tablespoons oil in a frying pan and sauté the onions gently until soft and golden. Add the reserved tomato pulp, herbs, seasoning and optional nuts. Bubble up, reduce the heat and simmer gently for about 10 minutes. Stir in the rice and the soaked, drained sultanas. Cook for another 5 minutes or so, until most of the liquid has been absorbed – the grains should still be quite nutty and firm.

Fill the hollowed-out tomatoes with the rice. Replace the tops and pour the watered-down tomato paste and the remaining oil into the gaps between the tomatoes. Cover with foil, shiny side down.

Bake for 40–50 minutes, until the rice is perfectly tender and the tomatoes are bathed in a very little aromatic oil. Leave to cool. Serve at room temperature.

Good with . . . grilled fish; mussels opened in a little white wine; crisply fried aubergine fritters with *skordalia* (page 41); a dish of Kalamata olives and slices of kefalotiri or feta cheese.

Ratatouille
Provençal vegetables with garlic and oil

This needs no introduction – unless it be a reminder that a ratatouille should never be mushy. The secret is to cut everything into same-size pieces, remembering that small cooks quicker than large, precook all separately, and marry them only at the end.

Serves 6–8

about 150ml / ¼ pint olive oil
1 large onion, finely sliced
2–3 cloves garlic, chopped
500g / 1lb aubergines, diced
500g / 1lb courgettes, diced (if very small, slice thickly)
500g / 1lb red peppers, deseeded and cut into strips
1kg / 2lb ripe tomatoes, skinned and roughly chopped
1 sprig thyme
1 sprig rosemary
salt and freshly ground black pepper

Have ready a sieve set over a basin and an empty casserole.

Heat about 4 tablespoons of the oil in a heavy sauté pan. As soon as it's lightly hazed with blue add the onion and garlic and fry until they are soft and golden – don't let them brown. Remove with a slotted spoon and transfer to the sieve to drain.

Return the drippings to the pan, add a little more oil and fry the aubergines – they soak up oil like a sponge but release much of it again as they cook. Meanwhile, empty the contents of the sieve into a roomy casserole. When the aubergine is perfectly soft, transfer to the sieve to drain. Add the drippings back to the pan, reheat with a little more oil and fry the courgettes until soft and a little gilded. Add the aubergines to the casserole and transfer the courgettes to the sieve. Repeat the process with the peppers.

Finally, fry the tomatoes in the remaining oil, using a potato masher to squash them down as they cook and bubbling up the juices to make a thick sauce. Stir the sauce into the vegetables in the casserole, tuck in the herbs, stir and season. Bring to the boil, then turn down the heat, cover loosely and leave to simmer gently for 10–15 minutes to blend the flavours. Finally, remove the lid and bubble fiercely until the sauce is reduced to a sticky scarlet slick. Serve at room temperature, with bread for mopping.

Good with . . . Provençal broad bean omelette (page 78); charcuterie – maybe a good *saucisson cru*.

Bamies stofato
Greek stewed okra

2

Okra – ladies' fingers – are a popular vegetable in Greece. A member of the Mallow family, like so many of the more primitive green vegetables they're preserved for the winter by sun-drying – you'll see them strung on thread, like beads on a necklace, in the markets of Greece and the Middle East. The plants grow quickly and the season is short since the pods must be picked young, before they ripen and become fibrous. When choosing, pick pods that are bright green, look juicy and are free of any little brown patches.

Serves 4–6

750g / 1½lb fresh okra
4 tablespoons olive oil
1 large onion, chopped
3–4 fresh beef tomatoes, skinned, deseeded and chopped,
    or a 400g / 14oz tin of plum tomatoes
1 lemon, juice and finely grated zest
2 tablespoons chopped parsley
2 tablespoons chopped dill
1 small glass white wine
1 small glass water
1 teaspoon sugar
salt and freshly ground black pepper
quartered lemons to serve

Prepare the okra by trimming the stalks close to the pod. If you don't enjoy their glueyness – and lots of people do – don't hull, just trim off the stems, toss the pods with salt and a little vinegar and leave in a colander for an hour or two, by which time they will have yielded up their gloop; rinse well before using.

Warm the oil in a heavy pan or casserole and gently fry the onion until soft – don't let it brown. Add the chopped tomatoes and bubble up, squashing with a wooden spoon to encourage a rich sauce. Stir in the okra and all the remaining ingredients, and bubble up. Turn down the heat, cover loosely and simmer for 30–40 minutes, until the pods are perfectly tender and the sauce deliciously rich and sticky. Or transfer to one of the shallow earthenware casseroles Greek country cooks like to use for slow-simmered dishes, cover with foil and bake in the oven at 150°C/300°F/ gas 2.

Serve at room temperature, with quartered lemons.

Good with . . . *köfte* (page 234); *souvlakia* (page 230); grilled fish.

Roots & winter vegetables

Potatoes, carrots, onions, leeks, pumpkins, marrows, garlic – all these storable things provide the winter dishes of the Mediterranean. Of all the roots the potato, a post-Columbian vegetable whose adaptability to its new territory provided the rural poor for the first time with a reliable food source, is the most versatile. Easy to grow, needing minimal attention and able to thrive in the poorest soils, the potato took to olive oil like – well, ham to eggs, salt to pepper, needle to thread. Chips, crisp, hot, thoroughly salted and straight from the pan. Chips dressed in the Spanish way, with chilli and tomato. Chips sprinkled with grated cheese, as they like them in Greece. Chips in any and every way you like. Or potatoes dressed with almonds and saffron, in the Valencian manner.

But of all the flavours of winter, garlic – queen of the pot-herbs, maturing in summer, star of the winter storecupboard, essential flavouring of the Mediterranean kitchen – is both the most universal and the least understood in the northern kitchen. When garlics are first harvested, they look like fat white onions. The outer covering is very soft and thick and the cloves are practically invisible – if you search them out at the base of the bulb, tucked inside the coverings, they look like tiny seed-pearls. These fresh garlics are delicious roasted or grilled whole, like young onions. As the bulbs dry, the infant cloves suck the moisture from the covering and become plump and juicy, with crisp creamy flesh and an exquisite fragrance. Unfortunately, from this moment on it's downhill all the way. The cloves shrink in their papery coverings and begin to sprout. At first, this tiny scrap of green at the heart can be nicked out with a sharp knife. At this point, although the garlic will be stronger-flavoured than in the first flush of youth, the flesh will still be palat-able. Astonishingly rapidly, however, the seedling becomes a full-blown shoot and the flesh becomes bitter and rubbery. Once the shoots show above the cloves you have no choice but to plant them out and harvest the green – delicious in salads and to flavour pasta stuffings and risottos – or wait until they do what nature dictates and form a new bulb.

In this section I have also included pickled vegetables. Fresh pickles with a relatively short shelf-life are much appreciated in Mediterranean lands, the underlying purpose being as much to add flavour as to conserve, perhaps because seasonal deprivations are shorter and less acute than in northern Europe.

Aglio al forno
Roasted garlics

2

Gorgeous as the simplest of antipasti – just pop the cloves straight onto hot bruschetta. Or make into a paste to stir into pasta sauces, bean soups – roasted garlic has a deliciously sweet mild flavour after the long slow cooking has tamed its fierceness.

Serves 4

4 whole plump heads garlic
about 4 tablespoons olive oil

Preheat the oven to 180°C/350°F/gas 4.

First separate the garlic cloves: using a sharp knife, slice the little platelets off the root ends of the garlic cloves (leave the skin on). Place them in a large square of aluminium foil, shiny side inwards, drizzle with the oil and wrap securely as a parcel.

Bake for about an hour. Check after 40 minutes and if necessary sprinkle with a little water. At the end of the cooking the cloves should be perfectly soft and lightly golden but not browned – garlic tastes bitter if it's burnt.

Serve as they are, with grilled bread – popped out of their skins directly onto the crisp crumb. Or make a garlic paste: use the back of a knife to push cloves out of their skins and sieve the mush or liquidize with its own luscious juices. If you don't need it straight away, pack into a jar, cover with a little more oil, and store in the fridge.

Good with . . . finely sliced *prosciutto* and *salami*; *ciabatta* (page 48); *porcini in umido* (page 150).

Pantzaria salata
Greek beetroot salad

2

Greek cooks use both the root and leaves of young beetroot, dressing the roots with olive oil and the leaves with lemon juice. If you can't find beetroot with leaves, a few stalks of Swiss chard will supply the greens. For a surprising contrast of flavour and texture, finish with a handful of pickled hyacinth bulbs, volvi, the tulip-like bulbs of the wild grape hyacinth, Muscari commutatum, which have been used as food since the days of Dionysus. Greeks esteem wild-gathered foods for their vigorous flavours and the bitterness believed to be blood-cleansing.

Serves 4–6

1 large bunch young beetroot with leaves – 6–8 roots
salt

To dress
about 4 tablespoons lemon juice
1 clove garlic, slivered
about 6 tablespoons olive oil
salt and freshly grated nutmeg

To finish **(optional)**
Pickled hyacinth bulbs or small pickled onions, sliced

Trim the leaves from the beets, leaving an inch or so of stalk still attached to the root – if the root is cut, the scarlet juices will leach out into the cooking water and much of the colour will be lost. Reserve the leaves. Rinse the roots – don't scrub too hard – and put them in a roomy pan with enough cold water to cover. Bring to the boil, salt generously, turn down the heat and cook for 20–40 minutes, depending on the size of the roots, until they are perfectly tender. Drain and leave to cool.

Meanwhile, rinse and shred the leaves and chop the stems. Cook in a very little water, well salted, for about 10 minutes, until tender. Transfer to a colander and drain thoroughly, squeezing to extract all the water.

Toss the greens with the lemon juice and a little salt and pile up on a flat dish. Skin and slice the roots as soon as they're cool enough to handle. Pile the dressed greens in the middle of the dish and surround with overlapping slices of the deep crimson roots lightly dressed with olive oil, slivered garlic, nutmeg and the optional pickles.

Good with . . . aubergine fritters (page 111); well-spiced *köfte* (page 234). Traditionally served with garlic-and-oil *skordalia* (page 41).

Salata kiseo kupus

Croatian cabbage salad

2

A simple salad of shredded cabbage dressed with caraway, a spice much used in the German kitchen – a preference which reflects Croatian ethnic leanings. In summer the salad is made with lightly salted fresh white cabbage, in winter with sauerkraut – salt-pickled (therefore soured) cabbage.

Serves 4–6

1 small or ½ large white cabbage (about 750g / 1½lb)
2 tablespoons salt
1 thick slice streaky bacon, diced
about 6 tablespoons nut or seed oil (walnut, sesame, pumpkin)
about 2 tablespoons vinegar
freshly ground black pepper
1 teaspoon caraway seeds

Quarter the cabbage and cut out the core. Shred very finely with a sharp knife – or use the food processor. Salt thoroughly and leave for an hour in a colander to drain and soften.

Meanwhile, fry the bacon crisp in its own fat – it may need a little oil to help it along.

Rinse the shredded cabbage thoroughly and shake or pat dry. Toss with the crisp bacon, oil, vinegar, freshly ground pepper and caraway.

Good with . . . *torshi* – salt-pickled vegetables (page 28); fresh or kiln-dried walnuts; a few slivers of kashkaval, known in Italy as caciocavalo – small round cheeses tied in pairs for ease of transport over the saddle of a horse; or a slice of sirene, the local feta, with sliced tomatoes. On the same dish (in the Balkans, *mezze* are often presented on single platters, as with the Russian *zakuski*), any other simple salads that take your fancy – grated carrot with sesame, fennel with lemon, potatoes dressed with finely sliced onion and chopped dill. On a special occasion, a few slivers of *salami* or *prosciutto* – *prsuta* is the Balkan name for wind-dried salt-preserved meats, although in the relatively damp climate the ham might well be mutton and smoking is added to the salting as an additional preservative.

Salatet jazar
Israeli carrot salad

2

Refreshing and delicious, this was the most popular mezze in the kibbutz canteen of an Israeli settlement down the Jordan valley I happened to visit when in a previous incarnation as a botanical painter, hot on the trail of a certain wild tulip in what happened to be a war zone. The kibbutzniks, while self-sufficient in most things, earned the income to pay for outside necessities from the cultivation of irises for French gardens. Being no more than a few miles from the border, the settlement endured nightly shelling from cross-border gun emplacements, making life somewhat hazardous for the field-workers obliged to negotiate unexploded shells. The kibbutzniks took turns in the kitchen, all food was home-grown and the cooking was, by necessity, of the simplest. Since this recipe is of Lebanese origin, no doubt their assailants were enjoying exactly the same dish. Choose organic carrots – sweeter and far less watery than those that have been plumped up with fertilizer and stored under refrigeration.

Serves 3–4

500g / 1lb well grown organic carrots
2 tablespoons raisins or sultanas
1 orange, juice and zest
4 tablespoons oil (sunflower, corn)
juice of 1 lemon
1 tablespoon runny honey
1 teaspoon ground cinnamon

To finish
1 tablespoon sesame seeds or flaked almonds, toasted

Grate the carrots finely and leave to drain in a sieve. Meanwhile, put the raisins or sultanas to soak in the orange juice.

Toss everything together and pile it up in a dish. Finish with the toasted nuts.

Good with ... freshly baked *pitta* (page 50); a dish of finely sliced cucumber dressed with lemon juice and parsley; a salad of finely shredded white cabbage, blanched, lightly salted and dressed with yoghurt whisked with a little lemon juice and oil.

Patates bamya salatas

Turkish potato and okra salad

2

Choose yellow-fleshed potatoes and okra pods that are perfectly green and plump without any little brown bits or stringy ends. If the okra is either not in the first flush of youth or un-obtainable, use fresh fava (broad) beans, podded and skinned, or young green beans. In summer, a diced peach is often included.

Serves 4–6

750g / 1½lb new potatoes, scrubbed
500g / 1lb okra, topped and tailed
4 tablespoons olive or sunflower oil
2 cloves garlic, finely chopped
1 small onion, finely chopped
2 tablespoons chopped coriander
salt and a pinch of crushed chilli
2 tablespoons pomegranate or lemon juice

Cook the potatoes in plenty of boiling salted water. Drain as soon as they're tender, and slice thickly.

Meanwhile, rinse and dry the okra. Warm the oil in a frying pan. Add the chopped garlic and onion and let them sizzle gently until they soften – 3–4 minutes – taking care not to let them take colour. Turn up the heat, add the okra and toss over the heat for 5 minutes or so, until the okra has softened a little but is still fresh and green. Turn down the heat, stir in the potatoes, turning to mix everything thoroughly. Season with salt and chilli, cover and leave to simmer gently for 5 minutes to marry the flavours.

Leave to cool before dressing with the pomegranate or lemon juice. Serve at room temperature.

> **Good with . . .** Turkish pancakes stuffed with greens (page 54), *pitta* (page 50) or whatever Middle Eastern flat-bread takes your fancy; rice-stuffed mussels (page 182); crisp little *böreki* (page 96) or maybe the Tunisian *brik* (page 75).

Salade de pommes de terre
Provençal potato salad

A variable recipe: possible inclusions are diced cucumber, hardboiled egg, tomato, diced apple, walnuts, toasted pinekernels, tinned tuna, anchovies. Don't omit the marjoram (oregano is the wild variety of the same species) – it has a warm earth fragrance which gives it a particular affinity with potato.

Serves 4–6

1kg / 2lb small waxy new potatoes, scrubbed
4 tablespoons olive oil
1–2 slices yesterday's bread, cubed
1 clove garlic, crushed with a pinch of salt

To dress
2 tablespoons mild French mustard
2 tablespoons wine vinegar
4 tablespoons olive oil
150ml / ¼ pint white wine or chicken stock
freshly ground black pepper
a pinch of salt

To finish
1 tablespoon capers, drained
1 tablespoon small black olives
1 small bunch spring onions, chopped
1 heaped tablespoon chopped marjoram or oregano
a handful of rocket, dandelion leaves or any other mustardy, bitter greens,
    roughly shredded

Cook the potatoes in plenty of well salted boiling water for 15–20 minutes, until perfectly tender. Drain immediately, then return the potatoes to the heat for a moment to dry them off.

Meanwhile, heat the oil in a frying pan. As soon as it smokes – a blue haze, nothing more – drop in the bread cubes and fry until they are crisp and golden. Remove, toss with the crushed garlic and reserve.

Set the frying pan with its oily drippings back on the heat and stir in the mustard, vinegar, wine or stock. Bubble up for a moment and whisk in the oil and seasoning – if you're lucky they'll form an emulsion; if not, no matter. Tip the dressing into the bowl in which you mean to serve the salad. Slice in the potatoes, skin and all, and turn them in the hot liquid. The potatoes will drink it all up as they cool. Toss with the reserved croûtons and the finishing ingredients.

Good with . . . roast rabbit or chicken, jointed into bite-sized pieces.

Papas fritas
Spanish potato crisps

2

A feria treat, cooked on the spot to order, bagged up in impossibly thin plastic bags. The difference in flavour if you fry your own fresh is quite remarkable. Olive oil – non-virgin, no sense in using the expensive leafy green stuff when the pure, rectified olive oil is better for the purpose – imparts a deliciously nutty flavour. As for the potatoes, every region has its preference. Wilja and Pentland Dell give good results – unless you can get hold of the Scottish Golden Wonder, the perfect tattie for the frying vat.

Makes about 500g / 1lb crisps

2kg / 4lb old potatoes
olive oil for deep-frying
salt

Peel the potatoes or not, as you please – if you don't they'll be better food-value, but the skins are undeniably tough. Slice finely either in the processor or with a mandoline, a wooden instrument shaped like a miniature washboard into which is set a pair of sharp steel blades. Rinse off the surface starch from the potato slices, drain and dry thoroughly in a clean cloth.

Heat the oil in the deep-fryer or a roomy pan. Watch for a faint blue haze to mist the surface. Scatter in the potato slices – only a handful at a time or the temperature of the oil will drop too abruptly. Stir and turn them as they fritter to a golden brown. Remove and drain thoroughly on kitchen paper. Continue until all are done.

To make the French *pommes soufflés*, cut the potatoes into slices of double thickness. Rinse, dry and give them a preliminary gentle frying (catch the oil just before the surface hazes blue). Remove when they're soft but only lightly gilded. Drain on kitchen paper and leave to cool. Bring the oil back to a high frying temperature. Refry the potatoes, a few at a time. Magically they will puff up into plump crisp hollow pillows.

Crisps keep well, unsalted (salt draws water), in a tightly lidded tin or in well sealed plastic bags. If they go soggy they can be crisped up again in a warm oven.

> **Good with . . .** any of the Middle Eastern dips – *hummus* (page 34); *taramosalata* (page 190); *melintzanosalata* (page 105); *tsatsiki* (page 36); *bessara* – Egyptian broad bean purée (page 254).

Patatas bravas
Spanish chilli potatoes

2

Literally, potatoes with the bravery of a fighting bull, a reference to the hot little sauce with which they are dressed. At its simplest, patatas bravas is chips served with tomato sauce spiked with a few drops of tabasco. Although this version is undeniably classier, the principle is the same – the bright red jacket packs the kick. In the spring, make it with plain-boiled new potatoes dressed with fresh breadcrumbs – migas – fried crisp in olive oil with garlic and a little fresh chilli, finished with a good dusting of pimentón – Spanish paprika. Make the sauce as mild or fiery as you please. In the bull-ring it takes all sorts.

Serves 4–6

750g / 1½lb potatoes, cubed small
1 teaspoon salt
olive oil for shallow-frying

For the sauce
2–3 cloves garlic, finely chopped
3 large tomatoes, skinned, deseeded and chopped
1 fresh red chilli, deseeded and chopped or 1 teaspoon chilli powder
1–2 tablespoons *pimentón* or paprika
salt and freshly ground black pepper

Sprinkle the potatoes with the salt and leave them to drain in a sieve for about 10 minutes. Shake to remove excess moisture, but don't rinse.

Heat the olive oil in a frying pan until a faint blue haze rises. Slip in the potatoes and fry gently, a batch at a time, until they are soft. Remove, drain, reheat the oil and fry them all again, until they are crisp and golden.

Pour out all but a tablespoon of the frying oil (you can use it again). Add the garlic and fry for a moment, until it softens. Add the tomatoes and chilli and paprika. Bubble up, squishing down the tomatoes, until they have melted into a sticky little sauce. Dress the potatoes with the sauce – or hand separately, for dipping.

Good with . . . something crisp such as shrimp fritters (page 167) or salt cod fritters (page 193); something soft and soupy such as meatballs (page 234/235); spiced oxtail casserole (page 242); olives; thinly sliced *jamón serrano*; grilled *chorizo* – all the good things of the Spanish table.

Patatas frescas a la valenciana

Spanish new potatoes with saffron

In this sunny little saffron-scented dish from Valencia, new potatoes are cooked in a wine-flavoured soffrito, *the basic flavouring of the Catalan kitchen; the secret lies in the long, gentle cooking of the onions, the only essential ingredient. The finishing touch is a* picada, *a spicy little paste of nuts, fried bread and garlic.*

Serves 4–6

1kg / 2lb new potatoes, scrubbed
6 tablespoons olive oil
2 large onions, finely sliced
500g / 1lb tomatoes, skinned and chopped (or tinned plum tomatoes)
1–2 bayleaves
12 strands saffron
1 small glass moscatel (or white wine plus 1 teaspoon sugar)
salt and freshly ground black pepper

To finish
25g / 1oz almonds, blanched and finely chopped
2 tablespoons fresh breadcrumbs
½ teaspoon cumin seeds
2 cloves garlic, finely chopped

To serve
quartered lemons and crisp lettuce leaves

If the potatoes are large, cut them into bite-sized pieces.

Make the *soffrito* first. Warm 4 tablespoons of the oil in a roomy pan or casserole, add the onions and fry over a gentle heat until they soften and gild a little – have patience, allow at least 20 minutes. Add the tomatoes, bayleaves and 6 strands of the saffron, turn up the heat, squash down the tomatoes to soften and bubble up into a rich, thick sauce.

Add the potatoes, the wine and enough water barely to cover, and season with salt and pepper. Bring to the boil, turn down the heat, cover loosely and leave to cook gently for 20–30 minutes, until most of the juices have been absorbed and the potatoes are perfectly tender. At the end of the cooking, remove the lid and bubble up to evaporate excess liquid.

Meanwhile make the *picada*: heat the remaining 2 tablespoons oil in a small frying pan and fry the almonds with the breadcrumbs until they are golden and crisp. Sprinkle in the remaining saffron, the cumin seeds and garlic, remove immediately from the heat and stir into the potatoes. Serve warm – about the temperature of a sunny day on a Spanish beach – with the quartered lemons and crisp lettuce leaves for scooping.

Good with . . . anchovies fried in fans (page 163); grilled sardines.

Sarmale
Serbian stuffed cabbage rolls

 Sarmale *are to the Balkans as* dolmades *to the Greeks and* dolmasi *to the Turks. In Serbia the wrapper is more likely to be cabbage than vine-leaves, the filling a well spiced rice pilaf – no changes there.*

Serves 6–8

1 small green cabbage
2 carrots, finely chopped
2 sticks celery, finely chopped

For the filling
4 tablespoons oil
1 medium onion, finely chopped
2 cloves garlic, finely chopped
250g / 8oz round (risotto or 'pudding') rice
salt and freshly ground black pepper
1 tablespoon finely chopped parsley
1 tablespoon finely chopped marjoram
1 teaspoon ground cumin
1 teaspoon ground cinnamon
1 egg, lightly forked (optional)

Settle the cabbage in a roomy bowl and pour over it a kettleful of boiling water – leave it just long enough to soften the bases of the leaves. Drain. Remove about eighteen of the large outer leaves and lay them flat, ready for stuffing, pressing down with the flat of your hand. Cut out the hard stalk and discard, shred the remaining inner leaves and put them in a roomy casserole with the carrot and celery.

Heat 2 tablespoons of oil in a frying pan and fry the chopped onion and garlic until soft and golden – don't let it brown. Add the rice and stir it over the heat until the grains turn translucent. Season and add enough water just to submerge the grains. Bring to the boil, turn down the heat and simmer for 10 minutes, at which point the grains will be chewy but most of the water will have been absorbed. Tip the contents of the pan into a bowl. Work in the herbs, spices and egg thoroughly with your hand, squeezing to make a firm mixture.

Drop a tablespoonful of filling on the stalk-end of each leaf, tuck the sides over to enclose, roll up neatly and transfer to the bed of cabbage in the casserole. Continue until all the leaves are used up. Add enough water to cover, bring to the boil, turn down the heat, lid and simmer gently for about an hour, until all the liquid has been absorbed.

Good with . . . Turkish filo triangles with parsley (page 118); anything crisp.

Topinambours en daube

Provençal root artichoke casserole

2

Jerusalem or root artichokes, topinambours, have a delicately sweet flavour quite at odds with their knobbly potato-faces. In French, they were named for the Brazilian tribe who first brought the tubers to the Portuguese colonizers' attention. Their English name comes from their membership of the daisy family, a genus which includes the bright-faced sunflower, known in the Latin languages as girasol ('turn-to-the-sun') – hence Jerusalem.

Serves 4–6

4 tablespoons olive oil
1 large onion, chopped
2–3 cloves garlic, chopped
1kg / 2lb root artichokes, peeled, cut into walnut-sized pieces
1 teaspoon grated nutmeg
salt and freshly ground black pepper
1 small glass white wine
1 small glass water
bouquet garni: bayleaves, rosemary, thyme

To finish
2 tablespoons chopped parsley
1 tablespoon chopped black olives

Heat the oil in a casserole or saucepan and fry the onion gently until soft and golden. Add the garlic and the artichokes, season with nutmeg, salt and pepper, cover and let everything sizzle gently, loosely covered, for about 15 minutes, shaking the pan every now and again to avoid sticking, until the sugar in the roots has caramelized a little.

Add the wine and an equal volume of water, tuck in the *bouquet garni*, bubble up, turn down the heat, cover and leave to simmer until the artichokes are tender – 15–20 minutes. Add a little more boiling water if necessary.

When the roots are perfectly soft, remove the lid and bubble up to evaporate all but the last little drops of the cooking juices. Stir in the parsley and chopped olives. Serve at room temperature.

> Good with . . . something for mopping – Provençal pork-crackling bread (page 57) or *focaccia* with sage and onion (page 49) or a plain *ciabatta* (page 48); a plate of charcuterie and one of the exquisite southern French cheeses – *picodons* or any little goaty treat that comes your way; *tapenade* – green or black (page 27).

Koloketes

Cypriot cinnamon pumpkin pies

The Cypriots are particularly fond of the variety of pumpkin known as butternut squash – very sweet, with bright orange flesh and a dense texture, for which cinnamon (the real stuff, not cassia bark) is the perfect partner. You can of course use any other pastry for the casing – puff or shortcrust.

Makes about 2 dozen

For the filling
750g / 1½lb pumpkin or butternut squash, peeled, deseeded and grated
1 medium onion, finely chopped
2 tablespoons coarse burghul (*pourgouri*)
150ml / ¼ pint oil – olive, but peanut or corn oil is preferred
1 teaspoon freshly ground cinnamon
¼ teaspoon ground cloves
salt and freshly ground black pepper

For the pastry
500g/1lb filo pastry
oil for brushing

Mix all the filling ingredients and leave them overnight to marry the flavours.

Preheat the oven to 200°C/400°F/gas 6. Cut the pastry into 30 x 10cm/12in x 4in strips. Pile and cover with clingfilm to prevent their drying out. Brush a strip with oil and lay another strip on top of this to give a double layer of filo. Place a line of stuffing (about a tablespoonful) along the short end, fold over a margin on either side of the pastry to stop the filling falling out, and roll up into a neat little bolster. Seal with a wet finger and transfer to an oiled baking tray. Continue until all is used up. Sprinkle with water from the tips of your fingers.

Bake for 10 minutes, then reduce the temperature to 180°C/350°F/gas 4 and bake for another 20 minutes or so, until the pastry is puffed and golden. Transfer to a wire tray and serve warm – the temperature of a sunny day on a Mediterranean hillside.

> Good with ... *laban*, the Middle Eastern yoghurt drink (page 66); *tsatsiki* for dipping (page 36); chunked tomatoes dressed with feta and oregano.

Tumbet

Mallorcan baked vegetables

Spicy and comforting, this dish can be prepared on the top of the stove in a heavy frying pan, or, as here, baked in the oven. The finishing touch is a few crisply fried slices of longaniza – *one of the island's fine pork products. The best of these are homemade with the meat of the local black pigs fattened – or so you will be told by those who keep and slaughter their own – on a diet of figs, yams and prickly pears. Small wonder they taste so good.*

Serves 6–8

1kg / 2lb medium potatoes, scrubbed
500g / 1lb pumpkin, peeled, deseeded and chunked
500g / 1lb small onions
2 whole heads garlic, soaked in water to swell the papery covering
4 tablespoons olive oil
1 teaspoon fennel or anis seeds
1 small stick cinnamon, crushed
salt and freshly ground black pepper

To dress
3–4 tablespoons olive oil
2–3 tablespoons wine vinegar
salt and freshly ground black pepper

To finish
2 tablespoons drained capers
1 tablespoon chopped marjoram
a loop of *longaniza* or *chorizo*, chunked into bite-sized pieces and fried in its own fat,
or bread cubes fried with garlic and paprika

Preheat the oven to 180°C/350°F/gas 4.

Spread the vegetables on a baking tray and sprinkle with the olive oil, spices, salt and pepper. Bake for about 1¼ hours, until all the vegetables are tender. Skin the onions and potatoes as soon as they are cool enough to handle, and chop roughly. Squeeze the garlic cloves either with your fingers or by exerting pressure with the back of a knife: they should pop out of their skins like little pearls.

To make the dressing, mash the garlic cloves with the drippings from the pan, the oil, vinegar, salt and pepper. Use this aromatic paste to dress the hot vegetables. Taste and adjust the seasoning. Finish with the capers and a good sprinkling of marjoram, *longaniza/chorizo* or bread cubes fried in fresh lard or olive oil with garlic and paprika.

Good with . . . toasted Andalusian sourdough bread (page 47).

Ailazan

Middle Eastern spiced vegetables

Baked vegetables, delicately spiced and flavoured with mint, a dish of Armenian origin. This version is made with winter roots – possible alternatives are jerusalem artichokes, leeks, turnip, butternut squash. Or, in summer, make it with aubergines, peppers, tomatoes, courgettes. The sweetness of the vegetables is sharpened with the touch of acidity provided by sumac, *the dried crushed berries of* Rhus coriaria, *a somewhat risky genus that includes poison ivy. Look for it in Middle Eastern grocers, or replace with lemon juice.*

Serves 4–6

1 large sweet potato, peeled and chunked into bite-sized pieces
1 large baking potato, peeled and chunked
500g / 1lb pumpkin, peeled, deseeded and chunked
2–3 mature carrots, scraped and chunked
2–3 parsnips, peeled and chunked
12 pickling onions, skinned, left whole
about 6 tablespoons oil (olive, sunflower)
1 tablespoon dried mint
1 tablespoon powdered *sumac* or juice and grated zest of 1 lemon
1 small stick cinnamon, broken into small bits
1 teaspoon cardamom seeds, roughly crushed
1 teaspoon cumin seeds
4 tablespoons sesame seeds
salt and freshly ground black pepper
lemon quarters to serve

Preheat the oven to 230°C/450°F/gas 8.

Spread the prepared vegetables in a single layer in a large roasting tin, trickle with oil and sprinkle with the mint, *sumac* or lemon, the spices, sesame, salt and pepper, turning the vegetables to coat. Roast in the hot oven for 10 minutes.

Turn the vegetables in the oil and cover loosely with foil. Reduce the heat to 180°C/350°F/gas 4 and leave to steam in their own rich juices for an hour or so, until they soften. Remove the foil, stir them again, sprinkle with a little water and leave to roast uncovered for another 20–30 minutes, turning them whenever you remember, until they are deliciously tender and coated with an aromatic crust.

> Good with . . . Turkish pancakes (page 54); lamb or minced meat kebabs (page 231).

Mushrooms & wild fungi

All fungi recipes can be made with any cultivated or wild mushroom – a troublesome area, since those that are eaten with enthusiasm in one region are shunned in another. The most widely available variety in Mediterranean markets as elsewhere is the *champignon de Paris*, a descendant of the field mushroom first cultivated in caves outside the French capital. The best are the ones with pinky-brownish caps and sandy feet – for some reason these have more flavour and a firmer flesh. If you are gathering mushrooms for the first time, go with someone who knows the territory and who understands local rules and regulations. Learn to read the landscape. Take a good fungi manual with you and err on the side of caution – if the thing looks right but it's not growing where you would expect to find it, leave it alone. As with all wild-gatherings, habitat is the key. Use a sharp knife to slice off the fruit-body just above the base so that you don't disturb the fine mycelium that provides the parasite with its life-support system. Gather into a basket or container that allows air to circulate freely – never a plastic bag, which acts as a microclimate in which the fungi quickly rot or can even become toxic. If you want to have the fungi identified (a service French chemists offer), you'll need the whole thing, including the root-bulb.

Opinions differ on the relative merits of white and black truffles. The Italians are passionate about the white and don't much rate the black. In France, passion swings to the black and the white is of no particular moment. Whether this is because there is genuine difference in the flavour of the tubers cropped in one place or another I cannot judge – and nor, it seems, can anyone else. In Spain the black truffle was eaten only in times of hardship. Within living memory – during the famines of the Civil War – it was poor man's food, a cause for shame, a meat-substitute to be used only when there was not even a ham-bone to flavour the broth. In recent years the arrival of the dealers from Périgord has made the gatherers more enthusiastic. Several other species – mostly belonging to the less-prized group loosely known as summer truffles – are to be found throughout the region. One, the desert truffle, crops prolifically after rain and is sold in Middle Eastern markets. Another, *criadillas de tierra* ('earth testicles', for those who like to know), is cropped in Extremadura, where it's cooked like potatoes.

Fungi most frequently encountered in Mediterranean markets

Agaricus campestris/augustus/macrosporus/bisporus (field mushroom, *champignon*). Needs no introduction: *A. bisporus* is the parent of the cultivated varieties first grown in caves near Paris, and is often known as *champignon de Paris*. Button mushrooms, sliced and dressed and allowed to marinate, make an exquisite little *antipasto*. When I lived in Andalusia, gypsy children gathered and sold the big black-gilled *A. macrosporus*, which appeared overnight after rain and was most prolific in the bare black earth blitzed by bushfires.

Amanita caesarea (Basque: *ous de reig*; Catalan: *oronja*; Caesar's mushroom). Fetches very high prices in Basque markets, Catalonia and northern Italy, where its pursuit can become an obsession. Firm, white fleshed, keeps its shape and texture, delicious scrambled with eggs.

Boletus edulis (Italian: *porcini*; French: *cèpe*; Spanish: *seta*). The obvious fungi for small boys to kick. Lumpy, reddish-brown cap (shiny only when wet), underparts spongy, pale cream to ochre, stalk bulbous, it is quite excellent in all its parts: the cap is firm-fleshed and glaucous with a pronounced mushroom flavour; the sponge is soft textured and gluey; the stem is fine flavoured and floury. Possessing a nutty, chewy, pronounced woodland flavour and a firm aftertaste, it is particularly delicious grilled or fried in olive oil with parsley and garlic. Popular all over the northern shores of the region – southern shores have some weird African hybrids, so take local advice. A friendly group of fungi, a few might give you a tummyache, but none are fatal. The best mushroom for drying.

Cantharellus cibarius (*chanterelle*, *girolle*). A buttercup-yellow fungus with beautifully fluted gills, like a Gothic cathedral – the most visually appealing of all the fungi. Popular in northern Europe, particularly Scandanavia, in our area only the Provençaux seem to value it highly. Chewy texture, flavour delicately peppery, bland if the weather has been wet. It is said to have a faint scent of apricots, although I think this must owe more to its colour than to its fragrance. Keeps colour and volume in cooking. *C. infundibuliformis* ('yellow-legs', also billed in French markets as *chanterelle* or *girolle*) is found in the same habitat but looks leggier, with thinner flesh, and the stalks are yellow, the cap dark – almost black. Good in ragouts, and rice dishes.

Cortinarius purpurascens (French: *violet*). Small blue-violet mushroom on a long stalk, which looks like everything Mother told you not to eat. Cap, gills and stalk are all the same colour; the stalk is woody and best removed. It fries neatly, losing volume but retaining most of its colour. Pleasantly tender like a button mushroom. It has no distinctive flavour, but it is decorative.

Hydnum repandum ('hedgehog' or 'tooth-fungus'). Has a cap white to yellowish; its gills are tiny little teeth or spines, white to pinkish in colour. It has deliciously peppery, meaty, firm white flesh which holds its shape, and a joyously dense woodland flavour. Gives a peppery kick to a fungi mix. Delicious in an omelette. For an exquisite little *antipasto* combine with sliced *chanterelles* and fry lightly in olive oil with *pancetta*, parsley and garlic.

Lactarius deliciosus/saunguifluus (saffron milk-cap, orange tear; Spanish: *seta*, Catalan: *escalat-sang*). Found under pines or spruce, the milk-cap has a convex cap, salmon to creamy yellow colours, and is marked lightly with darker concentric circles; the gills are salmon to orange. It bruises olive to blue and drips a milky juice when cut. The flavour is meaty and fine, firm when cooked. Excellent on the grill, in a *pipérade*, or simply, as in the Balearics, fried in oil with a *picada* of garlic and parsley. Absolutely top of the heap in Catalonia.

Marchella esculenta/vulgaris (morel, *morille*) is the spring mushroom par excellence (St George's, the other spring-fruiting edible fungi, is rarely encountered in the market). I've always found it in association with ground-orchids in pastures cropped by sheep. Volume imports come from Turkey – possibly because they've been picked out elsewhere. The dark cap is very distinctive, deeply wrinkled, like a heavily indented sponge; the inside is hollow and pale; the stem white to cream. Exquisite fresh but just as delicious dried – being hollow they dehydrate quickly with no loss of flavour. If you're buying by weight, pick out the drier-looking specimens: you get more for your money and lose nothing in flavour. Big flavour, chewy texture, wonderful with scrambled eggs, as a flavouring for rice, stuffings.

Pleurotus eryngii (Spanish: *seta de cardo*). An oyster mushroom whose host-plant is a thistle, the wild cardoon. Very sought after in Catalonia and Apulia. As might be expected, the fungi takes its physical characteristics from its host: the cap is blue-grey, the flesh firm, texture chewy, flavour distinctly artichoke. Delicious cooked in olive oil with garlic, or in a stuffing – particularly for artichokes and tomatoes.

Chanterelles en persillade

Provençal chanterelles with parsley and garlic

2

The chanterelle, Cantharellus cibarius, is the most easily identified of all edible wild fungi – never found singly but always in a bright necklace of sunny yellow frills hidden in the leaf mould in the woods in late summer. It is also known as the girolle (and don't let anyone persuade you otherwise), although the 'yellow-leg', C. infundibuliformis, which has a dark cap and thinner flesh, is sometimes identified as one or the other. The gills are like miniature gothic arches which slip smoothly into the cap. The scent is mossy and a little spicy; the flavour delicate, more pronounced if the weather has been dry; the texture firm, almost chewy. They keep both colour and volume in cooking.

Serves 4

500g / 1lb chanterelles (or oyster mushrooms)
4–5 tablespoons olive oil
salt
2–3 cloves garlic, finely chopped
2 tablespoons chopped parsley
1 tablespoon wine vinegar or lemon juice

Trim and brush the fungi, removing the woody bases of the stalks, and, if necessary, wipe with a damp cloth, but don't rinse. Slice thickly.

Heat the oil gently in a frying pan and add the sliced fungi. As soon as they begin to cook, sprinkle with a little salt and fry until the juices have evaporated and the edges are lightly caramelized. When cooking fungi (particularly if you have gathered them from the wild in damp weather), you'll notice a three-part process: first they appear to fry, then they go watery, finally they begin to fry again. The length of time this takes depends on the species and maturity of the fungi, and the dampness of the day they were gathered. This second frying is the pay-off – the juices become concentrated and the mushrooms acquire a deliciously roasted flavour.

Stir in the garlic and parsley and fry for another couple of minutes. Finish with a little vinegar or lemon juice, bubble up and pile onto thick slices of *pain de campagne* or any other sturdy country bread, toasted, rubbed with garlic and trickled with olive oil.

> **Good with . . .** plain boiled new potatoes as an alternative vehicle for the fungi; eggs scrambled in the mushroomy juices; little slivers of *bottarga* (salt-dried roe); a matched pair of tapenades (page 27).

Croustade aux morilles

Provençal morel mushroom quiche

Any wild or cultivated fungi can be substituted for the morels — a late summer crop found under beech trees, in birch woods — look for the bright orange frills in the leaf mould. In the autumn choose a mixture of pied-de-moutons, cèpes and oyster mushrooms.

Serves 4

For the pastry
250g / 8oz plain flour
4 tablespoons olive oil
warm water
½ teaspoon salt

For the filling
2 tablespoons olive oil
250g / 8oz morels or chanterelles (or other wild or cultivated fungi), brushed and sliced
1 large onion, finely sliced
1 sprig thyme
2 tablespoons chopped black olives
4 eggs
100g / 4oz fresh goat's cheese
salt and freshly ground black pepper

Work all the pastry ingredients together vigorously with the hook of your hand, adding enough warm water to form a smooth ball which comes away from the sides of the mixing bowl. Flatten the ball a little, cover with clingfilm and set it to rest for 30 minutes, while you prepare the filling.

Heat the oil gently in a frying pan, add the morels, onion and thyme and fry gently until the fungi yield up their juice and begin to sizzle. When it all begins to brown a little, stir in the chopped olives. Remove from the heat, pick out the thyme and leave to cool.

Preheat the oven to 200°C/400°F/gas 6.

Roll out the pastry to fit a 25cm/10in tart tin. Prick the base and bake for 10–15 minutes, until the pastry is set. If the pastry bubbles during the cooking, prick it again. Reduce the oven to 180°C/350°F/gas 4.

Beat the eggs with the cheese, plenty of black pepper and a little salt. Stir in the fungi mixture. Spread into the tart case and bake for 35–40 minutes, until it is almost set but still a little trembly in the middle.

Good with . . . wild asparagus; anything based on artichokes.

Crostini di porcini secchi e fegatini

Italian dried porcini mushrooms with chicken livers on toast

2

A delicious combination of flavour and texture. Boletus edulis – fungi porcini – dehydrates with minimal loss of its basic virtues: 20g / 1oz dried replaces 250g / 8oz fresh. Should you happen to come upon a decent crop in the woods, pick on a dry day, wipe, trim, discard the spongy underparts from mature specimens, and slice the caps as thick as a pound coin. Spread on newspaper in a single layer and set to dry in the airing cupboard or on a drying rack away from direct heat (a dehumidifier does the job in no time). As soon as the slices are perfectly brittle, store in an airtight jar. And if you should happen to have any dried fungi left over from last year, reduce them to a powder in the processor and use instead of a soup-cube – the flavour is amazing.

Serves 4–6

50g / 2oz dried *porcini*, soaked in hot water to swell
2 tablespoons olive oil
salt and freshly ground black pepper
1 clove garlic, finely slivered
100g / 4oz chicken livers, picked over and sliced
1 tablespoon chopped parsley
1 teaspoon chopped thyme
salt and roughly cracked black pepper
1 teaspoon balsamic vinegar

For the crostini bases
rounds of country bread cut as thin or thick as you please
1–2 cloves garlic
a little olive oil or butter

To make the *crostini*, rub the bread slices with garlic, brush with olive oil or butter and either grill or bake in a hot oven until crisp.

Simmer the *porcini* mushrooms in their soaking water with 1 tablespoon of the olive oil until the water has completely evaporated, returning its flavour to the fungi. Season and reserve.

Warm the remaining oil in a heavy frying pan, add the garlic and let it sizzle for a moment or two. Add the chicken livers, parsley and thyme, season with salt and plenty of pepper, and toss over the heat until the livers are lightly cooked – they should still be pink in the middle. Stir in the mushrooms, sharpen with a little balsamic vinegar and pile onto the *crostini*.

> **Good with ...** broccoli with chilli (page 91); anything with leaf or Jerusalem artichokes; any game recipe (pages 195–220).

Porcini in umido

Italian porcini in broth

2 *A modest little dish but good. The best cultivated substitute for the porcini is the bronze-capped portobello, otherwise known as the brown mushroom, which has firm flesh and a pronounced flavour that can stand up for itself.*

Serves 4–6

500g / 1lb fresh *porcini* mushrooms
4 tablespoons olive oil – more if needed
2 cloves garlic, finely sliced
2 tablespoons chopped flat-leaf parsley
25–50g / 1–2oz chopped *prosciutto* or *pancetta* (optional)
1 small glass white wine
about 100ml / 4fl oz mushroom or chicken stock
salt and freshly ground black pepper
crostini to serve (see page 59)

Pick over, trim, wipe and slice the *porcini*. Unless they're very mature don't, as some manuals instruct, strip off the spongy underparts – they make just as good eating as the caps, albeit a little slitherier.

Warm the oil in a roomy frying pan – stop before it heats to smoking point – and add the *porcini*. Salt them lightly to make them release their juices. Fry very gently for about 10 minutes, longer if the fungi were picked on a wet day and need to be dried out. When they have yielded up their moisture and begun to fry again, stir in the garlic, parsley and optional *prosciutto* or *pancetta*. Let the additions feel the heat, then add the wine and stock. Bubble up until the juices have mostly evaporated and the steam no longer smells of raw alcohol. Taste and season – you might need a little sugar if the wine was on the sharp side. Serve piled onto *crostini* – toasted country bread.

For a fancier finish, spread in a gratin dish, top with breadcrumbs tossed with grated Parmesan and chopped herbs – thyme, parsley, garlic – drizzle with oil and bake in a moderate oven to crisp the topping.

> Good with ... Ligurian *focaccia* with sage and onion (page 49); Neapolitan baked aubergines with cheese (page 107); a potato salad dressed with olives, olive oil, vinegar (balsamic if you have it) and very finely chopped raw onion.

Escalat-sang allioli
Catalan saffron milk-caps with oil and garlic

2

The saffron milk-cap, Lactarius deliciosus, is found in generous quantities throughout the autumn in the pine forests of Catalonia and the Basque country. It looks like an orange field mushroom but has a noticeably convex cap. A meaty mushroom, firm-fleshed enough to keep its shape in the cooking. Since it bruises blue and drips a milky juice when cut, the gatherer unfamiliar with its virtues might think it poisonous. In the Balearics they like it fried in oil with a picada of garlic and parsley. For the sauce, surely the most primitive of all dressings, choose the finest virgin olive oil with plenty of peppery leaf, and the most perfectly fresh garlic – simplicity deserves the best.

Serves 4–6

For the allioli
1 whole head of garlic (10–12 fat cloves), skinned
2 teaspoons salt
2 heaped tablespoons blanched almonds (optional)
juice of 1 large lemon
600ml / 1 pint olive oil
4 tablespoons hot water

For the fungi
About a dozen fine saffron milk-caps (or large cultivated mushrooms with pink underneaths and firm white heads)
olive oil for trickling
1–2 cloves garlic, finely chopped
salt and freshly ground black pepper

Crush the garlic with the salt in a pestle and mortar (or use a food processor), add the almonds and lemon juice and pound to a paste. Gradually trickle in the oil, as if you were making a mayonnaise, beating vigorously and adding the water as the emulsion forms.

Season the fungi, trickle with a little olive oil and sprinkle with chopped garlic. Grill or griddle until the juices run and the cap caramelizes at the edges. Serve with the *allioli* as soon as the mushrooms emerge from the heat. Provide fresh bread, naturally.

Good with ... plain-grilled vegetables; peppers in oil (page 121); anything fishy and simple; grilled lamb cutlets – favourites in Catalonia.

Setas a la parrilla

Catalan grilled mushrooms with garlic

2 *The Catalans eat a wide variety of wild-gathered fungi (including black truffles, which are to be found happily drawing sustenance not from the oak but from the modest little rock-rose) of which the favourite is the saffron milk-cap, Lactarius deliciosus.*

Serves 4–6

500g / 1lb wild fungi, or large flat cultivated mushrooms
4–5 tablespoons olive oil
2 cloves garlic, finely sliced
1 tablespoon chopped oregano
salt and freshly ground black pepper
1 small glass dry sherry
3–4 tablespoons fresh breadcrumbs
2–3 tablespoons chopped parsley

Shake any creepy-crawlies out of the mushrooms' gills and wipe the caps, but do not peel or wash them. Trim off the stalks close to the base.

Heat the oil in a shallow earthenware casserole or frying pan, toss in the garlic and let it fry for a moment or two. Lay in the mushrooms, cap-down, in a single layer. Sprinkle with oregano, salt and plenty of black pepper. Fry gently until the juice runs. Turn them over and fry the other side. Bubble up until the juice evaporates, at which point the fungi will yield up the oil they've absorbed and start to sizzle. Remove and reserve. Add the sherry to the oily juices, bubble up to evaporate the alcohol, and then stir in the breadcrumbs and parsley. Fry until golden, then spoon onto the mushrooms. Serve hot.

> **Good with . . .** Catalan bread and tomato (page 60); spiced kebabs (page 228). Finish with *leche frita* – Catalan cream fritters (page 278); pears in wine (page 274); junket with walnuts and honey (page 272).

Tortilla de setas y ajos frescos
Mushroom and garlic omelette

This is a popular summertime tapa *in Valencia, where it is made with wild-gathered orange milk-caps and fresh garlic. The summer garlics resemble white onions and have a mild flavour since they are used before the cloves have had time to form. Wild garlic grows throughout Europe, and many countries, including Britain, have similar recipes. I give here a combination of garlic cloves and spring onion as a replacement for hard-to-find fresh garlic.*

Serves 4–6

350g / 12oz mushrooms (saffron milk-cap, cep, button mushrooms)
4 tablespoons olive oil
2 cloves garlic, sliced
2 large spring onions (white part only), sliced
4 eggs
salt and freshly ground black pepper

Wipe (don't rinse) and slice the mushrooms. Heat the oil in a small omelette pan. Add the mushrooms and cook gently until all their moisture has evaporated and the oil is clear again. Remove and drain in a sieve over a bowl to catch the drippings.

Add the garlic and onion to the remaining oil in the pan. Fry them gently until they soften. Add them to the mushrooms in the sieve.

Beat the eggs lightly in a bowl and season with salt and pepper. Stir in the now-cooled vegetables.

Add the oil drippings to the pan, reheat and tip in the egg mixture. Cook as a thick pancake, turning once, as for the potato *tortilla* on page 76. Serve warm or cool, cut into bite-sized cubes.

> **Good with . . .** *patatas bravas* (page 136); any rice dish; sliced tomatoes dressed with olive oil.

Tian des pleurottes

Oyster mushroom tian

The Provençal tian is really a baked omelette or a pastryless quiche which takes its name from the shallow earthenware dish in which it's cooked. You can use any seasonal vegetable in a tian, lightly pre-cooked to get rid of excess moisture that would otherwise make the eggs soggy. A few spoonfuls of leftover ratatouille make an excellent summer tian. In winter, use spinach or chard – both the leaves and the stalks, well shredded – flavoured with a squeeze of lemon and finely grated lemon-zest.

Serves 4–6

350g / 12oz oyster mushrooms, wiped and sliced
2 tablespoons olive oil
1 clove garlic, crushed, or a handful of wild garlic leaves, shredded
1 tablespoon chopped ham or lean bacon
4 large eggs
1 teaspoon chopped marjoram or oregano
2 tablespoons grated Cantal (the local version of Gruyère)
½ teaspoon grated nutmeg
salt and freshly ground black pepper

Preheat the oven to 170°C/325°F/gas 3.

Oil an earthenware baking dish or *tian* (diameter about 20cm / 8in and at least two fingers deep).

Fry the mushrooms gently in the oil with the garlic and ham or bacon until they have yielded up their juices and fried a little. Remove from the heat and leave to cool while you beat the eggs in a bowl with the marjoram or oregano, the cheese, nutmeg, salt and pepper. Stir the contents of the frying pan into the eggs, and tip into the *tian*. Bake for 40–50 minutes, until the *tian* has just set, with golden bubbles round the rim and a softish middle which trembles a little under the finger.

Good with . . . *fougasse* (page 51) or *focaccia* (page 49); any dish involving artichokes, asparagus, fennel – complementary flavours since all three grow wild in oyster-mushroom territory.

▶ *Provençal chanterelles with parsley and garlic (page 147); Provençal morel mushroom quiche (page 148)*

Fish & shellfish

◀ *Catalan grilled monkfish and prawns with red pepper salsa (page 173)*

The fish of the Mediterranean make up in diversity what it lacks in quantity. Considering its size, the inland sea has never been heavily stocked, although migratory shoals can vastly increase the volume when they pass on their way to spawn in the sheltered waters of the Black Sea and its tributaries, or on their return to reach maturity in the open ocean. Reasons for this are various, not least – with the exception of the coast of Tunisia, the Adriatic and the Aegean – the narrowness of the coastal shelf: young fish need nursery slopes where they can feed in peace out of reach of larger predatory fish.

Throughout its length, the Mediterranean is relatively shallow and therefore warm, lacking the cool, deep waters and prolific sea-vegetation required by Atlantic fish. In addition, non-tidal waters do not easily rid themselves of effluent, and although this provides certain species – particularly crustaceans – with a food source, it reduces the available oxygen essential to life. The problem is exacerbated in modern times by the vast seasonal increases in the human population. Nevertheless, the cooks of the Mediterranean make good use of the available material: recipes are simple, reflecting the freshness of the catch.

When buying fish choose locally caught over flown-in every time – one white-fleshed fish is much like another. Small oily fish deteriorate more quickly than large white fish: fresh sardines and anchovies are not worth eating more than a few hours from their fishing grounds – hence the canning industry. In theory, never buy a fish you haven't looked in the eye and into whose gills you haven't poked your nose. In practice, most of the fish you're likely to find is already filleted. Fish is filleted in order to remove the main danger-zones and increase the shelf life – make your own judgement. If you are keeping filleted fish in the fridge overnight, salt it first – this firms the flesh and improves the flavour. Buy uncooked prawns and shrimps whenever you can; frozen is not ideal but it's better than precooked. Shellfish is best bought live and on the shell; mussels and oysters are widely available, scallops are usually shucked. Choose your fishmonger before you choose your fish – a knowledgeable fishmonger is worth his weight in silver.

Fish is best bought in the cool of the morning, preferably along the Quai des Belges on the Marseilles waterfront, where the business of the day starts around eight o'clock with the arrival of the eel-fishermen. Picture the scene: pale-flanked water-snakes squirm and snap while narrow-eyed housewives fold pink arms over large black bosoms, bargaining and bullying. The fishing boats dock one by one, most to throw their bulging crates directly into the whole-salers' expectant vans. Alongside others, the smaller vessels, the fishermen weigh out sand-freckled flatfish – sole, turbot and brill; silvery anchovies and sardines; small heaps of rainbow-coloured rockfish destined for soup. An octopus escapes from a bucket and slithers damply across the cobblestones. Under a striped umbrella a young man offers spike-shelled sea urchins for immediate consumption, scissoring off the lids to reveal the glowing corals. His neighbour sells shellfish: tiny purple-tinged *tellines*, spiny sea snails to eat with *aïoli*, oysters and mussels. One old woman presides over a pile of weed-whiskered rocks, which closer inspection reveals to be amber-fleshed *violets de mer*, to be eaten raw with a squeeze of lemon. Red mullet and monkfish rub aristocratic shoulders with the noble *rascasse* – the rockfish which separates the Sunday *bouillabaisse* from everyday's *soupe de poissons*.

Ensalada de mariscos

Spanish seafood salad

Vary the shellfish as you please. Lobster instead of prawns makes it particularly luxurious; queen scallops can replace the mussels. If fresh fish is hard to come by, make it with tinned tuna and anchovies. Possible extras are diced serrano ham, flaked salt cod (blister it on a dry pan first, then skin and debone), chopped hardboiled eggs, diced cucumber and homemade croûtons fried crisp in olive oil.

Serves 4–6

750g / 1½lb new potatoes, scrubbed (or old, peeled and chunked)
500g / 1lb mussels or clams in the shell
250g / 8oz squid, cleaned and sliced (see page 178)
100g / 4oz prawns
100ml / 4fl oz olive oil
2–3 tablespoons wine vinegar
½ mild Spanish onion, finely chopped
1 large beef tomato, deseeded and diced
1 red pepper, deseeded and diced
salt and roughly ground black pepper

To finish
2 tablespoons chopped parsley (flat-leaf, for preference)
2 tablespoons green olives
extra olive oil

Cook the potatoes in plenty of boiling salted water for 15–20 minutes, until perfectly tender. Drain immediately and shake over the heat to evaporate excess moisture.

Meanwhile, shake the shellfish in a little water or wine over a high heat in a lidded pan. Remove the meat from the shells – or not, as you please. Heat a tablespoon of the oil in a small frying pan and fry the squid, seasoning with salt and pepper; as soon as the flesh turns opaque, add the prawns and toss over the heat until they turn scarlet.

In the bowl in which you mean to serve the salad, whisk the vinegar with a little salt, then add the remaining oil with the chopped onion.

Turn the hot potatoes vigorously in the dressing, breaking them up a little with a spoon – while still hot they absorb vinegar and oil like sponges. Allow to cool and then gently fold in the shellfish followed by the tomato and red pepper. Taste and adjust the seasoning. Finish with the parsley and olives and serve at room temperature. Trickle over a little more oil just before serving.

> Good with . . . deep fried anchovy fans (page 163); salt cod fritters (page 193).

Sardines à la mode de Sète

Provençal sardines stuffed with spinach

A dish from the medieval port of Sète, gateway to the marshes of the Camargue, where flamingos build their muddy nests and wild white horses crop the meadows between the reedbeds. Sardines must be very fresh, with sparkling scales, bright eyes and firm flesh which, when prodded by an enquiring finger, won't keep the print.

Serves 4–6

1kg / 2lb perfectly fresh sardines, scaled

For the stuffing
500g / 1lb spinach or chard leaves, rinsed and shredded
1 tablespoon olive oil
1 medium onion, finely chopped
3 cloves garlic, finely chopped
1 teaspoon allspice
½ teaspoon grated nutmeg
3 tablespoons white breadcrumbs, soaked in milk
2 tablespoons chopped chervil
2 tablespoons chopped fresh chives
2 eggs
salt and freshly ground black pepper
olive oil for finishing
quartered lemons to serve

Preheat the oven to 240°C/450°F/gas 8.

Gripping the head of the fish, push your finger down the soft belly, pulling away the backbone along with the innards, severing the backbone just above the tail. Rinse thoroughly, making sure there are no loose scales.

Now make the stuffing. In a covered saucepan cook the spinach until soft in the water that clings to the leaves. Tip into a sieve, squeeze out excess moisture, chop finely and leave to cool. Meanwhile fry the onion and garlic in the oil until soft. Mix with the spinach and all the remaining ingredients.

Lay half the sardines – flattened, flesh side up – in a roomy gratin dish or baking tray, and spread each with about 1 tablespoon of the stuffing. Top with another sardine, skin side up. Season, trickle with a little olive oil and bake for 10–15 minutes – until the fish are cooked right through and the skin bubbles and browns. Serve with quartered lemons.

Good with . . . artichokes vinaigrette; braised fennel; potato salad.

Caballa escabechada

Andalusian pickled mackerel

 One of those delicious dishes devised in the days before refrigeration (a comparatively recent development – no more than a century old) and intended to preserve the fisherman's catch for a few more days in summer. So good that it remains on the menu.

Serves 4–6

1kg / 2lb mackerel, beheaded and gutted
2 heaped tablespoons of flour
salt
2 tablespoons olive oil
1 medium onion, finely sliced
1 clove garlic, crushed
1 small carrot, sliced
1 tablespoon chopped parsley
1 bayleaf, torn
1 teaspoon dried oregano or marjoram
6 peppercorns, roughly crushed
4 tablespoons sherry vinegar (or any wine vinegar)

Chop the mackerel straight through the bone to give three or four thick steaks per fish (your fishmonger will do this for you). Sprinkle the pieces with salt and dust with flour.

Heat the oil in a frying pan. When it's blue-hazed, put in the fish and fry gently until golden and firm (use your thumb to test – it should take 4–8 minutes, depending on the thickness). Transfer to a shallow dish.

Reheat the oil remaining in the pan – you may need a little more – and add the chopped onion, garlic and carrot. Fry gently for a few moments so that the flavours blend. Add the herbs, peppercorns, vinegar and a splash of water. Bubble fiercely for a few minutes, then pour over the fish. Turn the fish in the marinade, cover with clingfilm and leave overnight in the fridge.

Ready to eat in a day, good in two, best in three.

> Good with . . . a seafood salad (page 158); Catalan spiced crab pasties (page 172); Spanish salt cod fritters (page 193).

Boquerones en vinagre

Andalusian fresh-pickled anchovies

2

Straight from the net, the anchovy looks like a small, slender sardine. Look closer and you will notice the dark stripe down the flanks, the viridian sheen on the back, and the apparent absence of scales – conveniently, unlike the sardine, the anchovy's scales are tiny. Both anchovy and sardine are plentiful throughout the region, providing the bread and butter for the inshore fishing fleets who sell them fast and cheap in the morning market. A short shelf-life – the result of natural oiliness and relatively small size – means that the catch, unless salted or preserved in some other way, stays close to home. Methods of conservation – adding a few extra days rather than anything long term – involve salt or vinegar or, as here, both. Start 48 hours ahead.

Serves 4–6

500g / 1lb fresh anchovies
150ml / ¼ pint sherry or white wine vinegar
2 tablespoons water
1 tablespoon salt
2–3 cloves garlic, finely slivered

To finish
1 tablespoon olive oil
chopped flat-leaf parsley

Rinse the anchovies and drain thoroughly. Press lightly down the body of the fish to loosen the flesh from the bones. Holding the head firmly between your finger and thumb, pull it down through the belly towards the tail. The spine and ribs should slip easily through the soft flesh, gutting and splitting all in one movement. Continue until all the fish are done.

Open the fish flat and lay them flesh upwards in a single layer in a shallow dish. Mix the vinegar with the water and salt and pour over the fish – they should be well soaked. Sprinkle with garlic, cover with foil and leave in the fridge to marinate for 48 hours. To serve, drain and finish with a trickle of olive oil and a sprinkle of parsley. The pickled fish will keep for a week in the fridge.

Good with . . . crab croquettes (page 170); shrimp fritters (page 167).

Hut bin chermoula

Moroccan stuffed anchovies

A popular market-food in Casablanca, where the anchovy and sardine catch is plentiful and cheap. The marketing is done by the women, who then hurry home to prepare the midday meal – lingering in public places is a sign of loose morals – while the men are free to relax at the café tables, exchange news, set up one of the interminable games of chess and enjoy a taste of what's on offer from the food kiosks.

Serves 6–8

1 kg / 2lb fresh anchovies or small sardines

For the chermoula stuffing
2 handfuls parsley leaves
2 handfuls coriander leaves
2–3 cloves garlic, skinned
1 teaspoon salt
1 teaspoon ground cumin
juice of 2 large lemons, finely grated zest of 1

To finish
Oil for deep-frying
bread flour and a little semolina for dusting
coarse salt
quartered lemons to serve

First, butterfly the fish: rinse them thoroughly (if you are using sardines rub off the scales). Attending to the fish one at a time, press down the flank to loosen the flesh from the bones. Then, gripping the little fish head between your forefinger and thumb, pull it down through the belly, bringing the innards out with the skeleton. Sever the backbone just above the tail. Rinse again and reserve.

Now make the *chermoula* stuffing. Using a sharp knife, chop the leaves and crush the garlic with the salt and then blend with the cumin and the lemon juice and zest. Alternatively, pop all the ingredients in the processor and give them a good chopping.

Heat the oil for deep-frying (if you don't fry fish regularly you can use just enough to submerge the fish). Watch for the shimmering blue haze that tells you it's ready to fry.

Meanwhile, set out a plate of flour mixed with a little semolina and coarse salt. Sandwich the anchovies together in pairs with the *chermoula* and flip them quickly through the flour just before you drop them in the hot oil. Fry a few at a time – if the temperature drops, the coating will be soggy instead of crisp. Serve with quartered lemons.

Good with . . . shellfish opened in their own juices; any Arab bread.

Boquerones fritos en manojitos

Andalusian deep-fried anchovy fans

If the cooks of Andalusia have one skill universally acknowledged – and Andalusian culinary expertise is not much rated in the rest of Spain – it's an astonishingly light hand with the frying pan. The freshness of the raw materials, the quality of the flour, the purity of the salt, the clarity and ripeness of the oil, all contribute – but the real trick lies in the sleight of hand.

Serves 4–6

750g / 1½lb fresh anchovies or small sardines
bread flour and a little semolina for dusting
1 teaspoon coarse salt
oil for frying (a mixture of olive and sunflower is perfect)

Rinse and gut the little fish – you can do this just by running your finger down the soft belly and hooking out the innards. Behead them or not as you please. Anchovies don't need scaling, sardines do. Rinse under running water, shake off excess water, but don't dry.

Spread the flour mixed with the semolina and salt on a flat plate. Pinch the tails of the fish together in fans of three to five, depending on their size. Flip them through the flour, first one side, then the other, making sure the tails are firmly stuck together – a damp finger helps.

Heat the oil in a shallow frying pan – just enough to submerge the fish. Andalusian housewives fry in a minimum depth of oil – partly from frugality, but also because, as in life, a little bit of fresh is better than a whole lot of stale. When the oil is lightly hazed with blue, lay in the fish, head-first, only two to three fans at a time – the temperature must remain high, in spite of the small quantity of oil. Fry quickly, turning once – the little bunch of tails should be exquisitely crisp. Transfer to kitchen paper to drain and serve immediately.

Good with . . . prawns with garlic and chilli (page 166); clams in sherry (page 185); shellfish and potato salad (page 158).

Misto mare
Frittered fish

A Neapolitan name for the familiar fritto misto, a simple dish that depends on perfect raw materials, a light hand with the flouring, impeccable judgement with the frying. As for choosing the fish, your nose will tell you all you need to know: really fresh fish doesn't smell fishy, still less ammoniac. Find a good fishmonger, and trust him. Freshness is much more important than species – the closer to home the fishing fleet, the better. Baby cuttlefish and squid can be cooked whole, guts and all, but be warned: they spit oily juices all over the cooker. Cuttlefish are shoal fish: if they're there, you find plenty; if not, too bad. Flatfish are bottom-feeders – shy creatures, easily scared. Squid grow up to 2 feet long: the larger the tougher – aren't we all?

Serves 6–8

1–1.5kg / 2–3lb mixed small fish – choose among:
squid or cuttlefish, body cut into rings, tentacles in bunches (see page 178
    for their preparation)
small flatfish, gutted – heads left on if very small
anchovies, gutted unless very small, heads on
small sardines, gutted unless very small, heads on
small red mullet, ungutted, heads left on
any larger fish, in bite-sized chunks
shrimp or prawns, whole and unpeeled
flour for dusting, and a tablespoon of fine-ground semolina
oil for deep-frying (half olive, half sunflower)
quartered lemons to serve

Rinse the fish and shake – don't dry it or the flour won't stick. Sieve the flour onto a large plate and toss with the semolina and salt.

Heat plenty of oil in a deep-fryer. Wait until the surface is shimmering, then test with a cube of bread – it should take less than a minute to crisp and gild.

Meanwhile, flour the fish. Drop a handful of fish into the flour, toss lightly (using the tips of the fingers only), transfer to a sieve and shake to remove excess flour. As you finish each handful, drop it into the hot oil. Allow 1–2 minutes – just enough for the coating to brown, then remove with a draining spoon. Serve immediately, with lemon quarters.

> Good with . . . nothing at all. Keep frying until all are done and hunger is satisfied, then fry up some chips. Ice-cream to follow, and a wickedly black espresso. What else? This is Naples.

Gambas a la plancha

Andalusian grilled prawns

 A very simple way of preparing the fine fat prawns brought in by the inshore fishing fleets. The crustaceans must be perfectly fresh, the salt granular and crunchy. Salt on the prawns' skin enhances the natural sweetness of the flesh. Look for prawns that still have their heads: the juices are exquisite – just crush between the teeth and suck.

Serves 4–6

750g / 1½lb large prawns, with heads, unpeeled
1–2 tablespoons olive oil
1–2 tablespoons coarse salt – chunky crystals rather than flakes

To serve
quartered lemons

Rub the prawn shells lightly with olive oil and dredge generously with rough salt.

Preheat a *plancha* (a thick metal plate) or a heavy iron griddle. Or light the barbecue. You need a fierce, strong heat.

When you have a good heat, set the prawns on the grill and wait until the shells change colour from grey to bright scarlet (unless you have chosen the large deep-water prawns, which are naturally crimson in life). Let the shells blacken a little. Turn once, allowing 2–3 minutes each side – no longer – at which point the flesh will be firm but still juicy. Serve hot from the fire, with lemon quarters.

> Good with . . . Andalusian sourdough bread (page 47) for wiping your fingers and soaking up the juices; an ice-cold *gazpacho* (page 101).

Gambas al ajillo
Prawns with garlic and chilli

2
Tapa *bars that specialize in these mouth-scalding preparations have little wooden forks so that customers don't burn their lips. Crab is also excellent prepared in this way — it'll need an extra splash of sherry or brandy to keep it moist.*

Serves 4–6

500g / 1lb large, juicy raw prawns, peeled
4 tablespoons olive oil
1 clove garlic, sliced
1 teaspoon small dried red chillis, deseeded
salt

Pick over the prawns and remove any stray whiskers.

The important thing about this simple dish is that the prawns must be sizzling hot when they're served — ideally in the dish in which they're cooked. With this in mind, choose small individual casseroles capable of resisting a flame. Or use a frying pan to cook the prawns, and heat ramekins in the oven for serving.

Heat the oil in the casseroles or frying pan. When lightly hazed with blue, add the garlic and the chillis. Reheat until they sizzle, then add the prawns, which should turn opaque almost immediately. Serve as soon as the oil spits and bubbles, in the heated ramekins or their individual casseroles, with bread for mopping up the fiery oil.

> Combine with . . . grilled razor-shells (see below); vinegar-pickled anchovies (page 161); a potato and seafood salad (page 158).

To grill razor-shells – or any other bivalves: clams, mussels, small scallops. Soak the shellfish in cold water for an hour or two so that they spit out their sand – overnight is best. Preheat the grill or griddle, or heat the oven to maximum. Grill the shellfish until they open in their own steam. Remove immediately and serve without reheating. Accompany with lemon quarters – they'll need no other sauce.

Tortillitas de camarónes

Shrimp fritters

These crisp little fritters are sold hot from the frying vat on every street corner of the windswept port of Cadiz. They're made with the tiny shrimps, camarónes, that thrive in the long sandy shallows that edge the salt flats beyond the town. The shrimps are – or were – sold from buckets by small boys making a little money to spend in the fairground. The live shrimps jumped like fleas when stirred into the batter.

Serves 4–6

100g / 4oz chickpea flour or plain flour
1 teaspoon bicarbonate of soda
½ teaspoon salt
2 tablespoons olive oil
about 6 tablespoons water
1 teaspoon paprika
1 tablespoon grated onion
1 tablespoon chopped parsley
100g / 4oz whole tiny shrimp (or larger shrimp, chopped)
olive oil for frying

Toss the flour with the bicarbonate and salt in a bowl, and gradually blend in the oil and then the water, working in enough to give a runny batter, as for pancakes. Stir in the paprika, onion and parsley. Fold in the shrimps.

Heat two fingers' depth of oil in a frying pan. When lightly smoking, drop in the shrimp batter by the tablespoonful – not too many at a time or the oil temperature will drop. Fry until golden and crisp, turning once. Flatten the fritters with the draining spoon as they cook – the batter must be well spread out to allow the fritters to crisp right through.

Good with . . . grilled prawns (page 165); clams in sherry (page 185); fried green peppers – in Mediterranean markets you can find special thin-skinned green peppers for frying.

Aïoli de brochettes de crevettes roses
Provençal prawn brochettes with garlic mayonnaise

A speciality of Le Gallion, a restaurant on the waterfront of le Grau-du-Roi at the mouth of the Rhône. The recipe provides a generous amount of aïoli: if you have more guests than you have brochettes, cook up a panful of new potatoes for dipping and no one will mind going short on the fish.

Serves 6–8

1kg / 2lb large raw prawns, peeled, tails left on
2–3 tablespoons olive oil
juice of 1 lemon
salt and freshly ground black pepper
1 tablespoon dried oregano

For the aïoli
4–5 fat cloves garlic, roughly chopped
1 level teaspoon salt
3 egg yolks
1 tablespoon mild French mustard
2–3 tablespoons wine vinegar
600ml / 1 pint good olive oil

Thread the prawns on skewers and sprinkle with the oil, lemon juice, salt and pepper. Leave aside to marinate while you make the *aïoli*.

Crush the garlic with the salt in a mortar, using a pestle (or drop into the food processor). Work in the egg yolks, mustard and a little of the vinegar. Add the olive oil in a slow trickle at first, progressing to a steady stream as the emulsion forms and the sauce thickens. Add a little more vinegar, taste and add more salt if necessary.

Preheat the grill or light the barbecue – let it get really hot.

Drain the *brochettes* and trickle with a little more oil and a sprinkling of oregano. Grill for 4–5 minutes, no more, turning so that the heat reaches all sides, until the prawns are perfectly pink and firm. Serve immediately, with the *aïoli* on the side.

Good with . . . leaf or root artichokes; a warm salad of green beans, haricot or butter-beans cooked plainly with a ham bone and a little garlic.

To cook a crab

The seafood gourmets of the Mediterranean littoral hold the sweet white meat of *Maja squinado* – slender-clawed, spiky-carapaced spider-crab – in higher esteem than that of *Cancer pagarus*, our own heavy-clawed common crab. To cook from live – a dead crab is fit only for the seagulls – allow one pound per person. An hour or so before you mean to cook the creature, drop it into cold unsalted water to lull it to sleep. Without this preliminary attention crabs have an alarming habit of throwing off their legs and claws in the cooking – a traumatic experience for all concerned. Bring it gently to the boil, salt the water heavily and allow 15–20 minutes at a rolling boil, depending on size. Remove and drain. Loosen the lower half of the crab from the upper carapace to let the water drain out. Allow to cool. Pull apart to expose the interior. Remove the feathery grey gills that fringe the body. Pick out the meat any way that works.

Croquetas de centolla

Andalusian crab croquettes

2

An elegant little tapa, a bit more trouble than most, but worth it for the pleasure of the crisp coating and the melting, creamy interior. Any Andalusian housewife worth the name will have been making these since she was a little girl — but there's no doubt a little dexterity is required. The basis for all croqueta mixtures is a very thick white sauce — a panada. The greater the skill of the cook, the softer and less floury the mixture will be. The best stock for a fish croqueta is a concentrated broth made with shrimp and crab debris simmered with plenty of onion, carrot and green celery. Second best is a jar of ready-made fresh fish broth, the kind Mediterranean fishmongers sell as the basis for fish soups.

Serves 6–8

500g / 1lb prepared crabmeat
½ mild onion, grated, or 4–5 spring
**   onions, finely chopped**
1 heaped tablespoon chopped parsley

For the filling – the **panada**
4 tablespoons olive oil
100g / 4oz flour (more, if you're not
**   confident of your skill)**
about 600ml / 1 pint hot fish stock
salt and cayenne pepper

To finish
seasoned flour for dusting
1–2 eggs, lightly forked with a little milk
fresh breadcrumbs for coating
oil for deep-frying

Mix the crabmeat with the onion and the parsley.

Melt the oil in a heavy-bottomed pan and stir in the flour. Lower the heat and stir for a moment or two until it looks sandy (don't let it brown). Whisk in the hot stock in a steady stream, until you have a smooth, very thick sauce. Season with salt and cayenne pepper and continue to simmer for 5 minutes to cook the flour. Stir in the crab, spread in a shallow dish, leave to cool, cover with clingfilm and set in the fridge to firm — overnight is best.

Have ready a plate each of seasoned flour, forked egg and fresh breadcrumbs. Using a teaspoon, form the crab mixture straight from the fridge into neat little bite-sized bolsters — a bowl of warm water near by will be useful for dipping your hands. Dust the bolsters through the flour. Chill again for 30 minutes if you have time. Coat with egg and then press into the breadcrumbs, making sure they are well coated.

Heat enough oil to submerge the *croquetas*. Wait until it is faintly hazed with blue, then slip them in, a few at a time. If the coating splits open the oil is too hot. Remove and drain as soon as they are crisp and golden.

Good with . . . squid in sherry (page 178); fresh-pickled anchovies (page 161).

Centollas al horno
Catalan baked crab

The usual choice of crustacean for this dish is a spider-crab – a weird creature that looks like a large scarlet spider with a horny shell and slender claws. The meat is white and to be found only in the body; to get at the flesh use a sharp knife to chop the body in segments, following the line of the legs. If you can't lay your hands on crabs with shells – picked or not – allow 500g/1lb crab meat; you'll also need enough shallow earthenware dishes (cazuelas) to accommodate the volume.

Serves 4

4 cooked crabs, picked and with their shells
2 tablespoons olive oil
100g / 4oz butter
2 medium onions, finely chopped
2 medium leeks, white only, finely chopped
500g / 1lb tomatoes, skinned and chopped (or tinned plum tomatoes)
2–3 tablespoons brandy
a pinch of chopped tarragon
salt and cayenne pepper
2 tablespoons fresh breadcrumbs
1 tablespoon chopped parsley

Pick over the crab meat and remove any small bits of shell. Scrub the shells and oil the outside lightly.

Heat the oil and half of the butter in a frying pan and cook the onions and leeks gently until they are soft and golden. Add the tomatoes, squash them down and bubble up until they are well reduced and thickened. Stir in the crab meat and the liquor and turn the mixture over the heat until it bubbles again. Pour on the brandy, light it with a match and stand well back: the flames will burn off the alcohol and caramelize the crab meat a little. Stir in the tarragon, taste and add salt and cayenne pepper.

Preheat the oven to maximum: 250°C/475°F/gas 9.

Pack the crab mixture in the emptied shells or divide between the baking dishes, and sprinkle with breadcrumbs and parsley. Dot with the remaining butter and bake for 15–20 minutes, until beautifully brown and bubbling.

Good with . . . other fishy things such as pickled mackerel (page 160); salt cod with grilled red peppers (page 194).

Empanadas de centolla

Catalan spiced crab pasties

A popular little tapa in the sophisticated bars of Barcelona. The pastry is made with fresh pork lard in much the same way as a hot-water pie crust, but you can use an olive-oil pastry if you prefer. Or any other pastry, including ready-made puff-pastry (a Catalan favourite) or filo brushed with oil between the layers.

Serves 4–6

275g / 10oz prepared crab meat
2–3 tablespoons olive oil
2–3 shallots or 1 medium onion, finely chopped
1–2 cloves garlic, chopped
1 teaspoon paprika
1 teaspoon ground cinnamon
½ teaspoon ground nutmeg
1 large tomato, skinned, deseeded and diced
salt and freshly ground black pepper

For the pastry
275g / 10oz self-raising flour
½ teaspoon salt
125g / 4oz fresh pure lard
2 tablespoons white wine
about 150ml / ¼ pint milk or water
a little milk to glaze

Pick over the crab meat and remove any little bits of shell.

Heat the oil in a frying pan and gently fry the onion, garlic and spices until the onion softens. Add the tomato and bubble up, mashing to soften. Stir in the crab meat and bubble up again. Season and set aside to cool while you make the pastry.

Preheat the oven to 190°C/375°F/gas 5.

Sift the flour into a warm bowl and make a well in the centre. Sprinkle in the salt. Combine the lard, wine and milk or water in a small pan and heat until just warm – blood temperature. Pour the warm liquid into the flour, working dry and wet ingredients thoroughly to make a smooth, elastic dough. Roll out to a thickness of about 5mm/¼in and cut into small rounds using a wine glass. Spoon a dab of the crab mixture onto each round, wet the edge and fold the pastry over to make a semi-circular patty. Brush with milk and bake for 15–20 minutes, until crisp and golden.

Good with . . . a *pipérade* – *ratatouille* with eggs scrambled in the juices.

Rap a la brasa amb salsa romesco

Catalan grilled monkfish and prawns with red pepper salsa

The cooks of Catalonia have a highly sophisticated palate – not least because of their long association with Provence, trade-links that range from Italy to Istanbul, and the vigour brought by the capital and major trading port of Barcelona to an already well developed culinary habit. Salsa romesco is something of a cult in the city of Tarragona, its home territory, where annual competitions are held to discover the most exquisite recipe.

Serves 4–6

500g / 1lb filleted monkfish, cut into bite-sized pieces
250g / 8oz large prawns, peeled, tails left on
2–3 tablespoons olive oil
juice of 1 lemon
salt and freshly ground black pepper

For the salsa romesco
2 cloves garlic, crushed
1 teaspoon salt
2 tablespoons fresh breadcrumbs fried crisp in a little olive oil
2 tablespoons toasted almonds
2 roasted or fried red peppers, skinned and deseeded
2 large tomatoes, skinned, deseeded and roughly chopped
1 red chilli, deseeded and chopped
4 tablespoons red wine vinegar
150ml / ¼ pint olive oil

Thread the monkfish cubes and prawns alternately on skewers, and sprinkle with the oil, lemon juice, salt and pepper. Leave to marinate while you make the *salsa*.

Drop the garlic, salt, breadcrumbs and almonds into a food processor and grind to a paste. Add the peppers, tomatoes, chilli and vinegar and work it some more. Add the oil in a thin trickle, as you would for a mayonnaise, until the sauce is thick and shiny. (Alternatively, work by hand in a mortar.)

Preheat the grill or light the barbecue – let it get really hot.

Drain the monkfish and prawns and sprinkle with a little more oil. Grill for 4–5 minutes, no more, turning so that the heat reaches all sides, until the prawns are pink and the monkfish is opaque and the edges lightly caramelized. Serve with the sauce on the side.

Good with . . . white haricot beans cooked plainly with a ham bone.

Pez espada en seviche
Valencian marinated swordfish

Recipes for marinated raw fish have featured on Mediterranean menus since the first fisherman cast his net. Any firm-fleshed white fish will do instead of swordfish, but it must be very fresh. Oily fish such as mackerel, sardines and anchovies are better cooked before marination.

Serves 4–6

500g / 1lb swordfish steak, skinned and boned
juice of 3–4 lemons (enough to soak the fish)
salt
1 green and 1 red pepper, deseeded and diced
1 chilli, deseeded and diced (or 1 teaspoon chilli powder)
2–3 large tomatoes, skinned, deseeded and diced
1 teaspoon oregano or marjoram, chopped
4 tablespoons olive oil

To finish
½ tablespoon chopped parsley
½ tablespoon finely-chopped onion
½ tablespoon green olives, pitted and sliced

Dice the fish flesh into baby-bite-sized pieces. In a dish, combine with the lemon juice, sprinkle with a little salt, cover with clingfilm and set in the fridge for 5–6 hours, turning it every now and then, until the flesh turns opaque. Drain and mix with the remaining ingredients. Chill. To serve, finish with a sprinkling of chopped parsley, onion and olives.

Good with . . . Andalusian sourdough bread (page 47) or Mallorcan spinach pizza (page 56); Valencian potatoes with saffron (page 137).

Balik köftesi
Turkish fish balls

2

Fish köfte are easy, quick and can be made with any kind of filleted fish. Fresh is best, frozen will do – or you can make them with leftover cooked fish, salt fish soaked to soften (take a look at the Spanish recipe buñuelos de bacalao), even conserved tuna. The idea is universal, the spicing makes them Turkish. Swordfish, tuna and mackerel are the most likely candidates in Izmir and Istanbul, where they are a speciality of certain waterside kiosks. If the fish is really fresh – literally just caught – it will not need an egg to bind.

Serves 6–8

500g / 1lb fish fillets, skinned
4 tablespoons fresh breadcrumbs or cooked rice or mashed potato
1 egg, lightly forked
2 tablespoons finely chopped walnuts
2 tablespoons currants, soaked in a little water to swell
1 medium onion, finely chopped or grated
2–3 cloves garlic, finely chopped
2 tablespoons finely chopped parsley
2 tablespoons finely chopped dill
1 teaspoon ground cinnamon
½ teaspoon grated nutmeg
½ teaspoon chilli flakes or crushed pepper
1 teaspoon salt (omit if you're using salt fish)

To finish
bread flour mixed with a little salt and pepper
oil for frying

Mash the fish flesh thoroughly, checking for stray bones, then work it into a paste with the rest of the ingredients. Spread the flour onto a large plate and toss with a little salt. Break off little pieces of the fish paste the size of a walnut, and dust through the seasoned flour.

In a heavy frying pan, heat two fingers' depth of oil, enough to submerge the balls. When a faint blue haze rises drop the balls in batches into the hot oil – tiny bubbles should form around the edge immediately but the oil shouldn't splutter, a sign that it's too hot – and fry until they are firm and golden-brown all over, turning carefully. They'll take 5–8 minutes, depending on size.

Good with . . . *tsatsiki* (page 36). Just the thing for watching the sun set over the Bosporus.

Ochtapodi ladolemono
Greek octopus in oil and lemon juice

2

Lazarus, chef-patron of the best taverna on Ulysses' island of Ithaca, took it upon himself to instruct me in the manly art of preparing octopus. 'Do you know how to tenderize an octopus?' he enquired one lazy afternoon, spearing a chunk of rosy-fleshed cephalopod on a toothpick. I admitted I didn't. 'As a woman, it is not your business. As a foreigner in need of instruction, I shall tell you. First, you must capture your creature. For a skilled spearfisherman such as myself, this is not difficult. Now comes the work. You must pick it up without fear and throw it forty times against a rock. Less times are needed if it's small, more if it's large. First the flesh is hard, but slowly it softens. Now you must rinse it in sea water so that it foams. Unless you do this it will never soften. You'll know when it's ready because the tentacles will curl. You must not take off the skin as so many ignorant people do. The skin turns red when you cook it, and this is what tells you the ochtapodi is fresh and good. The tourists think the meat should be white, but that's not so. No Greek would eat a white octopus. To prepare it, put it in a pan and cook it gently with a ladleful of sea water until it's perfectly tender. Slice it carefully into pieces – all of it is good. Dress it with the oil pressed from the fruit of your own olives, and squeeze on it the juice from the lemons which grow on the tree in your own garden. Then you must shake over it a little of the oregano that you have gathered wild on the hills. Now all is ready. Set out the glasses with the ouzo and fetch water from the well, since you will also need to quench your thirst. Now you may call all your friends to share the feast.' Simple, when you know how.

Serves 6–8

1 medium octopus, prepared as above
150ml / ½ pint water
1 level tablespoon salt

To dress
about 6 tablespoons extra virgin olive oil
juice of 2 lemons
a handful of oregano, leaves only
salt and freshly ground black pepper

Drop the octopus in a roomy pan with the water and the salt. Bring to the boil, turn down the heat immediately, cover loosely and cook until tender – about an hour, longer if necessary. Keep the water just trembling – don't let it boil. Leave to cool. Drain, chop into bite-sized pieces and toss with the dressing ingredients.

Good with . . . a salad involving fennel and feta.

Ochtapodi stifado

Cypriot octopus braised in red wine

As an habitué of rocky coastlines, the eight-armed cephalopod is an inshore catch. Its capture is often a leisure activity for old boys home from the sea. Octopus fishermen have more rituals than Wimbledon tennis finalists. Those that accompany the tenderizing process – basically, a thorough beating – are many and various (see page 176). This dish can be made with dried octopus – a popular preparation all round the Mediterranean, sold as a leathery tangle of suckered arms.

Serves 6–8

I small octopus, weighing about 1kg / 2lb, ready-beaten (see page 176)
2 large onions, finely sliced
2 cloves garlic, finely chopped
6 tablespoons olive oil
300ml / ½ pint red wine
150ml / ¼ pint red wine vinegar
3 or 4 cloves
I small stick cinnamon
2–3 bayleaves
I teaspoon sugar
salt and freshly ground black pepper

Turn the octopus inside out and remove the intestines – eyes, mouthpiece, soft white innards, ink sac (those of a robust constitution should strain the ink and reserve it to thicken the sauce). Lift the fine veil of skin off the head or not – as you please. Scrape the little toenails from the suckers on the tentacles – leave the suckers themselves in place (no self-respecting Greek gets rid of a sucker).

Dip the octopus in a potful of boiling water three times. This ritual is traditional, no doubt with excellent reason, possibly because the flesh is naturally watery – it produces its own cooking juices – and the scalding stiffens the fibres. Chop into bite-sized pieces.

Gently fry the onions and garlic in the oil in a roomy casserole. When they are soft and golden, add the octopus chunks, the red wine, vinegar and spices, and season with a little sugar, salt and pepper. Bubble up, turn down the heat and leave to simmer gently until perfectly tender – 1½–2 hours. Remove the lid and bubble up at the end to concentrate the juices. Stir in the ink if you are using it. Discard the bayleaves and cinnamon bark and serve at room temperature.

Good with . . . country bread; Greek stuffed vegetables (page 124).

Calamares en jerez
Spanish squid in sherry

The squid is a cephalopod, a member of that delectable family of ivory-fleshed sea creatures whose distinguishing characteristic is the possession of tentacles and ink sacs. It can either be cooked for a few minutes – as here – or be gently stewed for a long time. There's nothing in between but rubber.

Serves 4–6

750g / 1½lb medium squid
2 tablespoons olive oil
1 medium onion, finely chopped
2 cloves garlic, finely chopped
1 small green pepper, deseeded and chopped
150ml / ¼ pint dry sherry or white wine
a pinch of saffron (6–8 threads) soaked in a splash of boiling water
1 bayleaf, torn
salt and freshly ground black pepper

To finish
chopped parsley

If the squid are not ready-prepared, wash them thoroughly: they're sandy creatures. Take out the clear quill and pull out the tentacles and innards from the body. Cut off and discard the eye section including the mouthpiece and soft innards, reserving the tentacles. Scrape off the speckled membrane of skin which veils the body. If the squid are large, scrape the tentacles to remove the hard little spiky rings in the suckers – they look like little toenails.

Slice the cap into rings, chop the tentacles and the rest of the body. Warm the oil in a heavy pan. Drop in the onion, garlic and chopped pepper and fry gently until they are soft. Stir in the squid and bubble up for a moment. Pour in the sherry and the saffron with its soaking water. Add the bayleaf, and season to taste. Bubble up again, turn down the heat, cover and let it all simmer for 5–10 minutes.

Stir in the parsley and serve at room temperature without reheating.

Good with . . . shellfish opened in a lidded pan or on the grill in their own juices; anchovies fried in fans (page 163); plain grilled sardines.

Calamari ripieni al finocchio

Italian stuffed squid with fennel

 Squid is the most delicious of the cephalopods – tender, white-fleshed, with a delicate flavour and the most convenient shape for stuffing. And while we're on the subject, I'm told the ancient Egyptians used the caps as a contraceptive device – well, you would, wouldn't you? Choose medium-sized squid with a body length of around 10cm/4in.

Serves 4–6

750g / 1½lb medium squid

For the stuffing
2–3 tablespoons fresh breadcrumbs or cooked rice
2 cloves garlic, finely chopped
2 tablespoons finely chopped parsley
1 tablespoon dried marjoram
1 tablespoon toasted pinekernels
salt and freshly ground black pepper

To cook
1 onion, finely sliced
1–2 fennel bulbs, trimmed and sliced
4 tablespoons olive oil
1 small glass white wine
1 small glass water

Rinse the squid. Take out the clear bone and remove the speckled veil. Scrape off any sharp little suckers from the tentacles. Trim off the fin flaps and reserve. Pull the tentacles from the body-cap and trim off the innards and everything above the eyes, including the beaky little mouthpiece, and discard. The rest is all edible.

Chop the tentacles, fin flaps and other reserved bits and bobs with the rest of the stuffing ingredients. Season vigorously. Use the mixture to stuff the bodies. Sew up their little mouths with cocktail sticks shoved through like darning needles.

Preheat the oven to 180°C/350°F/gas 4.

Spread sliced onion and fennel in a gratin dish to make a bed. Lay in the stuffed squid in a single layer, trickle with the olive oil and pour in the white wine and the water. Cover with foil, shiny side down, and bake for 50–60 minutes, until perfectly tender.

> **Good with . . .** *focaccia* (page 49); deep-fried baby artichokes.

Sepia con habas gaditanos
Cadiz cuttlefish with broad beans

The fishermen of Cadiz – gaditanos – rate cuttlefish more highly than squid. On the slab, you can tell the difference between cuttlefish and squid quite easily: cuttlefish are round-bodied and their 'bone' is a chalky wedge of softish material much appreciated by caged birds; the squid has a longer, cone-shaped body, with a 'bone' that is pretty much indestructible and looks as if it's made of clear plastic. Generically, the cuttlefish is a smaller beast – though if you have large examples of one and small of the other, this is by no means obvious. The combination of cuttlefish with fava or broad beans, the only native European bean, is about as ancient as you can get. Variations on the dish are to be found throughout the region.

Serves 4–6

750g / 1½lb cuttlefish or squid
2 tablespoons olive oil
2 cloves garlic, sliced
350g / 12oz shelled broad beans, skinned
1 small glass dry sherry
1 small glass water
1 teaspoon chopped oregano or marjoram
salt and freshly ground black pepper

Rinse the cuttlefish and pull out the chalky cuttle and the soft innards with the tentacles. Discard the cuttle, the innards and the eyes and chop up the rest, including the body. If the cuttlefish are large you'll need to scrape the spiky little toenails off the tentacles. Squid should be treated in the same way.

Heat the oil gently in a shallow heatproof earthenware casserole or a heavy frying pan. Throw in the sliced garlic cloves and let them soften. Slip in the cuttlefish and let it cook gently in the oil until it yields up its own juices – about 10 minutes. Add the beans, the sherry and the water and let it all bubble up. Sprinkle in the chopped oregano or marjoram, season, cover and leave to simmer for 20 minutes or so, until the cuttlefish is tender. Remove the lid, turn up the heat and bubble up the liquid until there's only a slick of oily juices left.

Good with ... Andalusian fresh-pickled anchovies (page 161); thin slivers of *mojama* (salt-dried tuna) dressed with a little olive oil – a wonderfully primitive flavour; crab *croquetas* (page 170).

Seppie in umido

Sicilian cuttlefish stew

 Many of the inshore fishermen working from the ports of the Italian Riviera are not locals at all but Sicilians following the shoals. They live on their boats and cook what they cannot sell. When you dip into a shoal of cuttlefish you catch plenty. Squid or octopus can be substituted for the cuttlefish in this recipe.

Serves 4–6

750g / 1½lb cuttlefish
3–4 tablespoons olive oil
4–5 cloves garlic, chopped
1 small red chilli, deseeded and finely chopped
a handful of celery leaves (or green celery stalks), finely chopped
1 teaspoon dried oregano (it dries naturally on the stalk, just shake it in)
1 teaspoon dried thyme (or a handsome sprig of fresh)
2–3 bayleaves
a knife tip of saffron (about a dozen threads)
½ bottle red wine
salt and freshly ground black pepper

Rinse the cuttlefish thoroughly. Pull the tentacled innards from the cap-like outer body and cut off the soft bits, including the eyes and the hard little beak-like mouthpiece. Squeeze out the cuttle, an oval bone made of chalky material, from the interior pocket and save it for your budgie. Pick through the innard debris and rescue two or three of the silvery little ink sacs, crush these into a sieve and reserve the liquid. Depending on the maturity of the cuttlefish, the tentacles may have little toenails embedded in their suckers which should be scraped off. Slice the cap into rings and chop the tentacles. If you rinse your hands in *cold* water after handling raw fish, they won't smell fishy. I've no idea why this should be so, but it works.

Warm the oil in a roomy saucepan and add the garlic. When it begins to sizzle, add the prepared cuttlefish. Turn up the heat and stir until the flesh stiffens and turns opaque. Add the chilli, the celery leaves, the herbs and the saffron, and a generous amount of freshly ground pepper. Pour in the wine, bring to the boil, turn down the heat, cover loosely and leave to simmer gently for about 40 minutes, until the flesh is perfectly tender and the juices well reduced. Stir in the reserved ink, taste and season – maybe a little sugar if the wine was a bit rough?

Good with ... grilled polenta (page 265); Italian rice and cheese balls (page 263).

Midye dolmase

Turkish stuffed mussels

2

Fresh mussels stuffed with an elegantly spiced rice pilaf which includes pinekernels and raisins – very much in the Ottoman style. The dish is a speciality of the itinerant food-peddlars of the Bosporus, where the mussels are fatter and sweeter than anywhere else.

Serves 4–6

2 dozen large fresh mussels
125g / 4oz round (risotto or 'pudding') rice
2–3 tablespoons olive oil
2–3 shallots or small onions, finely chopped
2 cloves garlic, finely chopped
1 tablespoon pinekernels
1 large tomato, skinned and chopped
1 tablespoon currants
1 tablespoon chopped dill and/or parsley
1 teaspoon ground allspice
½ teaspoon ground cinnamon
½ teaspoon crushed chilli
salt and freshly ground black pepper
quartered lemons to serve

Scrub the mussels well and pull away the 'beard' (seaweed-like threads). Discard any that are cracked or remain open when tapped. Open them with a short, strong knife. Put the rice to soak in warm, salted water for 20 minutes, then drain.

Heat the oil in a frying pan, add the chopped onions and garlic and cook until they soften and take a little colour. Push the onions to the side of the pan and fry the pinekernels until gilded. Add the tomato and currants and bubble up. Add the herbs, spices, rice and enough water to cover, season and bubble up again. Turn down the heat a little and cook for 12–15 minutes, until the liquid is all absorbed but the rice is still nutty in the middle. Remove from the heat and leave to cool.

Pack each shell with the rice mixture and close again. Wedge the stuffed shells tightly into a steamer so that the halves are pressed shut: if necessary tie with a thread. Steam over boiling water for 20–25 minutes, until the mussels are perfectly cooked and have added their fragrant juices. Serve at room temperature, with quartered lemons.

Good with . . . oysters *au nature* (page 188); scallop kebabs (page 187).

Midye tavasi

Turkish mussels in batter

Bosporus mussels are huge, dredged up by the ton, and provide one element of the peripatetic mezze feasts for which the inhabitants of Istanbul will cheerfully travel the strait from end to end. The fritters are prepared by the fishermen themselves, who moor their boats by the quayside, touting for custom. I have included a spoonful of roughage in the batter since our fine-sifted modern flours are far too smooth. Tarator – a walnut-and-garlic sauce – is the traditional accompaniment. It's very pungent, but it cuts the richness. Start the batter 24 hours ahead.

Serves 4–6

1kg / 2lb live mussels on the shell
100g / 4oz strong bread flour plus 1 tablespoon semolina
1 teaspoon salt
1 tablespoon olive oil
300ml / ½ pint cold water
oil for deep-frying

For the tarator sauce
6 cloves garlic, roughly chopped and crushed with a teaspoon of salt
100g / 4oz shelled walnuts
1 slice bread, torn into small pieces
2 tablespoons water
300ml / ½ pint olive oil
juice of 2 lemons

To make the batter, sieve the flour into a bowl, toss with the semolina and salt and mix to a smooth cream with the olive oil and water. Cover with a clean cloth and leave it in a warm corner overnight to ferment and lighten. If you need it the same day, make it with beer instead of water.

Prepare the tarator sauce before you embark on the frying. Drop the crushed garlic, walnuts, bread and the water into the food processor. Or pound to a paste in a mortar. Gradually trickle in the oil, as if you were making a mayonnaise, until it thickens. Add the lemon juice as you go.

Open the mussels with a knife (or shake over a high heat in a lidded pan until the shells open) and thread the meat onto wooden skewers.

Heat the oil until you can see a faint blue haze rising. Dip each skewerful in the batter and deep-fry – not too many at a time. Drain on kitchen paper. Serve piping hot, accompanied by the sauce.

Good with . . . grilled sweetcorn; roasted pistachios; dried figs.

Tellines provençales

Provençal shellfish

 In Provence the little purple-tinged clams known as tellines are the preferred mollusc, although the larger palourdes or any other bivalve can be prepared in this way. Serve without reheating – shellfish harden if overcooked.

Serves 6–8

2kg / 4lb live shellfish (clams, mussels, cockles, razor-shells, queen scallops)
a pinch of saffron (6–8 threads)
4–6 tablespoons olive oil
I large onion, finely chopped
3–4 cloves garlic, finely chopped
Ikg / 2lb ripe tomatoes, skinned, deseeded and chopped (or tinned plum tomatoes)
I bayleaf
a sprig of thyme
I tablespoon pitted black olives, chopped
salt, pepper, a little sugar
I small glass white wine

To finish
chopped parsley

Rinse the shellfish and leave them in a bucket of cold water for a few hours – overnight is best – to spit out their sand. Scrub the shells and beard the mussels.

Toast the saffron in a dry pan for a minute or two until it releases its scent – don't let it burn or it will be bitter – and drop it into a little boiling water. Leave it to infuse for 15 minutes or so. This preliminary toasting of the saffron is a refinement designed to enhance the flavour – I'm not entirely convinced, but try it for yourself.

Heat the olive oil in a roomy frying pan and fry the chopped onion and garlic until soft and golden – don't let them brown. Add the tomatoes and bubble up, squashing them down until they soften. Add the herbs, chopped olives and the saffron with its soaking water. Bubble up again, then turn down the heat and leave to bubble for 20 minutes or so until the sauce is thick and rich. Season with salt, pepper and a little sugar. Add the wine and the raw shellfish. Bubble up again, cover loosely and let the shells open in the steam, shaking the pan every now and again to allow the top layer to drop to the bottom. Take the pan off the heat as soon as the shells gape open – 4–6 minutes, depending on the size of the pan and the thickness of the shells. Finish with plenty of chopped parsley.

> Good with . . . oysters, raw or grilled (page 188 and 189); prawn brochettes (page 168).

Almejas en vino de jerez

Andalusian clams in sherry

2

Spanish housewives expect to buy their shellfish live on the shell. Bivalves have a relatively long shell-life, surviving for as long as they can keep water in their shells – hence the need to reject those with cracked shells or which remain closed when cooked. Recipes are of the simplest: when the fish is fresh there's no need to mask the flavour.

Serves 4–6

1kg / 2lb clams, cockles, mussels – live on the shell
2 tablespoons olive oil
2 cloves garlic, chopped
1 large glass dry sherry or white wine
2 tablespoons chopped parsley
salt, freshly ground black pepper, a little sugar

Rinse the shellfish and leave them in a bucket of cold water for a few hours – overnight is best – to spit out their sand. Discard any that are broken or weigh unusually heavy – they're probably dead and filled with sand.

Heat the oil in a saucepan, add the garlic and let it soften for a moment. Tip in the shellfish, add the wine, parsley, sugar and seasoning, and turn up the heat. As soon as steam rises, cover and leave to cook, shaking the pan to re-distribute the shells. Allow 3–4 minutes for all the shells to open – check and turn them over if necessary. Remove the pan from the heat as soon as the shells are open. Delicious hot or cold. Don't reheat or they'll be rubbery.

> **Good with . . .** chicken livers with sherry (page 217); *patatas bravas* (page 136); crisp-fried chips.

Vongole al pomodoro
Italian clams in tomato sauce

 The warm waters and sheltered inlets of the Mediterranean provide a home for an astonishing variety of shellfish, each of which has its own regional name and is eaten with relish in certain areas and disregarded in others. In Naples clams are served in every restaurant – in bianco, *without tomato, or, as here, in a rich tomato sauce.*

Serves 6–8

2kg / 4lb clams or mussels (or any other bivalves)
3–4 tablespoons olive oil
1 large onion, finely chopped
3–4 cloves garlic, finely chopped
1kg / 2lb ripe tomatoes, skinned, deseeded and chopped (or use tinned)
1–2 dried chillis, deseeded and chopped
1 small glass red wine
salt, freshly ground black pepper, a little sugar

To finish
chopped parsley

Rinse the shellfish and leave them in a bucket of cold water for a few hours – overnight is best – to spit out their sand. Discard any that are broken or are unusually heavy – they are probably dead and filled with sand.

Heat the olive oil in a roomy frying pan and fry the chopped onion and garlic until soft and golden – don't let them brown. Add the tomatoes and chilli and bubble up. Turn down the heat and leave to simmer gently for 20 minutes or so, squashing the tomatoes down, until the sauce is thick and rich.

Add the wine, taste and season with salt, pepper and a little sugar and bring back to the boil. Add the raw shellfish, bubble up again, cover loosely and let the shells open in the steam, shaking the pan every now and again to allow the top layer to drop to the bottom.

Take the pan off the heat as soon as the shells gape open – 4–6 minutes, depending on the size of your pan and the thickness of the shells. Finish with chopped parsley and serve without reheating – shellfish harden if overcooked.

> **Good with . . .** bread, naturally – *ciabatta* (page 48) or *focaccia* (page 49) if you feel like baking your own; Ligurian vegetable omelette (page 79); saffron rice cakes (page 262).

▶ *Italian stuffed squid with fennel (page 179); focaccia (page 49)*

Tarak sîs kebap
Turkish scallop kebabs

The scallop, unusually for a bivalve, is a swimmer capable of projecting itself through the water at considerable speed by opening and closing its shell – hence its reputation as a mysterious creature, and its alternative names: pilgrim shell, chariot of Venus. Choose live scallops with tightly closed shells – they should be really hard to open, closing quickly at the slightest disturbance.

Serves 4–6

12 scallops
juice of 1 lemon
2 tablespoons olive oil
1 teaspoon crushed chilli
1 teaspoon crumbled dried thyme
1–2 bayleaves, crumbled

To finish
1 tablespoon chopped dill
1 tablespoon chopped mint
1 tablespoon chopped flat-leaf parsley

To serve
flat-bread for wrapping – *pitta*
lemon quarters
salt

To prepare the scallops, scrub and leave them in fresh water for a few hours or overnight to spit out their sand. If it's still hard to prise the shells apart with a knife slipped behind the hinge, a few minutes in a bath of hot water, or in a warm oven, will encourage them to open. Once levered apart, slip the scallop off its shell with a sharp knife and remove the grey frill from the edge (edible but a little tough) and the sandy little intestinal sac. Cut the scallops into neat, bite-sized pieces, and toss them with the lemon juice, oil, chilli, thyme and bay. Don't salt. Leave to marinate for an hour or two in a cool place.

Preheat the grill or light the barbecue. It should be very hot.

Drain the scallops, reserving the marinade, and thread them onto fine skewers. Grill fiercely so that the edges caramelize a little, turning to cook all sides: 2–3 minutes is enough to firm the flesh. Meanwhile, strain the marinade into a small pan and bubble up to concentrate the flavours. Add a splash of water and stir in the fresh herbs. Bubble up again and pour over the kebabs. Serve with lemon quarters and salt.

Good with . . . *pitta* or any soft bread wrapper; stuffed mussels (page 182)

◀ *Italian rice and cheese balls (page 263); Provençal shellfish (page 184)*

Huîtres au nature, sauce verte

Provençal oysters with green sauce

 Oysters, being tidal creatures, can remain alive without water in a cool and damp place for ten days or more – as long as they can keep moisture in their shells. Here they're served with a hot sauce, deceptively green but packing a chilli-punch: perfect with each cool mouthful.

Serves 2–8 (appetites for oysters vary)

2 dozen oysters

For the sauce
1 fresh green chilli, deseeded and roughly chopped
a handful of parsley, de-stalked
2–3 shallots (or large spring onions), roughly chopped
150ml / ¼ pint white wine vinegar
1 tablespoon sugar

Set the oysters on a bed of cracked ice and leave them to cool.

Meanwhile, put all the sauce ingredients in the liquidizer or food processor and process them thoroughly – or use a sharp knife to chop everything very finely before blending with the vinegar.

Serve the sauce at room temperature, with the chilled oysters.

> **Good with . . .** crisply grilled spicy sausages (*merguez*, fresh *chorizo*, anything garlicky and chilli-spiked) and eat alternately, following each mouthful of the cool and smooth with a bite of the hot and rough. Exquisite. Provide a plate of raw vegetables with a selection of dipping sauces of the *hummus* variety, and you will surely be content.

To open an oyster: hold the more curved of the two shells firmly in a clean cloth, and slip the point of a short, strong knife in round the side of the hinge. If all goes well (and the oyster is a contrary creature) the shell will open with a gentle pop. Holding the blade parallel with the top shell, slide it across, severing the connecter muscle and taking care not to lose any of the precious juices. Slip the knife underneath the flesh and sever the bottom muscle. The oyster is now ready for eating: don't be tempted to rinse off any scraps of shell or it will taste of tap-water (a very good reason not to order them in a restaurant unless you can make your wishes perfectly clear).

Huîtres au gratin
Provençal baked oysters

The French love oysters, can buy them relatively cheaply and have no hesitation in eating them all year round. In summer, the breeding season, oysters are 'laiteuse' – milky with eggs – when they have a deliciously creamy flavour and a natural fattiness which makes them perfect for grilling. Always buy your oysters unopened and attend to them yourself – reject any that capitulate without a struggle: bivalves can only stay alive for as long as they can keep water in their shells.

Serves 2–8 (appetites vary)

24 oysters
2 shallots or 1 small onion, finely chopped
1 tablespoon finely chopped parsley
1 teaspoon fennel seeds
Pernod or any anis-flavoured *eau de vie*
at least 2 tablespoons freshly made white breadcrumbs
at least 1 tablespoon grated hard cheese – Cantal or Parmesan

Open the oysters with a short, strong knife (see page 188), slipping the blade in alongside the hinge – easiest done with an oyster-opener, a dagger-like instrument with a protective hasp. Grip the rough shell firmly in a cloth while you work.

Preheat the grill or turn the oven to maximum – 250°C/475°F/gas 9.

Leaving each oyster on the deepest of its two shells, arrange in a shallow gratin dish in a single layer – you can hold them in place on a bed of dishwasher salt. By now the oysters should have come up to room temperature – if not, wait until they do. Top each oyster with a little chopped onion, parsley and fennel seeds, a drop of Pernod and a sprinkle of breadcrumbs mixed with a little grated cheese; don't be too generous or you'll mask the fresh flavour of the shellfish.

Slip the oysters under the grill for 3–4 minutes, or in the oven for 6–8 minutes – just long enough to brown the topping. Serve immediately, while the topping is still crisp.

> Good with ... wine vinegar infused with a few dried red chillis; Provençal shellfish in tomato sauce (page 184); *tommes*, the robust little one-person goat's cheeses of Provence, popped under the grill and served on a croûton with a little salad; something crisp and chewy in the way of bread.

Taramosalata
Greek salt roe purée

2

Taramosalata is the dish most frequently encountered on the mezze table, and when properly made it is piquant, pungent and deliciously fishy. The commercially prepared stuff is familiar enough from every cook-chill cabinet – fluffy, pink, stabilized with whatever comes into the manufacturer's head – and weirdly unlike the real thing. It's not hard to make your own, and the difference will ensure you never buy it ready-made again. The traditional basis is tarama, the salted, pressed roe of the grey mullet – the blunt-nosed, grey-backed, white bellied fish that frequent Greek harbours and come up to be fed from the taverna tables, curious as cats. Nowadays, tarama is more likely to be salted dried cod's roe. Greek island cooks make a peasant version with mashed potato rather than bread, and will tell those who enquire that the potato thickening is more delicate. In Greece you can buy tarama in tubs by weight. Ask in your local fishmonger or delicatessen.

Serves 4–6

500g / 1lb organic potatoes, well scrubbed, chunked if large
2–3 cloves garlic, crushed with a little salt
250g / 8oz *tarama* or salted fish roe
150ml / ¼ pint olive oil
juice of 1–2 lemons
1 teaspoon cayenne pepper

To serve
extra olive oil
a black olive

Cook the potatoes in their jackets in plenty of boiling well salted water. Drain thoroughly, reserving a little of the cooking water, and skin as soon as they're cool enough to handle. Mash vigorously with the crushed garlic, *tarama* and enough olive oil to soften the purée. Season with lemon juice and cayenne pepper – you shouldn't need extra salt, but taste it to check. Swirl onto a shallow plate, trickle with a little extra oil and top with a black olive.

> **Good with** . . . any of the other Middle Eastern salad purées; bread and crisp Cos lettuce for scooping; crisp raw vegetables.

Salt fish

In Mediterranean grocery stores you can buy salt-cured, oil-conserved tuna and anchovies straight from the barrel: the latter need de-salting by soaking, usually in milk, and you'll have to strip out the whiskery little bones. Salt cod (split, salted and wind-dried cod known as *bacalao, baccala, morue, bacaliaros*) and stockfish (cod that has been wind-dried without salt, known in Italy as *stocaficada, stofinado*) started its gastronomic career as the sailors' staple, victualling the Viking longships and appearing on the bills of lading of both Magellan and Columbus. As a trade item with a long shelf-life it could be exchanged for other goods, accounting for its popularity in the inland villages of the Mediterranean, even though the fish itself is an Atlantic dweller never found in Mediterranean waters. Throughout the Middle Ages – when the Catholic Church required her congregations to abstain from meat not only on Fridays and throughout Lent but also on the eves of feast days and in the run-up to Christmas – resourceful cooks turned necessity into a virtue. Recipes evolved that tempered the harshness of the salt fish with olive oil and the sweetness of Mediterranean vegetables. The Norwegian fishermen who supply most of the world's salt and wind-dried cod will tell you the best recipes are those of the Mediterranean.

Salt cod can be bought ready-soaked and vacuum-packed in Portuguese or West Indian foodstores as well as in Mediterranean markets, particularly at Christmas in Provence where – as *brandade de morue* (a creamy salt cod dip, see page 192) or as part of the *grande aïoli*, a dish of plain boiled vegetables served with a thick garlic mayonnaise (see page 40) – it's the most important component of the Christmas Eve fasting supper.

To choose and soak your own salt cod, pick the thick middle cut of the fish, and check to see that there's no pink down the spine – a sign that it has not been thoroughly cured. Wash the salt cod and cut it into 3–4 pieces. Put it to soak in a colander set in a roomy basin filled with clean fresh water and change the water at least three times during this period. Best of all, leave the fish under a trickle of running water, until the flesh is completely rehydrated. Smoked haddock (the real thing, not those bright yellow fillets) is a possible substitute. Or you could use fresh cod, salted overnight, though the flavour's not nearly so raunchy.

Brandade de morue

Provençal salt cod purée

In the hills of Provence the réveillon's the thing. If you turn up in a Provençal village on Christmas Day you'll find the shutters up and everyone asleep, the main business of the festival long over and done with. All the excitement – the family gathering and the feasting – takes place on the eve. The most important dish is the brandade de morue, *the creamy salt cod purée that is the Provençal answer to the rigours of fasting imposed by the Catholic Church. At the festive season you can buy your* brandade *ready-made, or you might choose to select your salt cod ready-soaked. If it's not already soaked, you need to start preparations the day before.*

Serves 6–8

500g / 1lb salt cod
1 onion, skinned
2 bayleaves
3 fennel branches
1 strip orange zest (dried, if possible)
6 peppercorns

For the brandade
1 warm mashed boiled potato (optional, but it helps the emulsion)
2 cloves garlic, crushed
300ml / ½ pint warm olive oil
2–3 tablespoons warm cream
black olives, to decorate

Wash the salt cod and cut it into 3–4 pieces. Put it to soak for several hours or overnight in a colander set in a roomy basin filled with clean fresh water. Change the water as often as you remember or – best of all – leave the fish under a trickle of running water.

Drain the fish and put it in a saucepan with the onion and the aromatics. Cover with water and bring gently to the boil. Remove the pan as soon as the water gives a good belch and pour in a glassful of cold water. Leave for 5 minutes, remove the fish and drain and skin it.

Pound the fish with the potato, the garlic and a little of the oil. Do this thoroughly and vigorously. Beat in the rest of the oil gradually, as if you were making a mayonnaise, adding the cream towards the end, until you have a thick white purée. You can do it all in a food processor, in which case the *brandade* will come out smoother and whiter. Serve warm, decorated with black olives, with bread, as you would a pâté. It's very rich.

Good with . . . thick slices of grilled baguette; enough oysters for all.

Buñuelos de bacalao
Spanish salt cod fritters

The classic way with salt cod, also called mountain-fish since salt-dried fish was the only fast-day food available in the inland villages – an important consideration throughout the Catholic Mediterranean in the days when fast days were observed with rather more rigour. Call it the Mediterranean fishcake. Vary the flavourings to suit your taste: include finely chopped fresh green chilli instead of black pepper, dill instead of parsley, a little grated lemon zest or cheese.

Serves 6–8

500g / 1lb salt cod, presoaked (see page 191)
500g / 1lb floury potatoes, scrubbed
3 eggs
1 large onion, grated
4 tablespoons chopped parsley
freshly ground black pepper
olive oil for frying

Set the salt cod in a saucepan with enough water to cover, bring to the boil and cook until tender – about 20 minutes. In a separate pan boil the potatoes until tender. Drain thoroughly. As soon as they're cool enough to handle, skin the potatoes and mash well. Remove the skin and bones from the cod. Flake it with your fingers then mash it with a fork, to reduce it to threads. Beat the fish into the mashed potato. Let it cool a little before mixing in the eggs, one by one. Beat in the onion and parsley. Add a little potato-water or milk if the mixture's too dry – it should be stiff enough to support the weight of a wooden spoon. Add pepper and taste for salt – you probably won't need it. Allow to cool completely before shaping the mixture into balls the size of a walnut – a couple of spoons make the task easier.

Heat enough olive oil to submerge the balls – watch carefully until a faint blue haze rises and carefully slip in the balls a few at a time to avoid cooling the oil. Turn them as they cook to crisp and brown all sides. Drain on kitchen paper and serve piping hot.

Good with . . . a fresh tomato sauce spiked with chilli; *ratatouille* (page 125); potato salad; a seafood salad; oysters on the half-shell – deliciously cool and smooth with the hot fritters.

Pericana de bacalao
Valencian salt cod with grilled red peppers

This simple little recipe combines the sweetness of grilled red peppers with the salty punch of the fish. Choose the garlic carefully: it should be new-season, very plump and fresh, without a single green sprout – once a garlic has sprouted it's sure to be bitter and dry. Use sherry or balsamic vinegar – the older it is, the milder and sweeter it will be. Failing these, a handful of raisins soaked in boiling water will provide the necessary sweetness. The salt cod requires no presoaking: the heat of the grillpan will soften the flesh and draw the salt.

Serves 4–6

6 red peppers
250g / 8oz salt cod, chunked and unsoaked
I whole head garlic, new and fresh
I tablespoon sherry or white wine vinegar
I teaspoon crushed chilli
I tablespoon toasted pinekernels (optional)

To finish
extra-virgin olive oil

Grill the whole peppers on a high heat until the skin blisters black. Skin or not, as you please. Deseed and tear the flesh into strips. Shove a knife into the garlic head and turn it in the flame until the papery covering burns, a process that roasts the cloves a little, rendering them milder and sweeter; skin and slice.

Heat a *plancha* (griddle) or heavy iron pan until it is smoking hot. Slap on the salt cod and grill until it blackens a little. Remove the skin and bones and tear the fish into small flakes – use your fingers. Toss with the pepper strips, sliced garlic, vinegar and chilli and leave to infuse for an hour or so. Finish with a trickle of olive oil. Robust but good.

Good with . . . *pa amb tomaquét* (page 60) or Andalusian sourdough bread (page 47) and a salad of sliced tomatoes and mild onion.

Chicken & game

Chickens of the Mediterranean breed are small and muscular, closer to the bantam than our own barnyard birds, with the lean breasts and sinewy legs of their wild ancestor, the Malaysian jungle fowl. It is only recently that the large, heavy-breasted, pale-fleshed, battery-reared table-birds have been introduced, rapidly gaining popularity in city markets as a source of cheap protein.

In rural areas housewives still keep a flock of the small, sharp-beaked, aggressive little chickens of the old breed. These, unlike our barnyard hens, are more than capable of fending for themselves, scrabbling in the dirt for grubs and worms, picking up the household's leavings, gleaning behind the harvesters.

Loft-bred pigeon – squab – turkey and guinea-fowl are the alternative barn-yard birds, but since they are not prolific egg-layers they are regarded as something of a luxury. The goose and the duck, water-dependent fowl, are not particularly suited to the Mediterranean climate, although the Egyptians, having the advantage of the Nile's floodplain, are very fond of the former.

Any bird can be substituted for any other in any recipe, but the guinea-fowl is the closest in flavour and texture to the Mediterranean chicken.

Feathered game is in short supply these days, for which we have only our-selves to blame. Centuries of trapping, liming, netting and shooting have done for the bulk of the birds, while pressure on land for building, allied to modern farming methods – monocropping, lavish use of pesticides – are rapidly finishing off what little is left. In any recipe, replace the wild with the tame. Farmed quail, loft-reared pigeon (deliciously gamey) and guinea-fowl – least domesticated of all barnyard birds – make excellent alternatives. As always, domestic creatures are never in danger of extinction, which is more than can be said for the goldfinch and the figpecker.

Furred game – rabbit, hare, boar and several species of deer – are to be found throughout the region, and all of these make excellent eating. Wild meat is lean, sinewy and generally of indeterminate age, making it tough and dry if not handled with care. Once the animal has been skinned and jointed, use a sharp knife to lift off the tough membrane which covers the back and haunches of all but the youngest, and cook long and slowly, with plenty of enriching fat or oil. A friend of mine who cooks a great deal of game says it's much improved by a spell in the freezer – the meat is tenderer, the sinews less chewy.

As for small game – and by that I mean frogs and snails – frogs are off the menu and the French snail can be gathered only by licensed locals. Elsewhere, however, the succulent mollusc is never in short supply, as any gardener will tell you. The snail, although not exactly fast on its foot, is remarkably difficult to spot, unless you're out in the lettuce patch on a rainy day, when you'll find it by the hundred. I know of no species of land-snail whose meat is not both edible and good – it's the gut and its contents that give the trouble, hence the need for starving. The cooks of North Africa enjoy their own varieties of the succulent molluscs, including a particularly large species imported by the Romans for their vivariums. The French go to the trouble of digging them out of winter hibernation, when they are conveniently self-starved. In Provence, vineyard-owners simply harvest theirs directly from the vines and roast them like chestnuts on the fire. Andalusia gourmets rate the tiny snails that aestivate on thistles, and cook them in a dark broth flavoured with cumin and chilli; in Catalonia you'll find them finished in a tomato sauce, or combined, in autumn, with wild-gathered fungi. The Cretans, snail-experts of the eastern Mediterranean, fatten up their native molluscs on a diet of wheat grain and thyme, and cook them in broth flavoured with the herbs of the maquis.

To joint a chicken into 28 pieces

Reserve the neck and heart; slit the gizzard and rinse out any grain debris; inspect the liver and remove any little green streaks (they'll be bitter). Separate the legs from the carcass where they join the body and chop them into drumsticks and thighs, then tap a sharp knife through the bones to give you four pieces per leg. Cut off the wings, including a little chunk of breast, and divide each in two at the second joint. Separate the breast from the back at the base of the ribcage, and cut the whole breast in two through the wishbone and then cut each piece into four, to give eight pieces in all; chop the back in half, and again in two crosswise. Simple, when you know how.

Three classic chicken broths

2

To turn an informal summer meal into a winter feast, serve steaming bowls of chicken broth, fragrant and comforting, on the side. The basis is a homemade stock, best made with a boiling fowl, but failing this use chicken wings, which have plenty of bone and enough meat to give substance. The carcass from a roast chicken will do, but the broth will need to be de-fatted. A pig's trotter or ham bone – serrano or prosciutto – begged from the delicatessen counter will improve both texture and flavour. Additional flavourings – our grandmothers called them pot-herbs – are onions, carrot, leek, bayleaf, celery, fennel (sparingly), parsley stalks, peppercorns, allspice. If you include the skins of the onions they'll impart a golden tinge. For a clear stock, simmer very gently – the surface should tremble, no more – and allow a couple of hours to extract the maximum flavour and strength. Strain out the solids before you boil the stock down for keeping (the stronger the stock the better the keeping-qualities) and don't add salt until the end. To de-fat, let the stock cool in the fridge and then lift off the hat that forms – fat is lighter than water. If you mean to keep the stock for longer than a week in the fridge, leave out the flavouring vegetables. You can also freeze it in cubes. Great-granny would have boiled it down hard until it set as firm as a gum-drop – the first soup-cube. Now you know it all.

Serves 4–6

Souppa avgolémono (Greek egg-and-lemon soup). Bring 1 litre/scant 2 pints stock to the boil, stir in 2 tablespoons long-grain rice and simmer until the grains are tender – about 20 minutes. Meanwhile whisk 1 large egg with the juice of 1 large lemon. When the rice is soft, remove the pan from the stove and whisk a ladleful of the hot broth into the egg-and-lemon mixture. Whisk this back into the soup and serve. Don't reboil or it'll curdle.

Aigo bouillido (Provençal garlic soup). Simmer 8 finely slivered cloves garlic in 1 litre/scant 2 pints stock for 30 minutes. Five minutes before the end, add a sprig of sage. Bring back to the boil and stir in 2 tablespoons vermicelli – they cook in only 2–3 minutes. Take the pan from the heat and remove the sage. Wait for a moment and then whisk a ladleful of the hot broth into a well forked egg yolk. Whisk the egg mixture back into the broth. Don't reheat before serving. Finish each portion with a spoonful of olive oil.

Sopa cuarto de hora (Spanish quarter-hour soup). Heat 1 litre/scant 2 pints broth. Stir in 2 tablespoons vermicelli (or cooked rice), a handful of finely chopped *serrano* ham, a finely chopped hardboiled egg, and a good sprinkling of parsley. Reheat until boiling. That's all.

Pain de lapin
Provençal rabbit pâté

2

The Provençal hors d'oeuvre almost always includes a slab of rough pâté de campagne, made with well flavoured wild game, vigorously spiced and baked in a bread tin – no need to enclose it in a crust. Rabbits are plentiful everywhere on the northern shores of the region, but the farmers of Provence will often leave a patch of scrub between their fields to provide shelter for wild game, both feathered and furred. Wild rabbit needs a little more attention than domestic bunny. Boning-out is fiddly, and unless the animal is very young the clear membrane that covers the saddle and hind legs must be removed or the meat will never be really tender, however long you cook it. Use a sharp knife – you have to be brutal and waste a bit of flesh. The leanness of the meat is balanced here by the richness of the pork belly.

Serves 6–8

750g / 1½lb rabbit meat (could be chicken or any feathered game)
250g / 8oz fatty pork belly
3 eggs
300ml / ½ pint white wine
1 clove garlic, roughly crushed
1 teaspoon chopped thyme
1 teaspoon chopped rosemary
1 teaspoon crushed juniper berries
2–3 bayleaves
salt and crushed black peppercorns

Preheat the oven to 180°C/350°F/gas 4.

Chop the rabbit meat with the pork belly either with a sharp knife or briefly in the processor; don't mince – in a rough pâté you should be able to see the texture of the meat. Fork up the eggs with the wine and combine with the meat, garlic, herbs, spices (reserving the bayleaves), salt and pepper.

Pack the mixture into a small loaf tin (approx 20cm x 10 cm / 8 in x 4 in) – it should reach about two thirds of the way up. Top with the bayleaves and cover with foil, pleated down the middle to allow room for expansion. Set the tin in a *bain-marie* – a roasting-tin into which you have poured enough boiling water to come halfway up the sides of the pâté tin. Bake for about an hour, until perfectly firm and well shrunk from the sides. Test with a skewer thrust deep into the middle – the juices should run clear. Leave to cool, cover with a clean cloth and set a weighted board on top. Leave overnight before cutting in slices.

Combine with ... radishes; Provençal potato salad (page 134); Provençal chard quiche (page 92) or broad bean omelette (page 78).

Terrine de faisan aux noix

French pheasant terrine with hazelnuts

2 *The notion of combining the delicate, dry meat of the pheasant with the robust richness of hazelnuts is, one might think, the essence of French haute cuisine. Yet Circassian Chicken – a favourite dish of the Ottoman sultans – relies on the same elegant balance.*

Serves 6–8

2 pheasants (elderly birds are fine, or any feathered game), or 1 medium chicken

For the marinade
1 large glass red wine
1 small glass *eau de vie* or any white brandy
1 teaspoon ground allspice
1 teaspoon crushed juniper berries
1 teaspoon thyme
salt and freshly ground black pepper

Second day
100g / 4oz streaky bacon, de-rinded, diced
150g / 6oz belly pork, de-rinded, diced
2 egg yolks
50g / 2oz shelled hazelnuts, toasted
2 bayleaves

To line the terrine
3–4 fine sheets of pork fat or fatty bacon

Skin the birds and strip all the meat from the bones (which will make a delicious game stock). Set aside the breast fillets and dice the rest of the meat. Put all the meat into a bowl with the marinade ingredients, turning to blend. Cover and leave overnight.

Next day, preheat the oven to 180°C/350°F/gas 4. Remove the breast meat from the marinade and reserve, and put the rest through the mincer with the bacon and pork. Work in the egg yolks and the hazelnuts, plus enough of the marinade to moisten.

Line a terrine or loaf tin (approx. 20cm x 10cm/8in x 4in) with the pork fat or bacon – use the back of a knife to stretch them really thin – leaving flaps to be folded over the top. Pack in half the minced meat, top with the breast fillets, and finish with the rest. Arrange the bayleaves on top and fold over the flaps to enclose. Cover with foil and set in a roasting tin – *bain-marie* – pouring in enough boiling water to come halfway up the terrine.

Bake for about an hour, until firm to the finger and well shrunk from the sides. The length of time it takes depends on the shape of the tin. Test with a skewer thrust right into the middle – the juices should run clear. Weight with a heavy object and leave overnight to cool and firm. Slice thickly.

Good with . . . pickled gherkins, radishes, fresh bread – pork-crackling bread (page 51).

Rillettes de lapin

Provençal potted rabbit

2

Neither a pâté nor a paste but something in between, you'll find this succulent little preparation on sale in charcuteries and pork butchers throughout France – the recipe scarcely changed since the days of Charlemagne. In Provence, smallholding farmers take care to leave a bit of woodland as a sanctuary for game, both furred and feathered, in anticipation of wild meat for the pot. Elderly bunnies – those too long in the tooth for roasting – are included in the rillettes. The lard that lubricates the meat is either fat made with the rich leavings from the foie gras goose, or panne de porc, the soft white fat that surrounds a pig's kidney – take care to strip the little globules from the membranes and melt the fat very slowly with enough water to prevent it browning.

Serves 6–8

250g / 8oz goose fat or freshly made pork lard
1kg / 2lb belly pork, diced
500g / 1lb rabbit meat, diced
a *bouquet garni* of thyme, rosemary and bay
2 teaspoons salt
1 teaspoon freshly ground black pepper

Melt the goose fat or lard gently in a heavy pan (don't let it bubble), add the diced belly pork and stir over a very low heat until the fat runs. Add the diced rabbit and tuck in the *bouquet garni*. Cook very gently for 3 hours, or bake in the lowest possible oven, until the fat has completely melted and the meat is absolutely soft. Keep a careful watch for sticking – stir the pieces regularly with a wooden spoon. The fat mustn't bubble – the very low temperature throughout should prevent this.

Remove the *bouquet garni* and skim off a ladleful of the surface fat for sealing the pots. Season with the salt and pepper, then, using two forks, pull apart the meat and mix meat and fat until well blended. Taste and adjust the seasoning. Pot up in small jars and leave to cool. Seal under a layer of the reserved melted fat. The *rillettes* are ready immediately and keep for a month in the fridge so long as they're not disturbed, or almost indefinitely in the freezer.

> Good with . . . crusty bread – toasted or not as you please; raw baby artichokes or fresh walnuts in season; *saucisson sec*; a bunch of radishes with coarse salt for dipping; pickled gherkins; black olives.

Gibier en gallantine

French game terrine

2

Potted game – nothing simpler. You never can tell what the guns will bring in, and this is how a French chasseur likes to tackle a mixed bag of fur and feather. If you lack a good proportion of bone to meat, include a well scrubbed pig's trotter or a bit of veal shin to help the juices set into a firm jelly.

Serves 8–10

a mixed bag of game – 2–3kg / 5–6lb – on the bone
1 tablespoon *eau de vie* or Calvados
2–3 sprigs thyme
2–3 bayleaves
1 tablespoon crushed juniper berries
1 tablespoon salt
1 teaspoon crushed black peppercorns

To finish
4–5 very fine slices salt-cured ham – *de Bayonne, prosciutto, serrano*

Preheat the oven to 170°C/325°F/gas 3. Joint the game neatly if feathered; if furred, chunk it roughly. Pack all the bits into a large casserole or stone crock along with the *eau de vie* and the seasonings. Pour in enough water to cover the meat and cover very tightly – seal with a flour-and-water paste if the lid doesn't fit really snugly. Cook in the oven for 3–4 hours, until the meat is really soft.

Remove the meat from the pot and strain the broth into a pan. Boil down the broth to about half a pint – it needs to be really strong if it is to jellify properly. While the meat is still warm strip it off the bones and dice it.

Line a large loaf tin (approx. 23cm x 13cm/9in x 5in) with the finely sliced ham and pack in the meat – it should fill it right to the top. Pour in enough of the concentrated stock to wet the meat thoroughly. Fold the loose flaps of ham over the top, cover with foil, weight down and leave in a cool place overnight for the jelly to set. Serve cold, cut into slices. This keeps well in the fridge, but don't try to freeze it – the jelly will separate and there'll be no help for it but to bake it in a pie.

> Good with . . . bread, naturally; pickled gherkins and capers; olives – preferably the nutty little frost-cured black olives of Nyons; a plate of *charcuterie* – thin slices of *jambon cru*, lightly smoked salt-cured ham; *saucisson sec* – ring the changes with *saucisson d'Arles*, which includes beef with the usual pork, and *saucisson à l'ail* – with garlic – a cooked sausage for slicing.

Pollo chilindrón

Spanish spiced chicken with peppers

A speciality of Zaragoza in northern Spain. The aromatic scarlet sauce makes even frozen chicken-portions taste good. Like so many Spanish tapas, it's not exclusively designed as such but suitable since the chicken is jointed into bite-sized pieces that can easily be eaten with the fingers. To make the most of a small chicken, include the neck, liver, heart and gizzard, as well as the more obvious meat. This is good made a day ahead and served at room temperature.

Serves 6–8

I small free-range chicken, jointed into bite-sized pieces including bone (see page 197)
6 tablespoons olive oil
2 tablespoons diced *serrano* ham (or lean bacon)
I large onion, sliced vertically
3–4 cloves garlic, sliced
3 red peppers, deseeded and sliced into strips
500g / Ilb tomatoes, skinned and chopped (or tinned plum tomatoes)
I–2 bayleaves
2–3 cloves
I small stick cinnamon
2–3 dried chillis, deseeded and crumbled
salt

Wipe over the chicken joints and pat dry (particularly important if they were frozen). Remove any obvious fat and stray little feather hairs.

Heat the oil in a heavy iron casserole over a medium heat, lay in the chicken joints and fry gently until they brown a little – about 5 minutes. Push the joints aside (or remove and reserve, if the casserole is too small) and add the chopped ham, onion, garlic and peppers. Fry all gently, stirring regularly until the vegetables soften and caramelize a little – about 10 minutes. Add the tomatoes, bayleaves and spices, bubble up, return the chicken pieces (if removed), turn down the heat, cover loosely and leave to cook gently for about an hour, until the sauce is jammy and thick.

Serve at room temperature, with chunks of soft-crumbed bread for wiping the fingers and mopping the juices.

> **Good with . . .** broad beans with ham (page 89); crisp-fried chips; crisp lettuce leaves.

Pollo in padella
Italian pan-fried chicken

Pick a small free-range chicken, joint it ruthlessly, and give it the Italian treatment. Usually served after the pasta as a main course, this is also good left to marinate in its own deliciously oily juices and served at room temperature as an antipasto. Italy's rural housewives – those who maintain some measure of self-sufficiency – still keep barnyard fowl for eggs. The scrawny old hens past their laying go into the broth and the cockerels are fattened up for Sunday lunch.

Serves 6–8

1 small chicken, jointed into bite-sized pieces (see page 197)
6–7 tablespoons olive oil
3–4 cloves garlic, roughly chopped
2–3 sage leaves, shredded
1 sprig rosemary, leaves stripped from stalks
1 sprig thyme, leaves only
salt and crushed black pepper
1 small glass white wine

To serve
plenty of chopped parsley (flat-leaf for preference)
quartered lemons

Wipe the chicken joints, pat dry and remove any obvious fat and stray little feather hairs.

Heat the oil gently in a wide frying pan with the garlic. Add the herbs and let them fry for a moment to scent the oil. Add the chicken joints, season with salt and pepper and turn in the oil until they are nicely browned. Pour in the white wine. Turn down the heat and leave the chicken pieces to simmer for 20–30 minutes, until the wine has evaporated and the chicken is tender. Transfer to a bowl and leave to cool in its juices. Serve at room temperature, sprinkled with a good handful of chopped parsley. Hand with lemon quarters.

> Good with . . . good bread for mopping up the oil – bake your own *ciabatta* (page 48); ripe tomatoes sliced and dressed with olive oil, pepper and basil; plain-boiled artichokes with oil and lemon; artichoke hearts stuffed with peas (page 116).

Djej mechoi

Moroccan grilled chicken with salt-lemon

Salt-pickled lemons are the key to this simple dish – nothing fancy, just choose a lean little free-range chicken and let the flavours speak for themselves. If you can't find pickled lemons, make your own (see below). Or use fresh lemons instead, chopped small, pith and all – these will be a little chewier than salt-lemons.

Serves 6–8

1 small chicken, jointed into barbecuable pieces
2 tablespoons olive oil
1 salt-lemon, washed and chopped – skin and pith only
1 clove garlic, crushed
1 teaspoon ground cumin
1 teaspoon ground saffron (or turmeric)
1 tablespoon paprika
1 teaspoon crushed chilli

For the dipping sauce
4 tablespoons chopped coriander
4 tablespoons chopped parsley
3 spring onions, finely chopped
3–4 tablespoons lemon-pickling brine

Trim the chicken pieces neatly and combine with the rest of the marinade ingredients in a roomy bowl. Cover loosely and leave in a cool place for a few hours – overnight if possible.

Preheat the grill or barbecue. It should be moderately hot.

Shake excess moisture off the chicken joints and grill until the juices run clear – test through the thickest part with a skewer. Meanwhile, combine the ingredients for the dipping sauce, and leave to infuse.

Serve the grilled chicken with the dipping sauce on the side.

> **Good with . . .** a flat-bread, Moroccan *kisra* for preference. Never use a knife on Middle Eastern breads – it's considered disrespectful. Just tear off enough for one mouthful at a time.

Five-day pickled lemons (the usual method requires a month): choose unwaxed lemons and make 6–8 vertical incisions without cutting into the flesh. Cook in heavily salted water until the peel is very soft. Pack in a jar and pour in enough of the cooking liquor to submerge the lemons completely. Store in the fridge. Ready in five days – and best eaten within two weeks or so.

Pollo en camisa

Spanish chicken joints in a crisp jacket

Chicken joints, bite-sized, jacketed with herby breadcrumbs and fried crisp, just as they like it in Andalusia. Spanish barnyard chickens are small – monster poultry needs to be chopped into more pieces. Poultry is perfect tapa-material – the joints can easily be divided into bite-sized bits, and as long as everyone gets a joint it doesn't really matter which. Spanish butchers understand exactly what's required, but if you can't persuade your butcher to do this for you, chop the whole carcass into at least sixteen pieces, including the giblets if you have them.

Serves 6–8

1 chicken, jointed into bite-sized pieces (see page 197)
1 heaped teaspoon salt
freshly ground black pepper
1 egg, forked
4 tablespoons milk
about 100g / 4oz fresh breadcrumbs
1 heaped tablespoon chopped almonds
1 tablespoon chopped oregano or marjoram
1 tablespoon chopped parsley
1 teaspoon dried thyme
3–4 tablespoons flour
1 teaspoon paprika and a pinch of cayenne pepper
oil for deep-frying

Trim the chicken joints and season with salt and pepper.

Fork together the egg and the milk in a deep plate. Mix the breadcrumbs with the chopped almonds and herbs on another plate. Put the flour, paprika and cayenne in a large plastic bag, drop in the chicken pieces and shake the bag to coat them thoroughly. Then dip each joint into the egg mixture, turning to coat on all sides, and press into the herby breadcrumbs. Make sure that each piece is really well jacketed.

Heat enough oil in a roomy frying pan to submerge the chicken joints – wait until the oil is lightly hazed with blue before slipping in the pieces – cook them in at least two batches. The temperature should not be too high: a cluster of bubbles should form immediately round each joint, but they shouldn't boil and spit. Fry for 5 minutes, then turn. The drumsticks and thighs will be done in about 15 minutes in all, the breast and wings will take about 10 – test with a skewer to make sure the juices run clear. Remove to kitchen paper to drain. Test a thick piece with a skewer: if the juices still run a little pink, slip them in a moderate oven for 10 minutes to cook them all the way through.

Good with . . . chilled *gazpacho* (page 101). Perfect on a hot day.

Kotopoulo yachnia
Greek spiced chicken casserole with red wine and prunes

This recipe is from Thessaloniki, capital of northern Greece, only a day's march from the Turkish border. In this part of Greece the Ottoman influence remains strong, reinforced by the population exchanges between the two nations – ethnic cleansing by another name – which followed the establishment of the modern Turkish state in the years between the two wars. Although it can be hard to disentangle one culinary tradition from another – even the names of the recipes are similar – the Greeks use herbs where the Turks use spices. Here both are present, along with a little Persian-style sweet-and-sour in the inclusion of dried fruits. Very delicious, whatever name you care to call it.

Serves 6–8

I small chicken, jointed
salt and freshly ground black pepper
6 tablespoons olive oil
I large onion, slivered
3–4 cloves garlic, sliced
500g / IIb plum tomatoes, skinned and chopped (or use tinned)
4–5 cloves
I small stick cinnamon
½ teaspoon freshly grated nutmeg
300ml / ½ pint dry red wine
6–8 prunes, soaked in water to swell

To finish
I tablespoon chopped mint or I teaspoon dried mint

Season the chicken joints. Heat the oil in a roomy casserole (the Greeks have special two-handled roasting pans that can be started on top-heat and trans-ferred to the oven – a service once provided by the baker. Fry the chicken joints until they take a little colour, push aside and add the onion and garlic. Stir over the heat until they soften and gild. Add all the other ingredients and pour in a glass or two of water – just enough to submerge the chicken. Let everything bubble up, turn down the heat, cover loosely with foil and put in a low oven – 150°C/300°F/gas 2 – to cook very gently for 2–3 hours, until the meat is falling off the bone. Uncover for the last ten minutes or so to evaporate excess juices. Stir in the mint. Leave to cool and serve at room temperature.

> **Good with . . .** solid slabs of sourdough bread (page 47); olives; toasted almonds.

Tagine djej bin zafrani
Moroccan braised chicken with saffron

Sophisticated spicing for a Moroccan tagine, one of the stews which, throughout the region, takes its name from the pot in which it's cooked. The cooking vessels of the Mahgreb are round-bellied and made of unglazed earthenware which are tempered by filling with cold water and setting over hot coals until the water has evaporated. A well-tempered tagine can last the lifetime of a camel-driver.

Serves 6–8

I small chicken, jointed
I large mild onion, finely sliced
2 tablespoons clarified butter (see page 16) or oil
12 saffron threads, lightly toasted in a dry pan
I small stick cinnamon
I tablespoon crushed peppercorns
salt
600ml / I pint water
2 tablespoons raisins or stoned, chopped prunes

For the sauce
500g / 1lb mild red onions, sliced
2 tablespoons clarified butter (see page 16) or oil
salt
½ teaspoon ground ginger
½ teaspoon ground cumin
I tablespoon honey
2 tablespoons blanched, toasted almonds to finish

In a heavy casserole lay the chicken joints on a bed of the sliced onion. Dot with the butter, the saffron, cinnamon, pepper and a little salt. Pour in the water, bring to the boil, turn down the heat, add the raisins or prunes, cover loosely and simmer very gently for 40–60 minutes, until the chicken joints are tender – check occasionally and add a little more water if necessary.

Meanwhile, fry the sliced onions for the sauce gently in the butter until soft and golden. Sprinkle with a little salt, the ginger and cumin, stir in the honey and bubble up.

Remove the chicken joints from the broth and reserve. Strain the broth back into the pot and boil to reduce to 300ml/½ pint. Stir in the onion mixture, bubble up and spoon over the chicken. Finish with toasted almonds.

Good with . . . *pitta* (page 50), or any bread for scooping; crisp lettuce.

Capriolo
Italian spiced marinated venison

The Italians understand the cooking of game – lean meat which benefits greatly from a couple of days in a marinade and is well able to hold its own against a rich spicy sauce.

Serves 6–8

1kg / 2lb venison off the bone, cubed into bite-sized pieces

For the marinade
sliced carrot, onion and celery stalk, 1 teaspoon juniper berries, 1 teaspoon crushed peppercorns, 3 cloves
1 sprig each of rosemary, thyme, sage, 1–2 torn bayleaves
3 tablespoons olive oil
3 cloves garlic, crushed
1 bottle full-bodied red wine

To cook
4 tablespoons olive oil
2 tablespoons flour
50g / 2oz diced *pancetta* or streaky bacon
1 large onion, very thinly sliced
1 teaspoon ground cinnamon
½ teaspoon ground cloves
½ teaspoon crushed black pepper
150ml / ¼ pint double cream (optional)

Put the meat in a bowl with all the marinade ingredients. Mix well, cover and leave for 48 hours in a cool place.

Preheat the oven to 170°C/325°F/gas 3.

Remove the meat from the marinade and pat dry. Strain the liquid and reserve. Heat half the oil in a roomy frying pan and brown the meat very thoroughly on all sides. Remove and set aside. Sprinkle the flour into the pan and let it take a little colour, scraping up all the caramelized sticky bits. Pour in half the marinade and bubble up, stirring well, until the sauce thickens.

In a casserole, heat the remaining oil and fry the *pancetta* or bacon till the fat runs. Add the onion, salt lightly and cook until the onion is really soft. Add the meat, spices, the remaining marinade and the sauce from the frying pan. Bring to the boil, cover and transfer the casserole to the oven. Cook for about 1 hour, more if necessary, until the meat is absolutely tender and can be eaten with a spoon. Taste and adjust the seasoning. Stir in the optional cream.

Good with . . . soft or grilled polenta (page 265); a fennel salad.

Pato a la sevillana

Sevillan spiced duck

The marshes of the Guadalquivir delta south of Seville attract all manner of overwintering duck – once an attraction for the hunters, although nowadays most of the great delta is a nature reserve. Birdwatchers will be happy to hear that the domestic duck has largely replaced the pintails and wigeon on the Sevillan table.

Serves 6–8

2 wild duck (mallard), or I small domestic duck, jointed
2 tablespoons olive oil
2 tablespoons diced *jamón serrano* or lean bacon
2 large onions, finely chopped
I red pepper, deseeded and diced
2 cloves garlic, chopped
I small stick cinnamon
3–4 cloves
I small glass dry sherry or white wine
I whole bitter (Seville) orange or lemon, chopped small
2 tablespoons green olives
salt, freshly ground black pepper and a pinch of sugar

Wipe the duck joints and season.

Heat the oil in a large casserole and fry the *jamón serrano* or bacon, the onions, diced red pepper and garlic until soft. Remove and set aside, and add the duck joints – let them fry and take a little colour. Add the spices and the olives. Pour in the sherry or white wine and let all bubble up.

Add the chopped fruit, pepper and a pinch of sugar. Cover and leave to simmer gently for 30–40 minutes, until the duck joints are perfectly tender. At the end of the cooking time bubble up to concentrate the juices.

> **Good with** . . . Andalusian sourdough bread (page 47) or any dense-crumbed sourdough bread; toasted almonds; chips fried crisp in olive oil; a *tortilla española* (page 76) flavoured with a little finely chopped fresh marjoram.

Lepre in dolceforte
Italian hare in sweet-sour sauce

A speciality of Tuscany, dolceforte *simply means sweet-sour. Traditionally, the sauce is thickened with the blood of the hare and the crumbs of a Sienese spicy walnut biscuit (the Austrians thicken game sauces with crumbled gingerbread). In this recipe the chocolate serves instead of the blood and the nuts do duty for the biscuits.*

Serves 6–8

1 hare or 2 rabbits, membrane removed from the saddle and legs, jointed small
6 tablespoons olive oil
1 stick celery, finely chopped
1 clove garlic, finely chopped
1 carrot, diced small
1 sprig rosemary, finely chopped
2 tablespoons chopped *pancetta* or streaky bacon
1 bottle red wine
salt and freshly ground black pepper

For the dolceforte
25g / 1oz bitter dark chocolate, grated
1 tablespoon sultanas
1 tablespoon chopped candied peel
1 tablespoon crushed walnuts
1 teaspoon ground cinnamon
1 teaspoon ground ginger
1 tablespoon muscovado or dark brown sugar
4 tablespoons wine vinegar (or 2 tablespoons balsamic vinegar)

In a large casserole, fry the hare joints in the oil until lightly browned. Add the vegetables, rosemary and *pancetta*, sizzle until they take colour, and then stir in the wine. Bubble up, reduce the heat, cover and cook gently for 1–1½ hours, until the meat is perfectly tender and juices well concentrated.

Mix together the *dolceforte* ingredients until perfectly blended. Stir into the meat and bubble up to thicken. Taste and season.

Good with . . . *ciabatta* (page 48); fennel, cooked or raw, for the digestion.

Stufato de piccione

Italian stewed pigeons with orange and saffron

Nothing fancy, just the northern Italian way with older game birds – partridge, pigeon, pheasant. As a general rule, wild birds can either be plucked and eaten immediately or will need a week's hanging (ungutted, in feather) until they become tender again – in Italy, the former is preferred. Although in Italy woodpigeons have been pretty much shot out, those who stock their own barnyards still keep a loftful of squabs for the pot. The young birds – piccioncini – are wrapped in pancetta and roasted; older birds need longer cooking and a little acidity to tenderize the flesh, provided here by the juice of bitter (Seville) oranges. Sevilles are in season for only a few weeks in January and February – at other times, use a couple of lemons and one sweet orange.

Serves 6–8

4 pigeons or poussins, halved
3 bitter (Seville) oranges (or 2 lemons and 1 orange)
3 tablespoons olive oil
2 cloves garlic, roughly chopped
1 tablespoon diced *prosciutto*
1 teaspoon chopped oregano or marjoram
1–2 bayleaves
½ teaspoon freshly grated nutmeg
a knifetip of saffron (about 12 threads), soaked in 1 tablespoon boiling water
salt and freshly ground black pepper

Pick over the birds and remove any stray feathers. Pare a few strips of the zest from the orange, squeeze the juice and reserve.

Heat the oil in a heavy casserole and add the garlic and diced *prosciutto*. Let it sizzle for a moment, then add the birds. Turn them in the hot oil to gild them a little. Add the oregano, bay, nutmeg and saffron with its soaking water, along with the orange juice and zest. Season lightly with salt and generously with pepper, bubble up, turn down the heat, cover and leave over a low heat to simmer gently for 40–60 minutes, until the birds are perfectly tender, when the drumsticks should pull easily from the sides. Check after 30 minutes and moisten with a little water if necessary.

Remove and reserve the birds, and bubble up the juices to concentrate the flavours. Taste and adjust the seasoning – a splash of grape-brandy might not come amiss. Snip each bird into quarters and serve trickled with the juices.

> Good with . . . *focaccia* or *ciabatta* (pages 49 and 48); raw vegetables in season – peas, beans, baby artichokes.

Pigeons à l'ail

Provençal pigeons with garlic

In the days of self-sufficiency the rural housewives of Provence kept a loftful of pigeons for the pot. While the young birds – squabs – were tender enough for roasting, this recipe suited elderly birds that had outlived their usefulness as breeders, and birds of uncertain age that fed on the crops. If you can't get pigeons, replace them with poussins – baby chickens.

Serves 6–8

4 pigeons or poussins, quartered
I tablespoon flour
½ teaspoon crushed black peppercorns
4 tablespoons olive oil
I thick slice fatty bacon, diced
16 cloves garlic (with skin)
½ bottle red wine
I small glass water
I sprig rosemary
I sprig thyme
2 bayleaves
curl of dried orange peel (fresh zest will do)
salt and a little sugar

Toss the joints in the flour and crushed pepper – a light dusting, no more. Heat the oil in a heavy casserole and turn the joints over the heat until they take colour. Add the bacon cubes and garlic cloves and roast them a little – don't let them brown. Add the wine and the water and bubble up, scraping to loosen any little brown bits stuck to the bottom. Tie the rosemary, thyme and bay into a little bunch and throw this into the pot with the orange peel. Season with salt and a little sugar. Bring back to the boil, turn down the heat, cover tightly and leave to simmer gently for 40–60 minutes, depending on toughness, until the birds are perfectly tender. Check after 30 minutes and add a little more water if it looks like drying out.

Take off the lid towards the end of the cooking and bubble up to concentrate the juices. Remove the bunch of herbs and the orange zest before serving. Make sure everyone gets their share of garlic cloves – smooth and mild flavoured after the long cooking – to squeeze from the papery covering and mash into the sauce.

> Good with . . . Provençal pork-crackling bread (page 51) or any crisp-crusted bread for mopping; radishes; plain-cooked baby potatoes dressed with a little chopped onion and olive oil.

Ortikakia me maidanoskordalia

Greek grilled quail with parsley and garlic sauce

The Greeks, like the Italians, have managed to clear their hillsides of everything that has feathers and flies. Farmed quail fills the gap. To spatchcock a bird, split it right down the back and flatten it like a squashed frog.

Serves 6

For the birds
6 quails or 3 poussins, spatchcocked
2–3 tablespoons olive oil
1–2 cloves garlic, finely slivered
1 tablespoon dried oregano or marjoram
1 lemon, juice and finely grated zest
salt and freshly ground black pepper

For the skordalia
2–3 slices dense-crumbed bread, crusts removed, soaked and squeezed dry
3–4 cloves garlic, roughly crushed
6 generous handfuls parsley, destalked
1 small green chilli, deseeded and roughly chopped
juice of 2 lemons
150ml / ¼ pint olive oil
1 teaspoon salt

Thread the quails crosswise onto skewers to keep them flat. Sprinkle with the oil, garlic, oregano or marjoram, lemon juice, salt and pepper and set aside to marinate for half an hour at least – overnight is fine.

Preheat the grill or oven to maximum – 250°C/475°F/gas 9.

Grill or roast the birds for 10 minutes on one side. Turn, baste and allow another 5–8 minutes on the other side, until the flesh is firm and the skin beautifully browned. Test by pushing a larding needle or fine skewer into the breast and thigh of one of the birds – the juices should run clear. Poussins will take a little longer.

Meanwhile, make the *skordalia*. Put all the ingredients in the liquidizer, reserving a tablespoon of the lemon juice and half the oil, and process to a paste. Add the remaining oil in a thin trickle, taste and add more lemon juice if necessary. Serve with the little birds, as a dipping sauce.

> Good with . . . good country bread or *ciabatta* (page 48); beetroot salad (page 130); baked aubergines; stuffed vegetables (page 124).

Conejo al jerez
Andalusian rabbit with sherry

This is the Andalusian housewife's way with a young wild rabbit – and there're plenty out there in the cistus scrub. If the bunny was a bit on the elderly side – teeth long and yellow, nails hard, ears tough – remove the membrane that covers the back and legs, and allow at least an hour's gentle simmering. The recipe is also good made with a muscular free-range chicken – pay no attention to the heavy-breasted flab-artists, it's the skinny ones that have the best flavour.

Serves 4–6

I young wild rabbit or small free-range chicken, jointed small
I tablespoon seasoned flour
8 tablespoons olive oil
6 cloves garlic, roughly chopped
I small glass dry sherry (Manzanilla or fino)
2–3 small sprigs rosemary
I–2 bayleaves, roughly torn
salt and freshly ground black pepper

Rinse, pat dry and flip the joints through seasoned flour. Heat the olive oil in a heavy frying pan. Put in the meat and garlic and turn the pieces in the hot oil until well browned.

Pour in the sherry and bubble up. Add the rosemary and bayleaves, season and turn down the heat, cover loosely and leave to simmer gently for 30–40 minutes, until the meat is practically falling off the little bones and the juices have all evaporated, leaving a deliciously garlicky oil as the sauce.

Good with . . . thick slices of country bread – what else? a dish of fried peppers; salt cod fritters (page 193) – robust and crisp, just to show the rabbit who's boss; a plain *tortilla de patatas* (see page 76), maybe flavoured with a little marjoram. Snails any way you please – one wild thing deserves another.

Fatayer

Lebanese chicken pasties

Call it the Lebanese Cornish pasty – and who's to say the Phoenicians did not trade more than oranges for Cornish tin? In this recipe a well spiced savoury filling is enclosed in triangular scraps of bread dough. The everyday version is mutton. Chicken is strictly for best.

Serves 4–6

For the dough
350g / 12oz bread flour
25g / 1oz fresh or 12g / ½oz dried yeast
1 teaspoon salt
warm water
1 teaspoon oil

For the filling
2–3 tablespoons clarified butter (see page 16) or oil
2 skinned, boned chicken breasts, finely chopped
1 onion, finely chopped
2 tablespoons pinekernels
2–3 dried apricots, soaked and finely diced
1 teaspoon ground allspice
1 teaspoon ground cinnamon
salt and freshly ground black pepper
1 tablespoon pomegranate syrup (*debis roman*) or lemon juice

First make the dough: in a warm bowl mix the flour with the crumbled or dried yeast and salt and work in enough warm water to make a soft, elastic dough. Knead it into a smooth ball, slick with a little oil and set it in a covered bowl in a warm place to double in bulk.

To make the filling, heat the butter and fry the chicken and onion until cooked through. Stir in the pinekernels and apricots with a little of their soaking water, bubble up and sprinkle in the spices. Season. Simmer gently for about 10 minutes, add the pomegranate syrup or lemon juice, and check seasoning.

Preheat the oven to 180°C/350°F/gas 4.

Roll the bread dough out to the thickness of a pound coin and cut into 10cm/4in rounds, using up all the scraps. Place a teaspoon of the filling on each round, dampen the edges and bring them up to enclose the filling in the shape of a triangle, pinching the edges firmly to seal; leave a little air-hole at the top. Arrange on an oiled baking sheet and set aside for 10 minutes in a warm place to allow the dough to recover its volume.

Bake for 10–15 minutes, until well risen and golden.

Good with . . . any of the Middle Eastern salad-dips – *hummus* (page 34); *tsatsiki* (page 36).

Higados de pollo al viño de jerez

Andalusian chicken livers with sherry

2

Simple but good, and deservedly popular in the tapa bars of Andalusia. This is quickly prepared and requires only those supporting ingredients any Andalusian housewife keeps in the cupboard. Kidneys – veal, lamb or pork – sliced and soaked in a little vinegared water, can be given the same treatment.

Serves 4–6

350g / 12oz chicken livers
2 tablespoons olive oil
I clove garlic, chopped
salt and freshly ground black pepper
I small glass dry sherry (Manzanilla or fino)
I heaped tablespoon chopped parsley

Trim the chicken livers, removing any obvious veins and little green streaks of bile, which would taste bitter.

Warm the oil in a shallow earthenware casserole tempered to take the heat of the fire – or in a frying pan. Add the garlic first, then the livers. Season with a little salt and plenty of freshly ground pepper, and toss over the heat for 3–4 minutes, until the livers are firm on the outside but still pink in the middle. Add the wine and let the mixture bubble up until it no longer smells alcoholic – a minute or two over a fierce heat. Stir in the parsley.

If you have more guests than you expected, fry up a panful of chips and pile the livers on the top – the chips will soak up the sherry-flavoured juices.

Good with . . . country paella (page 261); thinly sliced *jamón serrano* and *chorizo*; Andalusian sourdough bread (page 47); peppers in oil (page 121); little glasses of well iced white *gazpacho* (page 100).

All about snails

All land snails are edible. It's only the excreta – which are contained in the little curl of intestine at the heart of the shell – that might contain toxic substances, and this is why you must starve the creatures before you clean and cook them.

If you are gathering from the wild, collect your snails after rain, when they climb the available vegetable and are thus easier to spot.

To prepare the snails you will need to control their diet for two weeks – if they are large; less if small. Keep them in a clean container that allows air to circulate and feed them up on whatever delicious goodies you would like to flavour them with. The Spanish favour pennyroyal, the Romans recommended beefsteak and milk, I prefer lettuce and mint. Clean them out every day – they make a lot of mess, for obvious reasons. French country dwellers go to the trouble of digging their snails out of winter hibernation, when they are conveniently self-starved and considered superior.

When you are ready to cook, wash the cephalopods in several changes of cold running water, salting them in between each washing and rinsing away the gluey froth that is their response to such unacceptable treatment. When the snails are clean – that is, when the frothing has subsided to a minimum – put them in a large pan with enough warm water to cover. Bring gently to the boil. Skim off the froth and add salt and a tablespoon of vinegar. Add a few peppercorns, a couple of bayleaves, parsley and thyme, and an onion cut in quarters. Simmer for 30–40 minutes. Drain, rinse in cold water and drain again (save the snail broth – it's a cure-all, thought to work wonders for everything from colds to rheumatism). Take the snails from their shells and pinch off the little dark curl of intestine at the end of the body. Now they are ready for finishing.

▶ *Moroccan grilled chicken with salt-lemon (page 205)*

Lumache alla salvia
Italian snails with sage

The Italians, as befits the heirs of the Romans – pioneers in the art of lumache farming – cook their snails in a hundred sophisticated ways. This is how they like them in Liguria. Those who cannot lay their hands on the real thing might like to know that the recipe works perfectly well with a combination of diced lamb kidneys and chicken livers – but don't tell the lumache-lovers, let 'em guess.

Serves 4–6

500g / 1lb shelled, cooked snails (see page 218)
6 tablespoons olive oil
1 medium onion, finely chopped
2 cloves garlic, crushed or finely chopped
1 teaspoon chopped rosemary
1 teaspoon chopped thyme
1 small glass grappa or any white brandy
2 tablespoons fresh breadcrumbs
1 tablespoon chopped parsley
salt and freshly ground black pepper

To finish
4–5 sage leaves, fried crisp (a minute or two in hot oil)
1 heaped tablespoon toasted pinekernels or slivered almonds

Pick over the snails and remove any bits of grit or shell.

In a roomy frying pan, heat the oil and fry the onions and garlic until they are soft and golden. Stir in the cooked snails, herbs and grappa. Bubble fiercely for 2–3 minutes to evaporate the alcohol, then turn down the heat and simmer, stirring throughout, for about 10 minutes. Stir in the breadcrumbs and parsley to absorb the juices, season and bubble up again.

Transfer to a hot dish and finish with a few deep-fried sage leaves and a sprinkle of pinekernels. Finger-licking wonderful.

Good with . . . Ligurian *focaccia* (page 49); grilled polenta (page 265).

◄ *Sardinian barbecued lamb (page 229)*

Caracoles en salsa

Spanish snails in spiced tomato sauce

The Spanish eat two kinds of snail: big and little. The tiny ones, which spend their summers sheltering on thistle skeletons, are cooked in a clear aromatic broth flavoured with pennyroyal, black pepper and cumin. The larger type – escargots de Bourgogne – are usually finished in an aromatic tomato sauce, as in this recipe from the venta in Pelayo, my local village when I lived in Andalusia. There's no need to shell the snails for this dish. The Andalusians are not dainty trencherpersons, don't mind the little black intestine – it's easy enough to avoid – and love sucking the juices out of the shells.

Serves 4–6

750g / 1½lb ready-cooked snails in their shells (see page 218)
4 tablespoons olive oil
50g / 2oz finely chopped scrag-end *jamón serrano*, prosciutto
1 onion, finely chopped
3–4 cloves garlic, chopped
1 red pepper, deseeded and chopped
1 glass dry sherry – Manzanilla or fino
750g / 1½lb ripe tomatoes, skinned and roughly chopped (or use tinned plum tomatoes)
2 dried chillis, crumbled
2 bayleaves
1 teaspoon cumin seeds
1 small stick cinnamon
salt and freshly ground black pepper

To finish
1 heaped tablespoon chopped parsley
1 clove garlic, finely chopped

Heat the oil gently in a heatproof earthenware *olla* or a sauté pan, and add the chopped ham or bacon, onion and garlic. Fry for a moment. Add the pepper and fry until the vegetables soften. Add the sherry and bubble up for a couple of minutes to evaporate the alcohol. Stir in the tomatoes, chilli, bayleaves, cumin and cinnamon, and cook uncovered for 10 minutes until you have a rich, thick sauce. Taste and add salt.

Stir in the snails and simmer all for another 10 minutes to blend the flavours. This dish will keep hot without spoiling. To finish, remove the cinnamon stick and stir in the parsley and garlic.

> Good with . . . chips fried crisp in olive oil or *patatas bravas* (page 136); chickpeas with saffron, garlic and almonds (page 258); fried artichokes – small ones, quartered.

Beef, lamb & pork

A Mediterranean butcher's shop is not a dainty sight: the carcasses on hooks and the anatomically unequivocal bits and bobs displayed without coyness can come as a bit of a shock to sensitive souls accustomed to sanitized supermarket packaging. Nor are the cuts recognizable. What is likely to be on offer is lean meat from any part of the animal, sliced on demand into thin steaks for frying, or diced for kebabs or stewing. Fat – suet, lard, fat bacon – is sold separately for enriching a stew, or for rendering and flavouring as a butter substitute. Variety meats – tripe, innards of various kinds – are popular *tapa* and *mezze* material, being cheap and quickly prepared. Mincing is carried out at the purchaser's request in any combination of meats, pushed through the mincer once or twice, depending on the requirements of the recipe, and can be stretched with some kind of grain food – breadcrumbs, rice, burghul. Up to half the total volume is perfectly acceptable.

Any meat can be exchanged for any other in most recipes. The main distinctions lie in religious prohibitions. In the lands where Muslim and Jewish religious prohibitions prevail and the tradition is nomadic, the main meat animals are sheep and goats. In Christian lands, pork is added to the menu – an animal that can be kept only by a settled peasantry, as anyone will confirm who has ever tried to herd a pig in any direction it does not care to travel.

Everywhere, meat is traditionally used sparingly, adding flavour and enrichment rather than substance. Only on feast days will anyone roast a joint, and then it is likely to be the entire animal – a young male kid or lamb – turned slowly on a spit over an open fire. Although peasants rarely roast meat, among shepherding communities who expect three crops from their flocks – milk, wool and meat – the runt of the flock can usefully be sacrificed to the herdsmen's hunger. Wild meat is appreciated whenever it can be got – boar in particular. Beef is the meat of the rich, making for some confusion when discussing recipes, since you will often be told that certain dishes are always prepared with beef, when in reality the meat is likely to be of the humbler sort. In Spain, mature beef is almost never encountered, while young bull meat is sold cheap in the marketplace on the day after a bullfight. In northern Italy, where cows are kept for butter and cream as well as cheese-making, young male calves are fattened for feasts.

In modern times, refrigeration has, in all but the most isolated households, solved the problems of conservation. Nevertheless, the fear remains that meat is vulnerable to spoilage and must therefore be consumed as fresh as possible.

Minced meat is invaluable as raw material for *mezze* and *tapas*, being cheap and infinitely tolerant of stretching with other foodstuffs. As with offal, mincemeat is traditionally the food of the urban poor: town dwellers had access to the tougher, fattier, less delicate cuts the butcher couldn't sell to his more affluent customers. Country dwellers rarely killed their domestic animals until they had outlived their usefulness as milk-producers, when they were fit only for the chopping knife. Meatballs, the Mediterranean hamburger, can be made with meat from virtually any part of any animal, and is often a mixture of more than one kind. You'll find mincemeat recipes throughout the region, variously spiced and herbed, and with the choice of meat animal taking account of religious taboos.

Mincemeat must be worked very well with the hands until it forms a doughy paste, a process that helps the balls keep their shape as they cook. Those who don't have the patience for such time-consuming labour can achieve the same effect with half the kneading and a raw egg. Over the centuries, clever cooks have taken the basic mix and used it in a number of innovative ways: for stuffing vine or cabbage leaves, enclosing in pastry, shaping round a skewer for grilling, slipping it into soups or stews. If a leaf or vegetable wrapper is used (*sarmale*, *dolmades*, hollowed-out vegetables including aubergines), the meat is likely to be bulked out with grain food (rice, breadcrumbs, bulghur), precooked or raw depending on the length of time needed to soften the casing. If the wrapper is pastry (*böreki*, *empanadas*, *kibbeh*) the grain-food is already present, so finely chopped vegetables are included for volume, flavour and balance. A simple thing, but capable of greatness.

Pâté de foie de porc
French country pâté

2

A country pâté, economical and easy to prepare, just like Maman used to make. And if Mother was too busy, she would certainly have prided herself on patronizing the only traiteur who could be relied upon to make his own – Faite à la maison? Mais oui, madame. Serve in the Provençal style with cornichons (pickled gherkins), a bunch of the little radishes the French like to eat with coarse salt, a bowl of pickled capers and fresh crusty bread.

Serves 6–8

500g / 1lb pork liver, cut into fine strips
1 medium onion, finely chopped
a walnut-sized lump of fresh butter
250g / 8oz lean shoulder pork
250g / 8oz fat belly pork
1 egg
1 teaspoon dried thyme
a dozen juniper berries, crushed
½ teaspoon grated nutmeg
¼ teaspoon ground cloves
salt and freshly ground black pepper
8 very thin slices pork fat or streaky bacon for lining the tin
2 bayleaves

Turn the liver and chopped onion in a hot frying pan with the butter until the meat stiffens. With a sharp knife or in a food processor mince thoroughly with the two pork meats. Work in the egg, herbs and spices, and season.

Preheat the oven to 170°C/350°F/gas 3.

Line a small loaf tin (approx. 20cm x 10cm/8in x 4in) with the bacon rashers, allowing them to flop over the sides. Pack in the meat, pop on the bayleaves and fold over the rashers. Set the loaf tin in a *bain marie* – a roasting pan with enough boiling water to come a third of the way up the loaf tin.

Bake for about an hour, until the top has browned a little. Cover with foil and continue baking for another 30 minutes or so, until the pâté has shrunk from the sides. Check for doneness by pushing a skewer into the heart of the pâté – the juices should run clear. Remove and leave to cool. Cover with a clean cloth, pop a weight on top and leave overnight in the fridge to firm. To serve, slice thickly with a sharp knife dipped in boiling water.

Good with . . . Provençal pork-crackling bread (page 51); a bunch of little red radishes; olives; pickled gherkins; baby tomatoes; capers.

Jambon cuit au four
Provençal baked ham

In southern France the hors d'oeuvre will often include a slice of ham carved from the bone. Unlike the salt-dried hams and dried sausages that fill the winter storecupboard, fresh ham is usually bought from the butcher – and it is only for a wedding or a funeral that the house-wife will contemplate cooking her own. A thorough soaking is necessary when you're baking a ham without preboiling; ask the butcher to soak it for you in advance, or take his advice on how long it needs. As for the bed of herbs that flavours the meat, it's best if they're the real thing, semi-dried from Provençal hillsides, not the soft-leafed stuff grown under glass.

Serves a large number – at least 30 as an hors d'oeuvre

1 salt-cured ham weighing 5–6kg / 10–12lbs, soaked to de-salt
a large handful of rosemary, oregano, thyme, dried fennel stalks

To finish
4–5 tablespoons toasted breadcrumbs

Preheat the oven to 170°C/325°F/gas 3.

Allow the ham to come to room temperature and settle it in a large roasting tin on a bed of the herbs. Cover loosely with foil, shiny side down. Bake until tender but still moist: allow 20 minutes per 500g/1lb for a 5–6kg / 10–12lb ham, plus 20 minutes. You'll know it's ready when the juices run clear right the way through to the bone and the meat feels firm. Remove from the oven and leave to cool.

As soon as it's cool enough to handle, lift off the skin with a sharp knife – it'll slip off quite easily. (Cut the skin into small squares and freeze it for later, to pop into the bean-pot.) Press breadcrumbs all over the creamy white fat. Slice with a sharp knife as you would a joint of pork.

> Good with . . . a butter-bean or new potato salad (page 134); a mustardy celeriac *rémoulade*; grated carrots dressed with olive oil, lemon juice and toasted sesame seeds; baby green beans dressed with olive oil and lemon zest.

Croquetas de jamón

Andalusian ham croquettes

2

The croqueta *is an art – you need neat fingers, patience, and the skill in frying that is the birthright of every Andalusian. The* panada *is a very thick white sauce – the basis of all croquetas. In the old days a young woman could find herself a good husband on the basis of a well made* croqueta. *These days you can buy them ready-made in the supermarket freezer – which misses the point, since this is a thrifty way with leftovers.*

Serves 6–8

For the **panada**
5 tablespoons olive oil
4 rounded tablespoons flour
100g / 4oz finely chopped *jamón serrano* **(or cooked ham)**
600ml / 1 pint well flavoured stock or broth
2 tablespoons chopped parsley
salt and freshly ground black pepper

To finish
3–4 tablespoons seasoned flour
1 large egg beaten with its own volume of stock or milk
100g / 4oz dry breadcrumbs
olive oil for frying

Heat the oil gently in a saucepan. Stir in the flour and let it fry for a moment without taking colour. Add the chopped ham. Beat in the liquid gradually with a wooden spoon. Cook over a gentle heat until you have a very thick, soft sauce. Add the parsley, taste and add salt and freshly ground pepper. Spread the sauce on a large dinner plate in a layer as thick as your thumb, cover with clingfilm and leave to cool and firm in the fridge – overnight if possible.

When you're ready to cook, spread the flour on one plate, the egg-and-milk on a second and the breadcrumbs on a third. Mark the filling into 20–25 short, stubby fingers. Roll each finger first in flour, then in the egg mixture, and finally press firmly into the breadcrumbs. Check that all surfaces are well coated. Continue until all is used up.

Heat two-fingers' depth of oil in a frying pan – just enough to submerge the *croquetas.* When the oil is lightly hazed with blue, slip them in a few at a time – not too many or the oil temperature will drop. Small bubbles should form immediately round the edges. If the bubbles are big the oil is too hot, if none appear it's too cool. Fry, turning them once with care, until they are crisp and brown. Drain on kitchen paper and serve immediately.

Good with . . . *tortilla española* (page 76); Spanish peppers in oil (page 121); fresh tomato sauce.

Lomo adobado a la plancha

Andalusian grilled paprika-crusted pork

One of those dishes that evolved as a way of prolonging the shelf-life of perishable foods in a hot climate – the meat is neither preserved nor fresh but something in between. The crust of mild, sweet paprika – pimentón – forms a protective covering intended to discourage winged invaders, a precaution no longer necessary since the marination takes place in the fridge. Spaniards do not actually grill food, but use la plancha, a heavy iron plate very much like the Scottish griddle, sharing with that useful instrument the advantage of distributing heat evenly.

Serves 4–6

500g / 1lb pork fillet
2 tablespoons Spanish *pimentón* (paprika)
1 teaspoon dried oregano
1 teaspoon dried thyme
1 clove garlic, well crushed
1 tablespoon coarse salt
2 tablespoons olive oil
oil for greasing the griddle
quartered lemons or bitter (Seville) oranges, to serve

Trim the fillet, rinse and pat it dry.

Mix the paprika, oregano, thyme, garlic and salt with the oil to make a thick paste. Spread the paste all over the meat, wrap tightly in foil and set in the fridge at least overnight – it can be kept for up to a week and will improve daily.

When you are ready to cook, slice the meat into medallions as thin as a pound coin, sliced on the diagonal if the fillet is slender.

Heat a *plancha*, griddle or heavy iron pan, and oil it lightly. As soon as the surface is smoking hot, drop on the medallions and cook for 2–3 minutes on each side. Serve with quartered lemons.

> **Good with . . .** Andalusian sourdough bread (page 47) or any dense-crumbed country bread; Spanish peppers in oil (page 121); broad beans with ham (page 89).

Pinchitos moruños
Andalusian spiced kebabs

Little kebabs – spiced in the Moorish style and never anything but meat – are my favourite of all the street-foods prepared during feria. They rarely appear on restaurant menus but are cooked to order on a little charcoal brazier by an itinerant pedlar resplendent in a scarlet fez. Algeciras, our local market town, held its feria in June – a week-long day-and-night fiesta of bullfighting, dancing and drinking during which the citizenry never seemed to sleep. In the morning there would be doughnut fritters – churros – to be dipped into a bowl of hot, thick cinnamon-infused chocolate. Every evening after the bullfight the pinchito-pedlar took up his post by the beer cellar and provided the revellers with fortification. His pinchitos were considered the best in town – no messing about with scraps of offal – and he gave good measure, threading the cubes of meat on long steel knitting needles, which his customers were honour-bound to return.

Serves 4–6

750g / 1½lb boneless pork or lamb, cubed small
4 tablespoons olive oil
2 teaspoons ground cumin
2 teaspoons ground coriander
2 teaspoons paprika
2 teaspoons turmeric
1 teaspoon salt
1 teaspoon freshly ground black pepper

Check over the meat – all the pieces should be neatly trimmed and no bigger than a baby's mouthful. Mix together the oil, spices and seasoning, and turn the meat cubes in this marinade. Leave in a cool place overnight.

Thread the meat onto skewers – 6–7 little pieces each. If you are using bamboo skewers, soak them in water first so that they don't catch fire.

Barbecue or grill over a high heat, turning them frequently, until well browned but still juicy. Serve on their skewers, with a cube of bread speared on the end of each to enable people to pull off the meat without burning their fingers.

Good with . . . chilled *gazpacho* (page 101); snails in spiced tomato sauce (page 220); *tortilla española* (page 76).

Furria-furria
Sardinian barbecued lamb

Unlike most island-dwellers, the Sardinians have traditionally seen no reason to entrust their lives to the uncertainties of the sea, preferring to herd their flocks in the safety of their in-hospitable mountain wildernesses – rock strewn, desert dry – wandering for weeks at a time in search of fodder. The herdsmen's diet was of the simplest: at midday, pecorino cheese eaten with pane carasau, *paper-thin disks of hard-baked unleavened bread which have to be softened in water. At dusk, a lamb or a kid – or, if fortune favoured the hunter, wild meat – spit-roasted over the campfire, which was always lit, even in summer. The cooking method – furria-furria, turn and turn again – gave the feast its name. Ask your butcher to bone out the lamb – or buy it boned and rolled and untie it.*

Serves 6–8

2kg / 4lb shoulder or leg of lamb, boned out (butterflied)
2–3 tablespoons olive oil
1 tablespoon red wine vinegar
1 tablespoon crushed juniper berries
chilli flakes or crushed black peppercorns
a generous bundle of mountain herbs: rosemary, thyme, sage, bay

To serve
coarse salt
quartered lemons or bitter (Seville) oranges
flat-breads for wrapping – Sicilian *pane carasau*, or *pitta*

Rub the cut side of the meat with the oil, vinegar, crushed juniper and chilli or pepper. Spread with the herb sprigs and roll up the meat tightly, securing it with skewers. Leave it to marinate for 2–3 hours – overnight if possible.

Light the barbecue (allowing time for it to heat up and die down). It should be very hot.

Unwrap the meat, remove the herb sprigs and spread them on the barbe-cue to make a fragrant bed. Starting cut side down and spreading it flat, roast the meat for 10–12 minutes, until the herbs char and the smoke permeates the flesh. Turn the meat, removing the protective bed of herbs, and allow 8–10 minutes to crisp the fat. Turn it again, allow another 3–4 minutes, and test with a skewer thrust into the thickest part: the juices should still run a little pink. How long it needs depends on the heat, the thickness of the meat and your own taste. Transfer it to a well scrubbed plank and carve into thick slices. Serve on a bed of the charred herbs, with salt, quartered bitter oranges or lemons and soft flat-breads for wrapping.

> **Good with ...** pecorino slivered onto vine tomatoes; fried green peppers.

Souvlakia

Greek kebabs

The Greek kebab differs from the Turkish in that the meat is neither marinated nor dressed in any way before it meets the fire. It's also likely to be pork rather than lamb or beef, making the point that this is a Christian rather than a Muslim community. The finishing herb is oregano – wild marjoram, one of the five scented sisters (the others being thyme, rosemary, sage and bay) free for the gathering on stony Mediterranean hillsides. Wild herbs, unlike their cultivated sisters, dehydrate naturally on the stalk, losing little of their flavour and volume when dried. You can, of course, stretch the meat with vegetables – peppers, tomato, shallot, courgette – but a Greek would see this as evidence of poverty, like the breadcrumbs in keftedes – all very well for tourists, but not for guests. The higher the proportion of meat, the greater the honour – the Greeks take pride in their reputation as the most generous of hosts.

Serves 4–6

750g / 1½lb pork, cubed into bite-sized pieces

To serve
juice of 2–3 lemons
dried stalks of oregano
salt and freshly ground black pepper
sturdy country bread, preferably Greek sourdough – *psomi horiatico*

Thread the chunks of meat onto skewers – metal is best because it takes the heat and contributes to cooking the interior. If you use wooden skewers, soak them first so that they don't catch fire on the grill. Pack the pieces tightly – the meat shrinks as it cooks. (Don't season the meat yet – that comes after the cooking – and no oil should be necessary, since pork is naturally fatty enough not to need basting.)

Preheat the grill or barbecue. When good and hot, grill the *souvlakia*, turning as they cook, until the meat is deliciously singed on the exterior, tender and juicy inside – being pork, it must be cooked right through. Remove from the heat and season immediately with salt and pepper. Sprinkle with lemon juice and dust generously with oregano.

Good with . . . bread. To eat the Greek way, hold the meat-laden skewer parallel to the mouth and pull off each chunk in turn with your teeth. Take a bite of bread between each mouthful.

Adana kebabi
Turkish minced beef kebabs

Adana, in southern Turkey, has given its name to the spiciest of kebabs, soldiers' food, made with beef – the military meat – and shaped round a sword like a sheath. The heat – hot-spiced food puts fire in the belly – comes from a liberal dusting of kirmizi biber, a peculiarly Turkish spice: chilli flakes rubbed with oil and sun-dried with salt.

Serves 4–6

750g / 1½lb finely minced beef
1 teaspoon freshly ground black pepper
1 teaspoon ground cumin
1 teaspoon dried mint
1 teaspoon dried oregano
**1 level teaspoon chilli flakes (*kirmizi biber*), chilli paste or finely chopped deseeded
    fresh red chilli**
1 egg white

To serve
coarse salt
thick strained yoghurt mixed with garlic, mint and grated cucumber (optional)

Combine the meat with the rest of the ingredients and knead thoroughly and patiently until you have a soft, shiny, very smooth dough-like paste. Leave for 10 minutes or so to develop the flavours.

Preheat the grill or light the barbecue (it should be very hot – allow half an hour for it to heat up and die down).

Wet your hands and form the paste round lightly oiled flat-bladed skewers – sword-handled skewers can be bought in any Turkish market. For maximum drama the Turks would use a ceremonial sword. For domestic consumption any metal skewer will do.

Grill until sizzling and well browned but still juicy – 4–5 minutes in all – turning once. To serve, slip the edible scabbards off their swords and divide into appropriate pieces. Serve with coarse salt for sprinkling and, for dipping, a bowl of thick yoghurt with or without garlic, mint and grated cucumber.

> Good with . . . any of the Arab flat-breads.

Merguez

Algerian spicy sausage

These little spicy sausages, Algeria's favourite fast food, are usually made with goat-meat or mutton. If you can get your hands on a hank of sausage skins, so much the better. Otherwise, the mixture is just as good made into patties. The secret ingredient is harissa, a fiery chilli paste. The quantities in the recipe below deliver enough to flavour a whole sheep. Whizz up a batch, pot it and keep it in the fridge – it's delicious in a tomato-based pasta sauce, gorgeous in a rouille to serve with a fish soup, and does wonders for a salsa.

Serves 6–8

750g / 1½lb minced lamb
2 heaped tablespoons chopped parsley
1 egg
2 teaspoons ground cumin
1 tablespoon *harissa* (see below)

Work all the *merguez* ingredients together. Form into small balls and pat flat. Either grill or barbecue, or slap them on a very hot greased griddle or heavy frying pan. Turn once. The fiercer the heat the better – the outside should be charred and the interior still juicy. Accompany with hot *pitta* or any Arab bread – *khubz arabi*.

> Good with . . . *tabbouleh* (page 84); raw oysters; Cos lettuce leaves; greeny-violet olives; Middle Eastern pickled vegetables.

Harissa

250g / 8oz deseeded dried red chillis, soaked in hot water to swell
8–10 cloves garlic, skinned
1 tablespoon ground coriander
1 tablespoon caraway seeds
1 tablespoon dried mint
3 tablespoons coriander leaves
1 tablespoon salt
1 tablespoon olive oil

Either pound in a mortar or put all the ingredients in a blender and whizz until you have a thick paste – you may need a little more oil to moisten. Pot up in a 500g/1lb jam-jar, covering the surface with a layer of oil. Lid tightly and keep in the fridge. Use to spark up anything that will benefit from a little fire in the belly. If you re-cover with oil every time you take some out, it'll keep for ages.

Hamburguesas de feria

Andalusian carnival hamburgers

Not so much MacDonald's as an Andalusian adaptation of the original German fast-food. With the retreat of self-sufficiency and the disappearance of the sharecropping landlord, the white villages of Andalusia – the pueblos, a word that embraces both people and place – depend on the wages of migrant workers. Germany's gastarbeiter return for feria – the all-singing, all-dancing festival of bullfights and general merrymaking staged by all Andalusian communities at some time during the summer months. The date, duration and extravagance of the festivities are dictated by the municipal purse, and can last for a day, a week or even longer. In Spain's southernmost provinces, where availability of water is the main preoccupation, feria is preceded by a romeria, a pilgrimage to fetch the guardian of the water-source to preside over the celebrations. Although the previous incumbent, the goddess-huntress Diana, was replaced in Christian times by the Virgin Mary, the objective remains the same: the placation of wilful gods through blood-sacrifice and carnival. Wine flows and frivolous foods are consumed – this is the only time of the year when preference is given to the unfamiliar and the foreign. Just as pinchitos – Moorish kebabs – are considered a feria treat, so with the Teutonic hamburger, blessed with Andalusian spicing.

Serves 4–6

500g / 1lb minced pork and beef
2–3 tablespoons fresh breadcrumbs
1 egg, forked
2 cloves garlic, finely chopped
1 tablespoon finely chopped onion
2 tablespoons chopped parsley
1 tablespoon *pimentón* (paprika)
1 teaspoon ground cumin
salt and freshly ground black pepper
olive oil for greasing
quartered lemons to serve

Work the ingredients together with your hands until you have a smooth, sticky mass. Work it some more. Divide into a dozen little balls. Flatten. Heat a griddle or a heavy iron frying pan and wipe it with oil. As soon as the oil smokes, lay on the hamburgers. Cook them quickly, turning once. Serve with quartered lemons and bread.

> Good with . . . Spanish chilli potatoes (page 136) or crisply fried chips; snails in spiced tomato sauce (page 220).

Köfte

Turkish meatballs

Every Mediterranean housewife has her own recipe for this thrifty little dish, which can be made with meat from an elderly beast too tough to be eaten in any other way. The impecunious, or those with more mouths to feed than anticipated, can stretch the meat with breadcrumbs. The basic mix is versatile: for dolmades, use as a stuffing for vine or young cabbage leaves, and cook according to the method on page 103. If böreki is what you have in mind, wrap in filo and fry, as in the recipe on page 118. For a party, make triple quantities of the meat mixture and serve all three recipes together: three different dishes is three times as festive as one.

Serves 4–6

500g / 1lb finely minced lamb or mutton
2 medium onions, very finely chopped or grated
1 tablespoon *kirmizi biber* (Turkish chilli flakes, oiled and salted – ordinary crushed chilli will do)
1 tablespoon ground cinnamon
1 tablespoon pinekernels
1 heaped tablespoon chopped mint (or 1 teaspoon dried mint)
1 heaped tablespoon chopped parsley
2–3 cloves garlic, crushed with salt
½ teaspoon freshly grated nutmeg
1 egg
2–3 tablespoons olive oil for frying
about 600ml/1 pint broth or tomato sauce (optional)

Mix, knead and work together all the ingredients (except the frying oil) until absolutely smooth – 5 minutes is good, 15 is three times better. When the mixture is perfectly stiff and no longer sticks to your fingers, form into balls the size of a walnut (dip your hands in water to stop the meat sticking).

Heat the oil in a frying pan and fry the balls over a gentle heat, shaking to turn them over and over until they are cooked right through.

Serve dry, with *caciç* – yoghurt stirred with cucumber and mint, or *keçup*, a thick tomato sauce spiced with cinnamon and cloves. To serve sauced (appropriate if the meat was really tough), add a ladleful of stock or tomato sauce and simmer for 20–30 minutes, until perfectly tender.

> Good with . . . bread; crisp lettuce leaves; spring onions for nibbling.

Youvarlakia avgolemono

Greek meatballs with lemon and egg

The Greeks like their lamb meatballs flavoured with mint – particularly on the islands – a taste like so many others shared with the Turks as well as ourselves. Several varieties of mint can be gathered from the hillsides, some of which are used medicinally and others for culinary purposes.

Serves 4–6

500g / 1lb finely minced lamb
1 small onion, very finely chopped or grated
2 tablespoons round (arborio or 'pudding') rice
2 tablespoons finely chopped parsley
1 tablespoon finely chopped mint
salt and freshly ground black pepper
flour for dusting
about 1 litre / 1¾ pints stock, or water with white wine (proportions 2:1)

For the avgolemono
2 eggs (3 if small), separated
juice of 2 lemons

Work together and knead the meat, onion, rice, herbs, salt and pepper. When absolutely smooth, shape into walnut-sized balls and roll lightly in flour.

Bring the stock or wine and water to the boil in a shallow pan and drop in the meatballs one by one. Cover loosely and simmer gently for an hour.

Just before you are ready to serve, whisk the egg whites in a roomy bowl. When they are quite stiff, whisk in the yolks. When the mixture is pale yellow and fluffy, whisk in the lemon juice. Then, little by little, whisk in the hot (but not boiling) juices from the meatballs (there should be about 300ml/½ pint). When it is all incorporated, pour the sauce over the meatballs and serve immediately with plenty of bread for mopping.

This meat mixture can also be used to stuff vine-leaves for *dolmades*. Scald the leaves first and use them to wrap little cylinders of stuffing, and cook as above.

Good with . . . crisp-fried chips; frittered deep-fried aubergines and courgettes (page 111); Greek stuffed vegetables (page 124).

Kibbeh

Lebanese mincemeat patties

Kibbeh – also known as köfte, a word derived from ancient Aramaic meaning shredded – is the Lebanese national dish, a kind of lamb tartar bulked with grain food, burghul wheat. To a nation proud to claim descent from desert nomads, it's not so much a recipe as a declaration of national identity. Lamb – very lean – is the most suitable, since it has an elasticity lacking in other meats. Those who don't fancy the notion of raw meat are perfectly at liberty to treat it like hamburger. Just cook the patties in a dry pan over a high flame, or wrap round a skewer and grill.

Serves 6–8

500g / 1lb burghul (fine-ground for preference)
350g / 12oz twice-minced lean lamb
1 tablespoon grated onion (or very finely chopped)
1 teaspoon ground allspice
salt and freshly ground black pepper

Soak the burghul grains in cold water for 10 minutes to swell – if the grains are coarse ground they'll need longer and the mix will be less desirably smooth. Drain thoroughly, spread in a dish and set in the fridge to chill and dry out some more.

Work the soaked burghul very thoroughly with the minced meat, onion, spice and salt. Keep working for at least 10 minutes until the paste is perfectly smooth. Dampen your hands in clean water and form the paste into neat little patties. It's the unctuousness of a woman's *kibbeh* – its smoothness and soft-ness, the delicacy of the spicing – that makes a woman a desirable mate.

> Good with . . . pitta pockets; crisp salad leaves for wrapping; pickled vegetables (page 28).

Köfte tarablousieh
Lebanese stuffed köfte

2

A refinement on the plain kibbeh *that takes its name from Lebanon's second city, Tarablous. The basic recipe is treated much like pastry, as a shell to enclose a spicy filling, formed into torpedo shapes and deep-fried, or baked as a pie, when it becomes kibbeh-bil-sanieh – minced meat baked in a tray. As with all such ancient recipes, there are as many variations as there are cooks.*

Serves 6–8

For the filling
4 tablespoons clarified butter (see page 16) or oil
1 medium onion, finely chopped
3 tablespoons pinekernels
250g / 8oz finely minced lamb or veal
1 teaspoon ground cinnamon
salt and freshly ground black pepper

For the shell
1 *kibbeh* recipe (see page 236)

To finish
oil for frying, or extra butter and pinekernels for baking

Fry the chopped onion in the butter or oil until it is transparent. Push aside and fry the pinekernels until golden. Add the minced lamb, season and sprinkle with cinnamon, and fry until the moisture evaporates and the meat begins to brown.

To fry: wet your hands and break off a walnut-sized piece of *kibbeh* dough and roll it between your palms to form a sausage shape. Push a hole through the middle with a wetted index finger, working your finger until the shell is as thin as possible. Fill the hole with the meat mixture. Close the open end with a wet finger. Roll gently – keep dampening your hands – to make a torpedo shape. Set on a lightly oiled tray. Repeat until all the ingredients are used up. Heat enough oil to submerge the torpedoes and fry until they are golden and crisp – 6–7 minutes. Transfer to kitchen paper to drain.

To bake: preheat the oven to 180°C/350°F/gas 4. Press half the *kibbeh* mixture in a round pie-dish, diameter 35cm/14in, cover with the filling, dot with little lumps of the remaining kibbeh and smooth flat with a wet hand. Mark deeply into bite-sized diamonds, pressing a pinekernel into the middle of each, and drizzle generously with melted butter. Bake for 30–40 minutes, until well browned.

> Good with . . . creamy yoghurt stirred with mint; crisp lettuce leaves.

Saltimbocca alla romana

Italian veal fillets with Parma ham and sage

 Translated literally, the dish means 'jump-in-the-mouth', which is indeed what these delectable little sage-scented morsels can be expected to do. A recipe from Rome – luxuriously simple, as befits the city to which all roads lead.

Serves 4–6

500g / 1lb veal escalopes (or pork, chicken or turkey)
100g / 4oz finely sliced *prosciutto*
about a dozen sage leaves
flour for dusting
salt and freshly ground black pepper

To finish
about 2 tablespoons each butter and olive oil for frying
1 small glass dry white wine
a small knob of cold butter

Flatten the escalopes with a heavy rolling-pin between two sheets of greaseproof paper or clingfilm – or have the butcher perform this service for you. Cut the flattened fillets into smaller pieces about the size of a child's hand and season with salt and pepper. Cut the *prosciutto* into slightly smaller pieces than the meat and lay a slice of ham on each escalope, top with a sage leaf and roll up to form a neat little bolster. Secure each with a cocktail stick, or tie neatly with a thread, and dust lightly with a little flour.

Heat the butter and oil in a roomy frying pan and lay in the little bolsters. Fry them gently on all sides until they are well browned and cooked right through: to test, prod with your finger – they're ready when they feel firm. Remove and reserve. Add the wine to the pan juices and bubble fiercely, scraping in all the little brown bits, until well reduced and no longer smelling of alcohol. Whisk in the cold butter to add a little gloss. Taste and season and return the *saltimbocca* to the pan. Reheat gently, spooning over the sauce.

> Good with . . . *ciabatta* (page 48); a warm salad of wild greens – rocket, chicory, dandelion, spinach, whatever mustardy leaves come your way – wilted in the water that clings to the leaves after washing and dressed with olive oil and lemon juice.

Caldereta de cordero
Andalusian braised lamb

 This is the dish prepared by the pilgrims of Almonte in the marshes of the Guadalquivir when they sleep under the stars on their annual visit to the shrine of their patroness, the Virgin of the Dew.

Serves 6–8

1kg / 2lb lamb off the bone, cubed
1 tablespoon seasoned flour
3 tablespoons olive oil
1 large onion, diced
1 red pepper, deseeded and cut into thin strips
2 cloves garlic, chopped
50g / 2oz *jamón serrano*, diced
1 teaspoon crushed peppercorns
1 small glass sherry
1 sprig each of rosemary and thyme
1 teaspoon dried oregano
2 bayleaves
12 saffron threads, soaked in a little water
salt and a pinch of sugar

To finish
1 clove garlic, finely chopped
1 tablespoon chopped parsley

Toss the meat with the seasoned flour. Heat the oil in a shallow earthenware heatproof casserole or a heavy frying pan, and fry the onion, pepper and garlic until soft and lightly gilded. Push aside and add the cubed lamb and ham, sprinkle with crushed pepper and turn to brown all surfaces. Add the sherry, herbs, saffron with its soaking water, and season with salt and a little sugar.

Bubble up, turn down the heat, cover loosely and leave to simmer very gently for at least an hour, until the meat is perfectly tender and the cooking juices have reduced to a shiny sauce. Check every now and then and add a little water if it looks as though it's drying out. Remove the lid at the end and bubble up to evaporate extra liquid. Stir in the garlic and parsley. Spoon-food, just right for sharing.

> Good with . . . a white *gazpacho* (page 100); rough chunks of sourdough bread (page 47) or any dense-crumbed country bread.

Arni stifado

Greek stewed lamb

For this recipe – a lamb stew, delicately spiced – I am indebted to the chef-proprietor of the Taverna Hierodytas at Fiscardo on Cephalonia, most southerly of the Ionian islands. Hierodytas says the spicing in the dish is Venetian rather than Turkish – probably correct, since the Doges held the islands through several centuries, although one stick of cinnamon is much like another. On a quiet day the proprietor amuses his guests with tales of the seafaring life on Aristotle Onassis's yacht. Meanwhile, while all are waiting for the charcoal grill to reach its perfect temperature, a ladleful of stew is served up as a little mezze to stave off the pangs of hunger. In Hierodytas's opinion, lamb is good for girls, mutton is for men, but for heroes it has to be beef – thick slabs, sold by weight, slapped on the grill.

Serves 6–8

1kg / 2lb boned lamb shoulder, cubed into bite-sized pieces
2–3 tablespoons olive oil (clarified butter if you mean to serve it hot; see page 16)
500g / 1lb pickling onions, skinned
1 green pepper, deseeded and diced
1 tablespoon raisins
3 cloves
a few coriander seeds, crushed
1 small stick cinnamon
salt and freshly ground black pepper

To finish
a dash of wine vinegar

Wipe the meat. Heat the oil in a roomy pan and fry the onions gently, shaking the pan over the heat until they take a little colour. Push to one side, add the meat and fry until it browns a little. Add the diced green pepper and fry for a moment longer. Add the raisins and spices, and enough water to cover the contents of the pan completely. Season with salt and pepper, bubble up, cover, turn down the heat and leave to simmer gently, loosely covered, for an hour or so, until the meat is perfectly tender and the juices cooked right down. Taste, adjust the seasoning, and sharpen with a dash of wine vinegar.

Serve at room temperature. No Greek likes his food piping hot. In winter, says the thrifty Hierodytas, when customers are scarce, the meat will go further if you include chunks of quince.

> **Good with . . .** crisp-fried chips sprinkled with salty kefalotiri cheese.

Chevreau aux amandes

Provençal kid with almonds

 An Easter treat in Provence, when milk-fed kid is on the menu. In non-Mediterranean lands your best bet is the halal butcher. A good substitute – which will yield the characteristically sticky gravy – is knuckle of veal, but shoulder of lamb will do.

Serves 6–8

1.5kg / 3lb shoulder or leg of kid, chopped across the bone into 6–8 portions
4 tablespoons olive oil
200g / 6oz whole unblanched almonds
20 cloves garlic, skinned
2 tablespoons chopped parsley
300ml / ½ pint white wine
salt, freshly ground black pepper and a little sugar

Wipe the meat and trim off any gristle. Heat the oil in a large, heavy sauté pan, add the almonds, let them take a little colour, remove and reserve. Put in the meat and turn the pieces in the hot oil until browned. Lower the heat, add the whole skinned garlic cloves and fry for a minute or two, until they are lightly gilded. Add the parsley, stir in the wine, bubble up and season with salt, pepper and a pinch of sugar. Turn down the heat, cover loosely and leave to simmer gently for 1–1½ hours, until the meat is absolutely tender. Or transfer to a casserole, cover tightly with a lid or foil, and cook in the oven at 180°C/350°F/ gas 4. Check after an hour and add a little more hot water if it looks as though it's drying out, but don't drown it – the success of the dish depends on the formation of a sticky, deliciously fragrant gravy.

Pound the almonds to a paste in a mortar, dilute with a little water, and stir into the sauce at the end, mashing to blend in the garlic cloves. Taste and check seasoning.

> **Good with . . .** bread and a little lightly dressed salad – leaves only – to dump into the delicious juices.

Rabo de buey cordobes

Andalusian spiced oxtail casserole

Wherever there's a tanning industry you'll find recipes for oxtails. The skins for the trade would come in with the tail of the animal still attached – affording a tasty free morsel for the worker's pot. This deliciously spicy oxtail stew comes from Córdoba, a centre for leatherwork since the days of the Moors.

Serves 4–6

I whole oxtail (weighing about 1.5kg / 3lb), cut into its natural sections
2 tablespoons olive oil
50g / 2oz diced *jamón serrano* or *prosciutto* scraps (bacon will do)
I large onion, chopped
I clove garlic, crushed with I teaspoon salt
I stick celery, chopped
I carrot, chopped
I tablespoon paprika
I teaspoon ground cinnamon
½ teaspoon salt
½ teaspoon freshly ground black pepper
3–4 cloves
I bayleaf
150ml / ¼ pint red wine

Wipe the oxtail and trim off excess fat.

Heat the oil in a casserole that will comfortably accommodate all the pieces. Turn the oxtail in the hot oil until it sizzles and browns a little, remove and reserve. Add the ham, onion, garlic, celery and carrot to the pan drippings and fry gently until the vegetables soften. Return the oxtail to the casserole. Add the spices, seasoning and the red wine and bubble up. Add enough water to submerge everything and bring back to the boil. Turn down the heat, cover tightly and leave to simmer very gently – or transfer to the oven at 150°C/300°F/gas 2 – for 2–2½ hours, until the meat is falling off the bones. Check from time to time, and add more boiling water if necessary.

If more people arrive for the feast, stir in ready-cooked chickpeas (tinned is fine, or keep some handy in the freezer).

> Good with . . . Andalusian sourdough bread (page 47); crisps; olives; crisp lettuce leaves; *tortilla española* (page 76) to fill in the corners.

Callos con garbanzos
Andalusian tripe with chickpeas

In Andalusia, what are delicately referred to as variety meats — sweetbreads, brains, tripe, intestines — are appreciated and valued for their distinctive flavour and texture. Since they're cheap — particularly when there's been a bullfight in the town and the six beasts from the ring are butchered and sold in the market the next day — much of the offal disappears into the tapa bars, where they make excellent eating. This is the most popular recipe for tripe — the chickpeas absorb the gluey texture of the tripe and the chilli cuts the richness. I much prefer it to Marseilles' pallid pieds-et-paquets, pale little parcels of tripe and trotters, a dish that has earned far greater fame. Since we can't buy unbleached tripe — although you can get it in halal butchers if you ask nicely — the chilli-spiked tomato sauce gives back some of the flavour to the sanitized over-bleached tripe that is all most of us can obtain. You can use tinned chickpeas if you prefer.

Serves 4–6

250g / 8oz chickpeas, soaked overnight in cold water
bayleaf, carrot, quartered whole onion, 6 peppercorns

For the tripe
3–4 tablespoons olive oil
2–3 cloves garlic, sliced
1 medium onion, chopped
50g / 2oz *jamón serrano*, diced small
500g / 1lb tomatoes, skinned and chopped (or use tinned plum tomatoes)
1 tablespoon paprika
2 bayleaves
1 teaspoon thyme
2–3 dried chillis, deseeded and chopped
500g / 1lb ready-cooked tripe, cut into small squares or strips
salt and freshly ground black pepper

Drain the chickpeas and put them in a roomy pan with the aromatics (don't add salt at this point), and enough water to cover to a depth of two fingers. Bring to the boil and keep at a steady bubble until the peas are tender — 1–2 hours. Add more boiling water if necessary. At the end of the cooking almost all the liquid will have evaporated.

Meanwhile, prepare the tripe. Heat the olive oil and fry the garlic and onion until soft. Add the ham, the tomatoes, paprika, herbs, bayleaf, thyme and chilli, and bubble up to make a thick sauce. Stir in the tripe, season and simmer for 10 minutes or so to marry the flavours. Add the cooked chickpeas, with enough of their cooking liquor to dilute the sauce.

> **Good with . . .** Andalusian sourdough bread (page 47); something crisp and fresh.

Higado con cebolla
Catalan liver and onions

A high proportion of onion to meat makes all the difference. This is a family favourite – the ingredients are cheap and easily found wherever you are. If you can afford calf's liver it will require only a few minutes' sautéing – it should be left pink and will need no further stewing.

Serves 4–6

500g / 1lb lamb or pork liver, trimmed and sliced into thin fillets
salt and freshly ground black pepper
4 tablespoons olive oil
500g / 1lb onions, finely sliced
1 tablespoon flour
1 tablespoon chopped *jamón serrano* scraps
300ml / ½ pint red wine

Season the liver with salt and pepper. Heat the oil in a wide, heavy pan. Stir in the onions and leave them to cook very slowly for 25–30 minutes, until they are quite soft and lightly caramelized. Push the onion aside or remove and add the strips of liver, lightly sprinkled with flour. Sauté them briefly, for no more than a couple of minutes.

Add the ham and wine and bubble up. Cover, turn down the heat and simmer for as long as it takes to tenderize the liver – 20–30 minutes. Remove the lid at the end and bubble to reduce the liquid to a shiny little sauce. Taste and adjust seasoning – you may need a little sugar.

> Good with . . . thick slices of Andalusian sourdough bread (page 47); a crisp salad of chopped Cos lettuce and slivered mild onion; grilled mushrooms with garlic (page 152).

Fideos a la catalana

Catalan pasta with pork, almonds and saffron

The Catalans cook small – angel-hair – vermicelli as if it were rice. This dish can be made with fish stock and include prawns, squid and shellfish. The almonds can be replaced by crisply fried bread cubes.

Serves 4–6

300g / 10oz vermicelli or any small soup pasta
250g / 8oz lean pork, diced
2 tablespoons olive oil
1 tablespoon blanched almonds
2 cloves garlic, chopped
1 tablespoon chopped parsley
1 tablespoon paprika
1 teaspoon ground cinnamon
½ teaspoon ground cloves
a knifetip of saffron strands (about 12 strands soaked in a little boiling water)
1 lemon, juice and grated zest
1 glass dry sherry or white wine
1 large onion, finely chopped
2–3 large tomatoes, skinned and chopped (or use tinned plum tomatoes)
1 small glass water

Set the pasta and the meat aside while you prepare the sauce.

Heat a tablespoon of the oil in a small frying pan. Fry the almonds and garlic until golden, stir in the parsley and let it sizzle and crisp. Tip the contents of the pan into the food processor or a mortar. Process or pestle-pound to a paste with the spices, the saffron and its soaking water, the lemon juice and zest. Dilute with the sherry or wine, and reserve.

Heat the remaining oil in a large frying pan, add the meat and the onion and fry gently until the meat is cooked through and the onions are soft and golden – 15–20 minutes. Push the meat and onions aside and sprinkle in the pasta. Let it sizzle and fry to a rich golden-brown. Add the tomatoes and bubble up, then pour in a glass of water. Bubble up again and stir in the almond sauce. Bubble up again, turn down the heat and leave to simmer gently until the pasta is perfectly tender and the juices have almost evaporated – about 10 minutes.

Set the pan in the middle of the table for everyone to help themselves – as with the *paella*, it is traditional to eat the portion immediately in front of you, working neatly from the outside to the middle. Very Moorish.

Good with . . . bread and crisp lettuce leaves for scooping.

Empanadas valencianas

Valencian spiced pork pasties

 Empanada literally means 'bread-wrapped'. The filling can be meat, fish, vegetables, cheese, so long as it's well and truly spiced.

Serves 4–6

For the filling
2 tablespoons olive oil
I onion, finely chopped
I clove garlic, finely chopped
I red pepper, deseeded and finely diced
50g / 2oz diced *jamón serrano* and /
  or *chorizo*
250g / 8oz lean pork, finely diced
I teaspoon dried thyme
salt and freshly ground black pepper
I small glass white wine or dry sherry
6 saffron threads, soaked in a splash of
  boiling water
I tablespoon chopped toasted almonds

For the pastry
300g / 10oz self-raising flour
½ teaspoon salt
4 tablespoons olive oil
2 tablespoons white wine
100ml / 4fl oz water

In a saucepan heat the oil and fry the onion, garlic and pepper until soft. Add the ham, *chorizo* and diced pork, sprinkle with thyme, season and fry gently until the meat takes a little colour. Then add the wine and the saffron with its soaking water and bubble up. Turn down the heat and simmer until the meat is perfectly tender and the liquid mostly evaporated – about 10 minutes. Stir in the almonds and leave aside to cool.

Preheat the oven to 200°C/400°F/gas 6.

Make the pastry: sieve the flour with the salt into a bowl. In a small pan, heat the oil, wine and water until just bearable to a finger. Pour the warm liquid into the flour, and knead to a soft, elastic dough-ball. On a well floured board form the dough into a roll and divide into twenty pieces. Roll out each piece into a thin round about 8cm/3in in diameter. Dot with a teaspoon of the filling, wet the edges and fold one half over the other to enclose the filling, marking with a fork to seal. Continue until you have twenty little pasties. Transfer to an oiled baking sheet. Bake for 15–20 minutes, until gorgeously puffed and brown. Or you can fry them.

Good with . . . iced *gazpacho* – red or white (pages 100 and 101); fresh tomato sauce.

Lahm Bi'ajeen

Lebanese lamb pies

These pasties are somewhat larger than Turkish böreki, but the idea's the same. The stuffing is diced lamb flavoured with cinnamon and a great deal of onion. Lebanese cooking is very exact – hence the unusual amount of attention paid to timing.

Serves 4–6

For the filling
500g / 1lb lean boneless lamb, diced small
2 tablespoons clarified butter (see page 16) or oil
1 tablespoon ground cinnamon
salt and freshly ground black pepper
300ml / ½ pint boiling water
500g / 1lb onions, sliced very thinly

For the pastry
about 12 sheets filo pastry – enough to make a dozen little packets
6–8 tablespoons clarified butter (see page 16)

Heat the butter or oil in a heavy pan and fry the meat for about 5 minutes, until it is lightly browned, stirring to avoid sticking. Sprinkle with cinnamon, season with salt and pepper and mix thoroughly. Turn the heat right down, cover tightly and cook very gently for 15 minutes, shaking the pan every now and again, until all the moisture has been completely absorbed, leaving only the oily residue. If it's still wet, unlid and bubble until dry. Pour in the boiling water, cover and simmer for about an hour, until the meat is perfectly tender and the juices cooked right down again. Add the onion, cover tightly and turn the heat right up for 15 seconds to build up steam. Turn off the heat and leave undisturbed for 5 minutes – if you take off the lid the onions will remain raw. Remove from the heat and leave to cool.

Preheat the oven to 200°C/400°F/gas 6.

Lay out one sheet of filo (keep the rest under clingfilm to prevent it drying out) and brush with melted butter. Fold in half to give you a rectangle as wide as your hand and three times the length (cut to size if necessary – filo comes in all lengths and widths). Spread 1 tablespoon of the meat mixture down the short edge of the pastry. Fold the long ends over the meat and roll up neatly into a tight bolster, sealing the final edge with a wet finger. Continue until all the meat and filo is used up. Transfer to a greased baking sheet and brush the tops with a little more butter. Bake for 15–20 minutes, until crisp and golden.

Good with . . . any of the Middle Eastern salad dips.

Sigara

Moroccan cigars

2

Think of these as sophisticated sausage rolls – children love them. In Morocco the pastry would be ouaka – very fine sheets produced by dabbing a ball of dough on a hot griddle, a skilled job requiring professional expertise. Housewives do not usually make their own – there's a ouaka stall in the corner of every Moroccan market.

Serves 6–8

For the filling
250g / 8oz lean minced lamb
1 small onion, finely chopped
1 clove garlic, finely chopped
1 tablespoon clarified butter (see page 16)
1 teaspoon ground cumin
1 teaspoon ground coriander
1 teaspoon ground cinnamon
1 small glass water
1 tablespoon finely chopped parsley
2 tablespoons finely chopped mint
salt and freshly ground black pepper
1–2 tablespoons fresh breadcrumbs

To finish
1 packet filo pastry (about 12 sheets)
oil for shallow-frying

First make the filling. Put the meat, onion and garlic in a small pan with the butter and spices and the glass of water. Bubble up, turn down the heat and simmer gently for 15–20 minutes, until the meat is perfectly tender. Stir in the herbs and season with salt and pepper. Remove the pan from the heat and leave to cool. Stir in sufficient breadcrumbs to take up all the remaining juice.

Cut the sheets of filo into rectangular strips three times as long as wide – about 7.5cm x 25cm / 3in x 10in. Cover with clingfilm until you are ready for each piece. Working with one strip at a time, lay a narrow cigar of filling along the short side. Fold the edges of the long side over the filling and roll up like a short, stubby cigar. Seal the end with a wet finger. Continue until all the filo and filling is used up. Heat a finger's depth of oil in a frying pan. When it is lightly hazed with smoke, fry the cigars, a few at a time so that the oil temperature does not drop. As soon as the pastry is crisp and brown, remove and drain on kitchen paper.

Good with . . . a dipping-sauce of thick yoghurt and mint.

Pulses & grains

This section is fairly short, mainly because grain-foods and pulses used in Mediterranean countries – lentils, chickpeas, beans, rice and wheat-based foods – are usually prepared as one-pot dishes designed to provide a substantial midday meal.

Pulses make an appearance on the *tapa* or *mezze* table as a leftover, as in the Greek butterbean recipe, where a soupy dish of beans is given a second incarnation in the oven, or in the form of fritters made with pounded beans, such as the Egyptian *falafel*. Beans are also eaten as scoopable purées, particularly in Arab lands, and it is in this form that they are most suitable as a *mezze*.

Rice is appreciated throughout the region, though more easily found on the northern shores. Although certain dishes such as *paella* use rice as the principal ingredient, it is more commonly presented in recycled form, as a stuffing for vegetables (look for these in the vegetable section) or bound with egg and fried as little patties, with or without extra flavourings. *Risottos* and *pilaf*s can be scooped from the dish with bread or crisp lettuce leaves, and this is how they are most conveniently served for sharing. Maize, the New World grain which replaced the chestnut as well as barley and oats in the porridge-pot, emerges as polenta – convenient finger-food only when grilled or fried.

Pre-prepared grain-foods served in combination with stews or soupy sauces, such as pasta, *trahana*, burghul and couscous – respectively the grain-foods of the western, eastern, south-western and south-eastern shores of the Mediterranean – also make their appearance in leftover form. Of these grain-foods, Italian pasta needs no explanation; the Balkan *trahana* is a tiny hand-rolled dried pasta used to make a nourishing porridge or to thicken a soup. Couscous, the staple grain-food of the Mahgreb, the lands which stretch from Egypt to Morocco, can also be classed as a miniature pasta since it is made with pre-cooked semolina, the hard heart of the wheat, rolled in fine-ground wheat-flour. Burghul, wheat kernels that have been pre-cooked and cracked, is the staple grain-food of what is sometimes called the Fertile Crescent, the Arab lands that reach from Lebanon to the Bosporus. All four of these preparations serve a single purpose: to overcome the natural

▶ *Algerian spicy sausage (page 232); Turkish pitta breads (page 50)*

tendency of grain to sprout. When milled, precooked and dried, wheat-seed becomes transportable, storable and not liable to put up little green shoots on a damp morning. In short, the perfect fast-food for nomads. Such wanderers, whether by land or sea, have little time for the more leisurely pleasures of the table.

Preparing pulses for the pot

Soak all beans and chickpeas overnight (6–8 hours) in cold water (lentils are the only pulses which don't need soaking). Don't leave them much longer for fear they'll ferment. Bring to the boil in fresh water without salt, skim off the grey foam that rises, then add garlic, flavouring meats, pot-herbs. Oil is best added at the end, as an enrichment. Fresh vegetables – leaves and herbs – can be stirred in to finish and balance the dish. If you mean to bake the beans as a layered casserole, cook them until they are tender before you transfer them with any finishing ingredients to the oven.

Beans mean flatulence, to put it delicately. A pinch of bicarbonate of soda in the soaking or cooking water is sometimes recommended to alleviate the problem, but soda tastes nasty. Since the beans that cause the problem are the ones cooked only until they are al dente, my advice is to cook them for as long as it takes to make them really soft. Chickpeas take the longest to cook – up to 4 hours if they're old and hard. Fava (broad) and haricot vary from 1½–2½ hours. Lentils will take 40 minutes. Chickpeas should remain at a boil throughout, and if you need to add extra liquid, make sure it's boiling.

To skin dried beans, pick up a handful at a time from the water in which they have soaked (overnight if possible) and rub between your palms. The skins will slip off and float when you drop them back into the water. Skim off the skins as they accumulate on the surface. A little more pressure is necessary to skin chickpeas. Soak and roll with a rolling pin – easiest if you drop them in a clean cotton bag first. To skin dried fava (broad beans), soak for 48 hours and then freeze until firm – they should pop out easily. If they do not, first slit the skin with a small knife. It's labour intensive, but there's no shortcut. The easy way is to buy them ready-skinned.

◀ *Turkish stuffed figs with bayleaves in rosewater syrup (page 271); Turkish saffron and cardamom ice-cream (page 301)*

About the fava bean

The fava or broad bean is the Mediterranean's only native bean. All the rest – haricot, runner, butterbean – are Johnnies-come-lately, unknown before Christopher Columbus set foot in the New World.

Acceptance of the newcomers was rapid on the northern shores of the Mediterranean, where ancient recipes were adapted to accommodate them, and the fava became the poor relation, taking its place as just another summer vegetable. In Italy fresh broad beans – podded or not, depending on maturity – are eaten as a simple *antipasto*, with a dish of coarse salt for dipping. And fresh baby broad beans go into the classic Provençal *tian*, a pastryless quiche which takes its name from its baking dish, a shallow earthenware casserole. In Morocco, where the French were the colonial power, the fresh beans are transformed into a delicate salad dip, *bessara*, although – more characteristically of the Middle East – it's also prepared in winter with dried beans.

On the southern shores of the Mediterranean, less influenced by incursions from the New World, or perhaps because ancestral habit is not so easily discarded, the fava remains the storecupboard staple. Cultivation is much as it has always been since the first gatherers decided to plant their surplus. The beans are planted in the early spring, allowed to grow to maturity and left to dry in tangled heaps in the fields until late autumn, when the pods are stripped and the beans left to finish drying on wire trays – separating bean from pod is a job for the old folk, sitting on the stoop in the last of the sunshine.

In Andalusia, where Moorish culinary habit has proved astonishingly resilient, dried favas remain a winter staple, sold by weight from open sacks in every village store. Nevertheless the Andalusians also appreciate the tender young pods, picked when the little beans are newly formed in their pale cottony beds, and cooked in one of the aromatic ham-flavoured, wine-scented broths that are a delight of the Iberian table. When I first moved to the area in the late sixties, all cooking was done in long-handled copper pans over a charcoal brazier set on the pavement outside the door. When the dish was cooked, the brazier would be tucked under the *mesa camella*, a circular table draped in a heavy blanket, round which the family would huddle, lower limbs snug in the warmth beneath, dipping chunks of bread into the aromatic broth, sipping a glass of wine, sharing the day's news.

Ful-medames

Egyptian brown beans

3

Ask any expatriate Egyptian, and he'll tell you with tears in his eyes that ful-medames *truly is the flavour of home. The preferred bean for this Egyptian national dish — you'll find the record in the pyramids — is the* ful hamam, *a small, brown, round fava which turns purple when cooked. The traditional cooking pot is the* dammasa, *a metal vessel with a narrow neck which ensures that the steam condenses and slides back into the pot, which is left to bubble away on a charcoal brazier (these days an electric element). Egyptians eat* ful-medames *for breakfast, lunch and dinner — and at any time between. When a stranger comes to call, the courteous host will send out to the* el-ful *shop for a portion to welcome the visitor. To refuse to partake would be like refusing to break bread — a terrible insult, only forgivable if you're a foreigner and can be expected to know no better. You'll find the raw materials in Cypriot as well as Egyptian groceries. If you can't get the dark beans, include a handful of brown lentils.*

Serves 4–6

500g / 1lb dried brown fava beans (pre-skinned), soaked overnight
150ml / ¼ pint olive oil
juice of 1–2 lemons
salt and freshly ground black pepper

Optional to finish
finely chopped garlic, onion, the diced flesh of a ripe tomato, chopped parsley, mint or coriander leaves, a sprinkle of powdered cumin, olives

Rinse the beans thoroughly in cold water. Bring 4 pints of fresh water to the boil in a large pan and add the beans. Bring back to the boil and cook at a rolling bubble for about 10 minutes. Reduce the heat to a gentle simmer, cover and cook for about 2 hours — or until the beans are perfectly tender. Don't add salt before or during the cooking, or the beans will never soften. If you need to add water, make sure it's boiling.

When the beans are tender, drain and leave them to cool. Dress with the olive oil, lemon juice, salt and pepper — and mash to a purée or not, as you please. Finish as you please.

Good with . . . bread for scooping; Egyptian preserved eggs (page 74) for fortification.

Bessara

Egyptian bean purée

*A garlicky purée for scooping up with bread, made with skinned dried broad beans (fava) –
the large, pale variety rather than the little dark ones used for el-ful. Elsewhere throughout
the region, it's made with any precooked pulse vegetable – haricot, kidney, butter, black-eyed
peas (an African native), chickpeas. In Apulia, the heel of Italy's boot, where the Arab culinary
habit has remained strong, it appears as fave e ciccoria – the touch of bitterness comes from
a handful of wilted wild-gathered greens (chicory is a general name for several varieties),
served separately to be swirled in by each diner, while the finishing garnish might be lam-
paschoni, the bulbs of the wild grape-hyacinth, boiled to tenderize and finished with oil and
vinegar.*

Serves 4–6

200g / 6oz dried beans (skinned fava, haricot, chickpea), soaked overnight
2–3 cloves garlic, roughly chopped
2 tablespoons white wine vinegar
4 tablespoons olive oil
I teaspoon ground cumin
I teaspoon ground paprika
I tablespoon dried mint (or 2 tablespoons fresh)
salt and freshly ground black pepper

To finish (optional)
2 tablespoons chopped, pitted green olives
2 tablespoons chopped coriander leaves
I small green chilli, deseeded and finely chopped
2–3 spring onions, finely chopped with their green

Drain the beans and transfer to a roomy pan with water to cover to a depth
of two fingers. Bring to the boil, lid loosely and simmer for at least an hour
until perfectly tender. If you need to add water it should be boiling. Drain and
tip everything into the food processor or blender and process until smooth,
or pound in a mortar with a pestle.

   To finish, taste and season, swirl on a plate or in a shallow bowl, and decorate prettily with the optional green things. The Egyptians like to include a
sprinkle of dried *melokhia* leaves – *Corchorus olitorius*, a member of the mallow
family, as is okra – for the colour rather than the flavour, which is mild and
hard to detect in small quantities.

> Good with . . . *aish*, Egypt's version of *pitta*, or *semit*, sesame-sprinkled
> bread rings; *torshi* – salt-pickled vegetables (page 28); slivered onion – raw
> if mild and young, fried to a melting caramel sweetness later in the year.

Gigantes plaki
Greek baked butterbeans

3 *Greek butterbeans make all others look like pygmies – truly gigantic, very meaty and the perfect partners for olive oil. Beans for winter use are grown on all the islands and by every rural community on the mainland. For storage they are spread in wooden trays to dry in the summer sun.*

Serves 6–8

500g / 1lb butterbeans, soaked overnight
1 teaspoon salt
6–8 peppercorns
3–4 allspice berries
1 small stick cinnamon
4 tablespoons olive oil
2–3 large ripe tomatoes, skinned and chopped
2–3 cloves garlic, sliced
1 mild red onion, finely sliced

To finish
2 lemons, quartered

Drain and rinse the beans in cold water, and transfer to a large saucepan with enough water to cover to a depth of two fingers. Bring to the boil, skimming the froth as it rises. Turn down the heat, salt lightly, add the peppercorns, allspice, cinnamon and olive oil, cover loosely and simmer gently for 1–1½ hours, adding more boiling water if necessary, until the beans are perfectly soft.

Preheat the oven to 150°C/300°F/gas 2.

Stir the remaining ingredients into the beans and spread them in a roomy earthenware dish. Cover loosely with foil, shiny side down, and transfer to the oven for another half-hour – as long as you like, within reason. Serve with quartered lemons for squeezing.

Good with . . . quartered hardboiled eggs; slices of feta dressed with a little oil and oregano; *saganiki* – roasted cheese.

Cocido con chorizo

Andalusian chickpea stew with chorizo

Spain's chickpea stews are many and varied, but they are always a meal in themselves and eaten with a spoon. Diced fresh pork or a slab of pork belly is sometimes included, or a boiling fowl.

Serves 4–6

350g / 12oz dried chickpeas, soaked overnight
1 whole small head of garlic
2–3 links *chorizo* (about 100g / 4oz)
a short length *jamón serrano* bone or bacon knuckle
1 carrot, scraped and diced
1 dried red pepper, torn into pieces, or 1 tablespoon *pimentón* (paprika)
1–2 bayleaves
1 teaspoon coriander seeds, roughly crushed
12 black peppercorns, roughly crushed

To finish
1 large tomato, skinned, deseeded and chopped
1–2 potatoes, peeled and chunked
a handful of spinach or chard, rinsed and shredded
salt
2–3 tablespoons olive oil

Drain the chickpeas and put them in a roomy pan with enough cold water to cover generously. Bring to the boil and skim off the grey foam that rises. Meanwhile, push a skewer or knife through the head of garlic and char it over a flame until the papery covering blackens and the air is filled with the exquisite scent of roasting garlic.

Drop the whole garlic and the remaining ingredients into the pot. Bring back to the boil, turn down the heat, cover loosely and cook for 1½–2 hours, until the chickpeas are quite soft. If they're old and hard, they'll take longer. Keep the broth at a rolling boil throughout – don't add salt or let the temperature drop, or the chickpeas will never soften. Add *boiling* water as and when necessary. When the chickpeas are quite soft – at this point they won't harden again – add the chopped tomato and chunked potatoes. When the potatoes are just soft but still whole, add the spinach, bring back to the boil and cook for another 5 minutes or so, until the leaves have wilted. Remove the ham or bacon bone, taste and add salt. Finally, stir in the olive oil and bubble up to emulsify the juices.

Good with . . . Andalusian sourdough bread (page 47); *pa amb tomaquèt* (page 60); a salad of Cos lettuce and mild onion.

Falafel

Egyptian fava bean fritters

2

Crisp little fritters made with pre-soaked but uncooked fava (dried broad beans – see page 251), variously spiced and herbed, a favourite of the mezze table. Although widely available in Middle Eastern fast-food outlets – you can buy a special falafel iron for shaping the patties – your own will be infinitely superior. The aim is a crisp shell enclosing a deliciously soft interior. The Egyptians are the experts, but you'll find variations made with other pulses in Lebanon, Syria and Jordan as well as on many of the islands. In Israel you can buy the local version (made in the Palestinian way, with chickpeas rather than fava) in any gas-station, stuffed into a pitta pocket with a hank of salad and a spoonful of garlicky hummus. You'll need dried ready-skinned fava beans from a Middle Eastern store (or see page 251). Vary the flavourings – more or less chilli, with or without coriander – to suit your palate.

Serves 4–6

250g / 8oz dried, ready-skinned fava beans, soaked for 24 hours
2–3 cloves garlic, crushed
¼ teaspoon ground chilli (cayenne) – more if you like it hot
I teaspoon ground cumin
I teaspoon salt
½ teaspoon baking powder
2 tablespoons grated onion or 4 spring onions, finely chopped
2 tablespoons finely chopped parsley
2 tablespoons leaf coriander
oil for frying – any vegetable oil will do

Drain the beans and dry thoroughly. Pound in a mortar or in the food processor until you have a very smooth paste; unless this is done very thoroughly with absolutely dry beans the paste will fall apart in the frying. Add the remaining ingredients in the order given, processing between each addition, until well blended. Leave the mixture to rest for an hour.

Break off pieces the size of a walnut and form into small patties about 4cm/1½in in diameter. Arrange on a plate ready to slip into the hot oil – they'll be too fragile to pick up in your fingers.

Heat the oil until it is lightly hazed with blue. Use a spatula to push the patties into the hot oil, a few at a time, and fry until crisp and brown. If they splutter and split, the oil is too hot. Turn once and transfer to kitchen paper to drain.

> **Good with . . .** any of the Middle Eastern dipping purées, *pitta* pockets.

Garbanzos ajimoli

Catalan chickpeas with saffron, garlic and almonds

2   *Almonds and saffron were established as crops in Spain during the Moorish ascendency. The method of cooking is more Arab than European: the dressing is first fried, then soaked with the cooking liquid, and finally allowed to evaporate until it fries again.*

Serves 4–6

4 tablespoons olive oil
4 tablespoons blanched almonds, finely chopped
I clove garlic, finely chopped
4 tablespoons fresh breadcrumbs
250g / 8oz dried chickpeas, soaked overnight and drained (or two 200g / 14oz tins)
a knifetip of saffron (about a dozen threads), soaked in a splash of boiling water
600ml / 1 pint good stock (chicken or ham)
salt and white pepper

Put the chickpeas in a pan with cold water to cover to a depth of two fingers. Bring to the boil, cover loosely and keep the pot bubbling for about 1½ hours, or until the chickpeas are perfectly soft. If you need to add water it must be boiling.

Heat the oil in a heavy sauté pan. As soon as it's lightly hazed with blue stir in the almonds, garlic and breadcrumbs and fry gently until lightly gilded – the breadcrumbs should be just crisp, but on no account let anything burn.

Add the chickpeas, saffron with its soaking water, and enough stock to submerge everything. Bring back to the boil, turn down the heat, cover and leave to simmer for 20 minutes. Remove the lid, turn up the heat, season and bubble up until all the remaining liquid has evaporated and the breadcrumbs and almonds begin to fry again. Let everything brown a little, turning the chickpeas over in the heat to coat them with the aromatic dressing.

Good with . . . shellfish opened in its own juices on the grill: try razor-shells – they look somewhat priapic but taste wonderful; oysters grilled or *au nature*; a pretty plate of thinly sliced *jamón serrano* and *chorizo*; *pa amb tomaquèt* (page 60).

Fagioli con la bottarga

Italian beans with salted fish roe

2

A simple salad of plain-cooked beans – usually borlotti, the small speckled pinkish beans that are Italy's favourite storecupboard bean – topped with thin slivers of salt-dried pressed roe of grey mullet or tuna, a speciality of Sicily and Sardinia. Bottarga – from the Arab batarkhah – is a popular mezze throughout the eastern Mediterranean and was known in Egypt in Pharaonic times. In Greece it's combined with gigantes, the outsize butterbeans you find in every Greek grocery store. In Catalonia and Valencia, a similar combination of haricot beans and mojama, salt-dried tuna, is served as a tapa. The gentle flavour and soft texture of the beans provides an elegant counterpoint to the chewy, salty slivers of fish. Possible alternative toppings are thin slivers of smoked salmon, salt herring or flakes of salt cod – don't soak it, just slap it on a hot griddle to draw the salt, then skin and bone it with your fingers.

Serves 4–6

250 / 8oz dried borlotti or haricot beans, soaked in cold water overnight
½ mild onion, finely chopped
2 tablespoons finely chopped dill or fennel fronds
3–4 tablespoons olive oil
salt and freshly ground black pepper or chilli flakes

To finish
a few drops balsamic vinegar
100g / 4oz *bottarga*, finely sliced
olive oil

Drain the soaked beans, cover with fresh cold water and cook at a steady boil for an hour, or until perfectly soft but still whole. Drain and dress with the onion, dill, oil, salt and pepper or chilli flakes. Leave to cool.

Sprinkle with balsamic vinegar, top with slivers of *bottarga* and finish with a trickle of olive oil.

> **Good with . . .** something crisp such as vegetable fritters (page 111); frittered fish (page 164); broccoli or cauliflower florets cooked until tender and dressed with oil and garlic; green olives; toasted salted almonds.

M'jaddas

Lebanese lentils and rice

 A fasting, therefore meatless, dish enjoyed by the Christian communities of the Middle East throughout Lent. The proportions of pulse to grain can vary to suit whatever the housewife has in the storecupboard. The same combination – dark lentils, white rice – is known in Spain as moros y cristianos, *Moors and Christians.*

Serves 4–6

250g / 8oz greeny-brown lentils
1 small stick cinnamon
½ teaspoon allspice berries, crushed
½ teaspoon black peppercorns, crushed
salt
250g / 8oz long-grain rice
6 tablespoons olive oil
2 medium onions, finely sliced (vertically)

To finish
2 tablespoons chopped coriander
1 lemon, quartered, to serve

Pick over the lentils, checking for tiny stones. Put into a roomy pan, cover generously with cold water, bring to the boil, add the spices and a little salt, and simmer for 45–50 minutes, or until the lentils are perfectly soft.

Meanwhile, rinse the rice in a sieve under cold water. Heat the oil in a heavy saucepan and fry the onions until they caramelize and crisp – they should be a rich chestnut brown, but don't let them blacken. Remove, drain on kitchen paper and reserve. Stir the rice into the oily drippings in the pan and turn the grains over the heat for a moment or two, until they turn transparent. Add enough hot water to cover the rice to a depth of one finger, season, bring to the boil, turn down the heat and simmer for 18–20 minutes, until the rice is perfectly soft.

Make a circle of rice on a warmed dish and ladle the lentils into the middle. Top with the fried onions and chopped coriander. Serve at room temperature, with quartered lemons.

You can, if you prefer perfect authenticity, cook the rice and lentils together in the same pan. Start with the oily juices from the onion, stir in the rice and lentils, add 1.5 litres/2½ pints water along with the rest of the flavouring ingredients. Simmer for 45–50 minutes, remove from the heat, cover the pan with a clean teatowel, put the lid back on and leave to rest for another 10 minutes.

Good with . . . sesame bread-rings (*semit*) or *pitta* (page 50) for scooping; salt-pickled vegetables (page 28).

Paella de campo

Andalusian country paella

This is a dish for the open air, cooked by Andalusian field-workers as the midday meal. The only essential ingredients are rice, oil and saffron. The cooking liquid is fresh water; all other ingredients are variable, with a strong preference for wild-gatherings – by the sea, fresh fish and shellfish; in the countryside, rabbits, freshwater crayfish, wild asparagus, young thistle-rosettes, snails. All must go in raw – the cooking juices must be absorbed by the rice. A purpose-made paella *pan – raw iron, double-handled, very shallow – is essential to the identity of the dish. If cooked in any other pan, even with identical ingredients, the* paella *becomes* un arroz *– a rice-dish. The heat-source – charcoal, a purpose-made wide gas-ring – must be broad enough to allow even contact with the entire base of the pan.*

Serves 6–8

3–4 tablespoons olive oil
4–5 cloves garlic, crushed with a little salt
1 large onion, chopped
1 red pepper, deseeded and diced
1 young wild rabbit or small chicken, jointed into bite-sized pieces
salt
750g / 1½lb round (risotto or 'pudding') rice
2–3 large ripe beef tomatoes, skinned and finely chopped or grated
a knifetip of saffron (about 12 threads), soaked in a little boiling water
a handful of thin asparagus or green beans, chopped small

Heat a *paella* pan of the right size – it should be broad enough to accommodate the dry rice in a single layer. As soon as the metal changes colour, add three tablespoons oil, let it heat, then add the garlic, onion and pepper and fry for a few minutes. Add the rabbit or chicken joints, salt lightly, and turn them patiently over the heat until they are cooked right through. When the juices no longer run pink, add the rest of the oil and sprinkle in the rice. Stir until the grains go translucent. Add the tomato and saffron with its soaking liquid, and enough water to submerge everything completely – roughly 2 measures of water to each measure of rice. Bubble up and add the asparagus or green beans. Leave to cook without stirring for 12 minutes, adding more boiling water as the surface dries out. At the end the rice should still look juicy and the surface pitted with tiny craters. Remove from the heat, cover with a thick cloth and leave for 10 minutes for the rice to finish swelling.

The true Andalusian eats the *paella* straight from the pan, tackling only the portion directly in front.

Good with . . . a rough salad of Cos lettuce and onion dressed with lemon juice, salt and olive oil.

Fritattini di risotto alla milanese

Italian saffron rice cakes

2 Risotto, *like the Spanish* paella *and the Turkish* pilaf, *requires that the grains be coated with hot fat before the cooking liquid is added. All other flavourings are secondary. The advantage of using short-grain rather than the long-grain favoured in oriental cuisines is that its spherical compactness permits the exterior to absorb the flavours of a cooking liquid while retaining a nutty little heart. The basic* risotto *can also be used to stuff anything suitably hollow: tomatoes, courgettes, aubergines, artichoke hearts, mussels.*

Serves 6–8

For the risotto
350g / 12oz round (risotto or 'pudding') rice
about 1.5 litres / 2 pints well flavoured stock (chicken or beef/veal)
50g / 2oz butter
2–3 shallots or 1 medium onion, finely chopped
a knifetip of saffron (about 12 threads), soaked in a little boiling water
salt and freshly ground black pepper

To finish
3–4 eggs, lightly forked
1 tablespoon grated Parmesan (or any grana cheese)
olive oil and a small knob of butter for frying

Pick over the rice. Heat the stock until simmering.

Melt half the butter in a heavy, wide pan and add the chopped shallots or onion. Fry gently until softened and gilded a little – don't let them brown. Stir in the rice and turn it in the hot juices until the grains turn translucent. Add the saffron and its soaking liquid, followed by a ladleful of the hot stock; season and let it bubble gently until all the liquid is absorbed. Add another ladleful and stir. Continue ladleful by ladleful (you may not need it all) until the rice is tender but still a little nutty in the middle – about 15 minutes. Cover it and leave it to rest and finish swelling for 10–15 minutes after you take it off the heat. The rice should be juicy but with the grains visibly separate.

Allow to cool. Stir in the eggs and grated Parmesan.

Heat a little olive oil with a scrap of butter in a roomy frying pan. When the butter is sizzling, drop in spoonfuls of the rice-and-egg mixture and fry until crisp on the outside but still soft inside. Transfer to kitchen paper to drain. Continue until all are done.

> Good with . . . a fresh tomato sauce for dipping; pan-fried chicken (page 204); sliced tomatoes and mozzarella dressed with capers

Suppli-al-telefono
Italian rice and cheese balls

Italian children love these crisp little balls – the melted hearts of mozzarella form telephone-line strings. Gorgeous made with saffron risotto (page 262).

Serves 4–6

about 350g / 12oz leftover risotto
2 eggs, lightly forked
75g / 3oz mozzarella, cubed small
1–2 slices Parma ham, chopped
100g / 4oz dried breadcrumbs for coating
oil for deep-frying

Tomato sauce
2–3 tablespoons oil
1 medium onion, chopped
2–3 cloves garlic, chopped
1kg / 2lb tomatoes, peeled and chopped (or tinned plum tomatoes)
4 tablespoons red wine
1 teaspoon crumbled dried thyme
1 teaspoon crumbled dried marjoram
salt and freshly ground black pepper

Mix the risotto with enough forked-up egg to form a thick paste. Dip your hands in warm water and squeeze the mixture into balls the size of a small fig. Using your finger, push a hole in each ball, tuck in a cube of mozzarella and a scrap of ham, then close up the hole and roll the balls in breadcrumbs, pressing to coat thoroughly.

Heat enough oil in a frying pan to submerge the balls completely – use a deep-fryer if you have one handy. When the surface is lightly hazed with blue, drop in a few *suppli* – not too many at a time or the temperature will drop. Remove when deliciously brown and crisp, drain on kitchen paper and keep warm. Continue until all are done.

Meanwhile, make the sauce. Heat the oil in a pan and fry the onion and garlic gently until they soften and gild, then add the tomatoes, wine and herbs. Bubble up, turn down the heat and leave to simmer gently for 20 minutes or so, occasionally mashing with a wooden spoon, until the sauce is perfectly thick and smooth. Taste and season – you may need a little sugar. Serve the sauce with the *suppli*. Be careful not to burn your tongue on the melted middles.

Good with . . . chips – shame to waste the deep-fryer.

Tikvishki so oriz

Macedonian rice patties with yoghurt

2

Little patties made with leftover rice combined with any seasonal vegetable – shredded spinach, chard, cabbage, beet-top – make an excellent mezze. You'll find similar recipes throughout the Balkans. Instead of rice you can use breadcrumbs or mashed potato. Balkan housewives, as with all those who live their lives under the threat of war, have frugal habits – nothing ever goes to waste.

Serves 4–6

250g / 8oz cooked rice – leftovers from a *pilaf* are perfect
2 eggs, lightly forked
2 tablespoons finely diced strong cheese (kefalotiri, feta, Cheddar)
I clove garlic, finely chopped
I green chilli, deseeded and finely chopped
olive oil for shallow-frying

To serve
I large tub (250ml / ½ pint) thick yoghurt
2 tablespoons chopped dill
3–4 spring onions, finely chopped

Mix the rice with the eggs and cheese, garlic and chilli. Divide the mixture into eight little mounds, roll each into a ball (wet hands make the task easier) and flatten into patties.

Heat the oil in a roomy frying pan and fry the patties over a moderate heat in oil until browned on both sides. Transfer to kitchen paper to drain.

Serve with the yoghurt whisked smooth and stirred with the chopped dill and spring onions (don't add salt – it hardens and separates the curd).

Good with . . . pickled vegetables – *torshi* (page 28); any of the spiced kebabs, hamburgers and sausages that fuel the evening stroll around the village square.

Crostini di polenta
Italian grilled polenta

3

This is a two-part process, much like converting bread into toast. Maize – the New World's corn, an amiable, soil-tolerant crop – quickly replaced wheat in the marginal lands of the Old World, slipping easily into the porridge pot and, in some areas, replacing bread as the universal staple. The traditional method of preparing polenta is to start with boiling water, adding the meal in a thin trickle while beating vigorously to avoid lumps, and cooking until it thickens – anything between 20 and 60 minutes, depending on the coarseness of the grind and the freshness of the flour. Although modern milling methods are more predictable, polenta remains a terrible lumper and sticker. The method below avoids all the usual pitfalls and tastes just as good. It's well worth the effort: instant or vacuum-packed ready-cooked polenta never seems to taste as fresh and sweet.

Serves 4–6

600ml / 1 pint cold water
125g / 4oz coarse-ground yellow cornmeal (polenta)
½ tablespoon salt
oil for greasing

Preheat the oven to 180°C/350°F/gas 4.

Put the cold water in a heavy pan, stir in the cornmeal and add the salt. Bring the pot to the boil, stirring constantly with a wooden spoon while the mixture thickens – about 5 minutes, a process much like making porridge. Tip it all into an oiled ovenproof dish, spread into the corners, cover with foil and bake for an hour. Leave to cool and then cut into squares or fingers.

Preheat the grill or heat a griddle or heavy frying pan.

If you are grilling the polenta, brush the slices with a little oil and toast until crusted and golden, turning once, as if making toast. If you are using a griddle, heat it first, oil it lightly and lay on the slices as soon as the surface smokes a little. If you are frying, heat a finger's depth of olive oil and slip in the slices a few at a time – turn once but carefully to avoid detaching the crust from the soft interior.

> **Good with . . .** aubergine chutney or any dish of slow-cooked vegetables; a tomato-based sauce of your own making for dipping; a *ragù* of wild mushrooms; grilled small birds – these days quail rather than songbirds; any rich, juicy stew of fish, meat or game; Gorgonzola; *prosciutto* and *salami*.

Fruit, ices & desserts

The shores of the Mediterranean are particularly blessed with orchard fruits – oranges, all the other citrus fruits, peaches, nectarines, plums, cherries, pomegranates, quinces, apples – as well as field fruits such as grapes, melons, strawberries. Country dwellers traditionally made sure to plant fruiting trees along the highways, where the trees need little or no attention – providing the closest thing to food for free. Among rural communities there is an unspoken agreement that a single fruit can be plucked and eaten from any tree along the verge. Sometimes this agreement is formalized as in Spain, where the strip of land on either side of the *camino real* – the network of roads under royal protection that serve as a highway for transhumant herds – is considered common property, free for the cropping by man and beast. For those walking to market or making their way to the fields, there is always something delicious to nibble along the way.

A by-product of this profligacy is a thriving population of bees. The blossom that appears in the early spring provides honey-makers with a source of nectar at a time when little else is available. Mediterranean bee-keepers often move their hives from one place to another, progressing up the mountain slopes as new sources become available. Until the advent of cheap, manufactured beet-sugar, a nineteenth-century innovation, honey was the main sweetener.

Among the profusion of fruits available, grapes, figs, apricots, cherries and mulberries are particularly suitable for drying. In the eastern areas, unripe fruit is made into spoon-sweets, very sticky, syrupy preserves that can be stirred into a glass of water, well iced, to make a sherbet. Apricots in paricular are preserved as fruit-leathers, the pulp spread in a thin layer to dry then rolled like a miniature carpet. Throughout the year, as the different fruits ripen, orchard owners pile up their crop by the roadside in multi-coloured pyramids for sale to passing motorists – often alongside jars of the honey made from the blossom. Even in the depths of winter the Mediterranean fruit basket is never empty. Fruit is always offered at the end of a Mediterranean meal, varied, in the early spring, by sweet-flavoured young vegetables – peas or fava beans – dumped on the table to be podded by the consumer.

Cakes, pastries, biscuits and ices are traditionally eaten on their own as a snack, a little treat. They're offered as a dessert only on special occasions, when they're usually ordered from an outside source, commercial or private, whose expertise is admired and valued. Custards and sweet fritters, children's treats, are the exception.

About lemons

The lemon tree bears fruit and flowers throughout the seasons, carrying its scented blossoms on the same branch as the ripe fruit. Left on the tree, the fruit can be harvested more or less at will. One of the essential flavours of the Mediterranean, the lemon is equally at home in dishes both sweet and savoury; it is valuable as an anti-scorbutic for sailors on long sea voyages, to the house-wife on shore, and is a source of vitamin C in winter.

In sweet dishes – cakes, puddings and creams – the lemon adds a welcome touch of bitterness to recipes that might otherwise be bland. The juice is used in a *ceviche*: left for a few hours to soak in lemon juice, raw fish will turn opaque and effectively cook. In Spain, the whole fruit, roughly chopped, is used to perfume the brine for home-pickled olives. In Greece, chunks of lemon are added to oven-baked meats to roast in the hot oil, and lemon juice is one of two diagnostic ingredients in *avgolémono* – a mixture of olive oil and lemon used to sauce everything from salads to grilled fish, even more fragrant if you include the finely grated zest.

When choosing your lemons, pick firm fruit with a thin skin. Before squeezing, bring to room temperature or warmer, and give them a good firm roll to loosen the juice. In recipes that call for the zest, look for organically grown lemons whose skins have not been treated with a wax-and-ammonia coating. Those that have been so treated should be given a good scrub under hot water to get rid of as much of the coating as possible. It will do you no harm, but the less you eat of it the better. The practice of waxing the skin (very common these days) is not entirely cosmetic: citrus oil is volatile, and a holdful of citrus fruit rattling around in a storm is perfectly capable of spontaneous combustion. I well remember, some twenty years ago when I lived in the hills above the Strait of Gibraltar with a fine view of the busy shipping lanes, a citrus boat that exploded in a mighty shower of burning oil. Months later the debris was still being washed up on the beach.

Membrillo

Spanish quince paste

Look for the golden, downy-skinned quince – rather like a large furry apple – in Middle Eastern stores. This is the apple supposed to have been offered by Eve to Adam, the fruit that landed Paris in trouble when he was called upon to judge the beauty of the goddesses of Mount Olympus: small wonder that quince paste is de rigueur at Mediterranean wedding feasts. Once you've made the basic paste, this is the simplest and easiest of desserts. You can do the same thing with plums or apricots, dried or fresh.

Makes about 1.5kg / 3lb paste

2.5kg / 5lb ripe quinces
7cm / 3in length vanilla pod or 2–3 drops vanilla extract
about 2kg / 4lb sugar

Peel, quarter and core the quinces and tie the peelings and cores in a clean piece of muslin. Put the fruit and the bag of debris into a preserving pan with enough cold water to cover. Add the vanilla, bring to the boil, turn down the heat and simmer gently for 20–30 minutes, until the fruit is perfectly soft.

Remove the bag of peelings and discard, lift out the solids with a draining spoon, and match their weight with the same weight of sugar. Return the fruit to the preserving pan with the sugar. Stir all well together over a gentle heat until the sugar crystals are completely dissolved, and continue to stir over a low heat until you have a thick, smooth paste: do this carefully – the pulp should not be overheated or it will caramelize. If you prefer, you can spread it in a baking tin and leave it in a very low oven overnight: the important thing is that the cooking should be gentle.

Spread the paste on a large china plate or a roasting tin lined with grease-proof paper – it should be no deeper than a finger's width. Leave in a warm place – on a shelf above the cooker or in the airing cupboard – for 5–6 days to dry out. Cut into squares, wrap in waxed paper and store in an airtight tin until needed.

> Good with . . . thin slices of manchego or any distinguished cheese; gorgeous with Cabrales, a pungent blue-veined cheese from northern Spain.

Incir tatlisi

Turkish stuffed figs with bayleaves in rosewater syrup

Dried figs are often sold mixed with bayleaves in Turkish and Greek markets – the spiciness of the bay balances the caramel richness of the figs. These nut-stuffed figs are delicious with fresh white cheese or thick strained sheep's-milk yoghurt – a little acidity cuts the sweetness. Rosewater can be found in Middle Eastern groceries, and in the deli section of some supermarkets.

Serves 4

250g / 8oz dried figs (ready-soaked is convenient – but you'll need 500g / 1lb)
2 tablespoons freshly shelled walnuts, roughly chopped
2 tablespoons freshly shelled almonds, roughly chopped

For the syrup
150ml / ¼ pint rosewater
2 tablespoons honey or sugar
finely grated zest of 1 orange or lemon
2–3 bayleaves

If the figs are not ready-soaked put them in a bowl and pour in enough boiling water to cover. Leave to soak and swell for at least 6 hours. Drain the figs, reserving the water. If the figs are ready-soaked you'll need 300ml/½ pint tea.

Bring the reserved liquid (or the tea) to the boil with the rosewater, honey or sugar, citrus zest and bayleaves and simmer for 10–15 minutes.

Preheat the oven to 180°C/350°F/gas 4.

Meanwhile make a small slit in the base (the non-stalk end) of each fig, and stuff the interior firmly with the chopped nuts. Arrange the figs in an oven-proof dish, stalks upwards. Strain the hot syrup over the fruit. Transfer to the oven and bake for 20–30 minutes, until the figs are plump and the syrup is dark and silky.

> Good with . . . saffron ice-cream (page 301).

Coajada con miel y nueces
Spanish junket with honey and walnuts

Junket is the first stage of the cheese-making process, the soft curds that form when fresh milk is 'turned' with rennet, a substance found in the digestive juices of any ruminant – cattle, sheep, goats. In its most primitive form, the renneting agent is simply a nugget of dried milk from the stomach of a new-born kid, calf or lamb, crumbled directly into the warm milkings. Fresh milk can also be turned – in essence, a process of digestion – with vegetable rennet, a substance found in a wide variety of plants, notably the young buds of thistles (including artichokes and cardoons), the sap from the fig tree, and, oddest of all, an infusion of the leaves and roots of members of the fly-trap family – insectivorous plants with glaucous leaves. So much for the vegetarian option. For a creamier junket replace a quarter of the milk with single cream.

Serves 4

600ml / 1 pint full-cream milk
1 teaspoon rennet

To finish
a little grated nutmeg or ground cinnamon
runny honey
**freshly shelled walnuts (in season use green or 'wet' fresh walnuts – these will need to
    be skinned)**

Warm the milk to finger temperature to reproduce the natural heat of the milk when fresh from the cow. Stir in the rennet, pour into little earthenware pots or individual ramekins and leave to set at room temperature – this will take at least a couple of hours.

To serve, sprinkle with a little nutmeg or cinnamon. Hand the honey and walnuts separately for people to add their own.

> Good with . . . slices of Valencian madeira cake (page 284); any crisp, nutty biscuits; meringues.

Skorupaça sa jagodama
Bosnian clotted cream with wild strawberries

An unusual little mezze of thick yellow cream flavoured, during their short season, with a handful of fragrant wild strawberries. Buffalo milk was the source of the cream in the days when that patient animal was the usual beast of burden. The mezze-habit was introduced by the Turks during the time of the Ottoman empire – the product of a leisurely lifestyle supported by the labours of others, an ideal to which their subject nations aspired when the colonial yoke was lifted. Among the ladies, at least, the liquid refreshment was non-alcoholic: fresh fruit juice; a little cup of Turkish coffee; in summer, a cool glass of frozen sherbet – fruit syrup poured over crushed ice (see page 299). Among the men the choice was – then as now – raki, that fiery anis-flavoured spirit that has somehow managed to side-step Muslim prohibitions. A distinguished Arab academic described this daily disregard of the mullah's rule as much like adultery: forbidden, but people do it anyway.

Serves 4

250g / 8oz clotted cream
125g / 4oz wild strawberries

To serve
plum brandy – pure, clear and unsweetened, as they take it in the Balkans – or iced lemonade

Gently turn the cream with the strawberries. No sugar. Pile in a pretty dish and provide little spoons. Serve with tiny glasses of plum brandy or tall glasses of freshly made lemonade.

Good with . . . a dish of mixed dried fruits and nuts – raisins, figs, prunes, apricots, almonds, walnuts, pistachios; Turkish cream cheesecake (page 281) – or any of the sticky spoon-sweets popular throughout the region.

Peras en viño con canela

Catalan pears in red wine with cinnamon

Choose round rather than elongated varieties of pears – William rather than Conference. The fruit should be just ripe but not yet soft. If the pears are large, you'll need only one per person; if small, allow two each. Use a drinkable wine as the poaching liquid – a Rioja, perhaps, since the spicing is Spanish.

Serves 4

4–8 pears (depending on size), ripe but firm
1 bottle light red wine
175g / 6oz sugar
a small stick of cinnamon
6 peppercorns
1 bayleaf
1 lemon, juice and finely pared zest

To finish
100g / 4oz shelled walnuts, skinned if fresh

Peel the pears, leaving the stalks in place, and arrange stalks up in a heavy saucepan just large enough to fit them comfortably. Pour in the wine and the remaining ingredients (reserve the lemon zest), bring to the boil, turn down the heat, cover loosely and leave to poach very gently for 30–40 minutes, until perfectly tender.

Remove the pears with a slotted spoon and set them in the dish in which you plan to serve them. Turn the heat up and boil the liquid fiercely to reduce to half the volume and make a shiny syrup. Strain the syrup over the pears and finish with a sprinkle of walnuts and a tangle of lemon zest.

Good with . . . *leche frita* – the sweet cream croquettes of Catalonia (page 278).

Naranjas con miel y almendras
Andalusian oranges with honey and almonds

Not so much a recipe as a reflection of a way of life. This is the way the owner of an orange grove down the Guadacorte river on the way from the coast to the hill town of Ronda in the heart of Andalusia likes to prepare his fruit. Since he also has the good fortune of an almond tree and honey from his own bees, he doesn't need to go far for the ingredients.

Serves 4

4–8 juicy oranges, depending on size
4 tablespoons runny honey – orange blossom, for preference
1 tablespoon blanched almonds, slivered

Wipe or scrub the oranges, pare off the zest very thinly and shred into fine strips. Trim the white pith from the oranges and slice them into rings through the equator (catch all the juice). Arrange in concentric circles on a pretty dish.

Put the shredded zest into a small saucepan with the honey and the juice from the cut oranges, and simmer it gently on a low heat for 10–15 minutes to soften the peel a little. Meanwhile, toast the slivered almonds in a low oven until they are delicately browned – don't let them burn.

Pour the warm honey and the lightly crystallized zest over the sliced oranges, and top with a sprinkling of almonds. Perfection.

Good with . . . Valencian madeira cake (page 284), and any crisp nutty biscuit.

Beignets de pommes

Provençal apple fritters

The favourite French apple is Golden Delicious – Le Golden – pressed for juice, eaten raw, baked in tarts or, as here, dipped in a wine-batter and deep-fried – crisp on the outside, soft and juicy on the inside. For frying purposes, the Provençal housewife prefers a non-virgin – heat-pressed, refined, rectified – olive oil. Such an oil lacks the peppery sediment that can turn to indigestible bitterness when heated to frying temperature. The same batter can be used to coat elderflower or acacia blossom – spring flowers, light and delicate, the subtle perfume preserved by the application of high heat for the shortest possible time.

Serves 4–6

4 apples, Golden Delicious for preference
juice of ½ lemon
1 large egg
4 heaped tablespoons plain flour
1 teaspoon ground cinnamon
a pinch of salt
1 large glass white wine
1 tablespoon Cointreau or other orange liqueur
light olive oil (not virgin) for deep-frying
caster sugar for dusting

Peel and core the apples, cut into thickish slices and sprinkle with lemon juice to prevent browning.

Crack the egg into a small bowl and whisk to blend. Sieve in the flour and cinnamon with a tiny pinch of salt. Whisk to a smooth paste, pressing out any lumps. Whisk in the wine and Cointreau gradually until you have a thick cream. If you prefer, process the batter in the liquidizer until it is smooth.

Heat the oil. When it's smoking hot, dip the slices of apple into the batter and drop them into the oil a few at a time. Turn once. Fry until crisp and golden, turning once. Drain on kitchen paper and sprinkle with sugar. That's all.

Good with . . . a glass of *vin d'orange*; a nip of Cointreau – whatever is orange-scented and alcoholic; a salad of orange segments macerated in orange blossom water; strawberries sliced and soaked in *vin d'orange*; for an exquisite contrast of crisp and hot with soft and cool, the best and creamiest of vanilla ice-creams.

Crema catalana
Catalan caramelized custard

The Catalan crème brûlée is flavoured with a twist of lemon zest and a stick of cinnamon – subtle and delicious. Catalan cooks can't resist reaching for the spice jar. The usual cooking dish for a crema catalana *is a shallow earthenware ramekin.*

Serves 6–8

300ml / ½ pint single cream
300ml / ½ pint milk
1 small stick cinnamon
1 small strip lemon zest
2 tablespoons caster sugar
1 heaped teaspoon cornflour mixed with a little milk
6 egg yolks

To finish
4 tablespoons caster sugar

Bring the cream and milk to the boil in a heavy pan with the cinnamon and lemon zest, remove from the heat immediately and leave to infuse for 30 minutes or so. Remove the cinnamon and lemon rind, stir in the sugar, then whisk in the cornflour and egg yolks. Stir over a gentle heat until the custard thickens enough to coat the back of a wooden spoon – about 10 minutes. (If it scrambles, tip it in the liquidizer and give it a quick whizz with a little cold cream.) Pour into individual ramekins and allow to cool before transferring to the fridge for a few hours to set – overnight, if possible.

When you're ready to serve, sprinkle the surface of each ramekin with a thin, even layer of sugar, which should cover the custard completely. Dip your hand in cold water and sprinkle with a few drops – only enough to dampen slightly.

Now comes the problem of how to apply a heat high enough to melt the sugar and avoid re-boiling the custard. Catalan housewives can buy a purpose-made instrument – a searing-iron – for the task. Failing this (or that joy of the modern pastry-chef, a kitchen blowtorch) either heat a metal spatula on the gas burner and apply directly to the sugar, or pop the ramekins under a *very* hot grill until the sugar caramelizes. The topping should be crisp and crackable while the cream beneath remains cool and soft.

Good with . . . Andalusian oranges with honey and almonds (page 275).

Leche frita
Catalan cream fritters

A sweet version of the croqueta, *Spain's favourite* tapa, *this is a very thick custard,* crema catalana, *egged, breadcrumbed and fried.*

Serves 4

600ml / 1 pint milk
25g / 1oz butter
75g / 3oz flour
1 pinch ground nutmeg
2 tablespoons caster sugar
3 egg yolks
1 strip lemon zest

To finish
1 whole egg
2 tablespoons milk
breadcrumbs for coating (fresh or dried)
oil for frying
sugar and ground cinnamon for dusting

Put all the ingredients except the lemon zest into the liquidizer and process thoroughly. The butter will make the mix seem somewhat lumpy, but no matter – it'll melt down. Heat the mixture gently in a saucepan over a low heat. Keep whisking and stirring so that it doesn't stick. Just before it comes to the boil, add the lemon zest, turn down the heat and simmer until the mixture is thick and no longer tastes of raw flour. Remove the zest and pour the custard into a lightly oiled dish in a layer as thick as your thumb. Leave to cool and firm – best under clingfilm overnight in the fridge.

Fork the egg up with the milk on a plate. Spread the breadcrumbs on another plate. Cut the custard into bite-sized squares. Dip the squares in the egg-and-milk to coat them, then press gently all over in the breadcrumbs.

Heat 2 fingers' depth of oil in a heavy frying pan. When lightly hazed with blue, test with a cube of bread – it should sizzle and gild immediately. Carefully slip in the squares, a few at a time. Turn them once, taking care not to break the crust. Remove with a slotted spoon and drain on kitchen paper. Pile on a warm plate and sprinkle with cinnamon and sugar.

Good with . . . pears in red wine (page 274); a fresh fruit salad – melon with grapes, peaches with raspberries, strawberries with orange juice.

Palaçinke cici
Serbian jam pancakes baked with cream

Jam-stuffed pancakes are the feast-day treat throughout the Balkans. In this recipe – the name means 'pretty pancakes' – they are bathed in cream and baked in the oven until irresistibly brown and bubbling.

Makes 15–20 small pancakes

For the pancakes
100g / 4oz plain flour
a pinch of salt
2 eggs
300ml / ½ pint milk
2 tablespoons brandy or vodka

To finish
butter for frying (clarified is best – see page 16)
500g / 1lb plum jam (homemade, for preference)
300ml / ½ pint thick double cream
1–2 tablespoons caster sugar

Sift the flour and salt into a bowl. Stir in the eggs and then beat in the milk gradually until you have a thin cream – a job easily done with an electric hand beater. Leave the batter to rest for 20 minutes. When you are ready to make the pancakes, add the brandy, whisk or whizz up the batter again, and transfer to a jug.

Heat a small frying pan – whatever utensil you use to make an omelette. When the pan is good and hot drop in a small knob of butter (clarified butter will not splutter and burn) and wipe round with kitchen paper (keep the buttery paper to wipe the pan each time, and melt a little more butter only when you need it). Pour in a couple of tablespoonfuls of the batter and roll it round to allow a thin layer to stick to the pan. If you add too much, just pour the extra back into the jug. Cook over a medium heat until the pancake edges are lacy and curl away from the pan. Flip over and cook the other side. Repeat until all the batter is used up. As each pancake is done, tuck it inside a clean napkin, one on top of the other.

Preheat the oven to 180°C/350°F/gas 4.

Spread a spoonful of jam down the middle of each pancake, fold the ends over the short side and roll up into a little bolster. Tuck the pancake rolls into a baking dish in rows. Bathe the pancakes in the cream, cover the dish with foil (shiny side down) and bake for 20 minutes. Remove the foil and sprinkle with sugar for the last 5 minutes to allow the top to brown and bubble. Serve immediately.

Petits pots au chocolat

Provençal chocolate pots

Not a mousse nor yet a custard, but something in between. An old-fashioned dessert but delicious. The Provençaux flavour with orange, the Italians prefer strong black coffee, in Catalonia the chocolate would be infused with cinnamon. Whatever you prefer, the secret of success lies in the quality of the chocolate. Choose the best – the cocoa-solid content should declare itself as over 70 per cent, so expect a price to match. The usual strictures about raw eggs apply: live dangerously.

Serves 4–6

150g / 5oz best-quality dark chocolate
4 tablespoons orange juice, heated to just below boiling
4 eggs, separated
1 teaspoon finely grated orange zest
caster sugar to taste

Break the chocolate into small pieces in a bowl set over gently simmering water. Add the orange juice and stir until the chocolate has melted and is perfectly smooth. If, as a result of too high a heat, the chocolate should go grainy (the *chocolatier*'s word is 'seize' – an exact description of what happens), beat in a little warm clarified butter or vegetable oil until the chocolate is smooth again.

Remove the bowl from the heat and beat in the egg yolks one by one – they'll cook and thicken a little in the residual warmth. Allow to cool to finger-temperature while you whisk the egg whites until they are perfectly stiff.

Fold the egg whites and the orange zest into the chocolate, and taste to make sure it's sweet enough – if not, fold in a little caster sugar. Spoon into individual soufflé dishes or, if you have them, special purpose-made chocolate pots. Set in the fridge for a few hours to firm. Beautiful stuff.

Good with . . . lime-blossom tea or a steaming pot of freshly brewed coffee and a little glass of Cointreau or Drambuie – both orange-based liqueurs.

Pasta kaymakli
Turkish cream cheesecake

A feast-day dessert from Anatolia, where dairy products – mostly eaten in the form of yoghurt and fresh white cheese – are an important part of the diet. Kaymak is a very thick ripened cream originally made with buffalo milk. Cream cheese blended with single cream makes a good substitute. You can also make it with thick strained yoghurt.

Serves 6–8

100g / 4oz caster sugar
50g / 2oz softened butter
1 tablespoon flour
500g / 1lb fresh cream cheese (*kaymak*)
150ml / ¼ pint single cream
2 tablespoons runny honey
5 eggs, separated
grated zest of 1 lemon
1 tablespoon sultanas, soaked in a little tea or orange juice

To finish
1 teaspoon ground cinnamon
1 tablespoon caster sugar
1 tablespoon flaked almonds

Preheat the oven to 170°C/325°F/gas 3.

Beat the sugar with the butter until white and fluffy. Fold in the flour. Beat the cream cheese with the cream and whisk in the honey with the egg yolks. Combine the two mixtures until smooth. Whisk the egg whites until they are perfectly stiff – stop before they go grainy – and fold into the cream with a metal spoon until well blended. Fold in the lemon zest and soaked sultanas.

Butter and line with greaseproof paper a 20cm/8in cake tin – the un-moulding will be easier if the tin is hinged. Tip the mixture into the tin, smooth the surface and sprinkle with a light dusting of cinnamon, caster sugar and a scattering of flaked almonds. Bake for 1 hour. Switch off the oven and let the cake cool in the oven for another hour. Turn it out so that the top side remains uppermost. Now you know why you needed a hinged tin.

> **Good with . . .** in summer, crisp buttery biscuits; a salad of sliced oranges; a handful of fresh strawberries or pitted cherries. In winter, serve warm with a hot apricot or plum compote flavoured with cinnamon.

Torta di polenta all'arancia
Italian polenta and orange cake

A sunny golden cake in which a proportion of the wheat-flour is replaced by cornmeal and the butter by nut or olive oil. Rough-ground polenta gives the crumb a nutty sweetness balanced by the acidity of the fruit. Marmalade – Seville – oranges are perfect. If the oranges are sweet, use a lemon and an orange – you really do need the acidity.

Serves 8

175g / 6oz self-raising flour
1 teaspoon baking powder
50g / 2oz coarse-ground cornmeal (polenta)
225g / 8 oz caster sugar
225ml / 8fl oz walnut oil (or mild olive oil)
4 medium eggs
2 Seville oranges, finely grated zest and juice

Preheat the oven to 170°C/325°F/gas 3. Lightly grease a cake tin about 18cm/7in square – a roasting tin is fine – and line the base with greaseproof or butter-paper. Brush the paper and the sides of the tin with a little of the orange juice.

Sift the flour into a bowl with the baking powder and add the polenta and sugar, tossing lightly to mix. Make a dip in the middle and pour in the oil. Drop in the eggs and, using your hand at first, then a wooden spoon, mix thoroughly until completely free of lumps. Add the orange zest and juice to give a mixture that drops softly from the spoon – you may need a little water if the mixture's too stiff.

Drop the mixture in the tin, smoothing into the corners and flattening the top. Bake for about 1¼ hours (check after an hour), until well risen, shrunk from the sides and firm to the finger. Let it rest for 10 minutes before gently transferring to a wire tray. Peel off the paper when cool.

> **Good with . . .** a cinnamon-spiced compote of winter fruits; pears in wine (page 274); Sicilian lemon ice-cream (page 300).

Reine de Saba

French almond and chocolate sponge

No cookbook is complete without its chocolate cake, and this – light, buttery, moist – is flavoured with rum imported from the sugar plantations of French West Indies. France's former colonies are actually an overseas département with the right to send representatives to parliament in Paris.

Serves 6–8

225g / 7oz dark chocolate (at least 70% cocoa solids)
1 tablespoon rum
150g / 5oz butter
150g / 5oz caster sugar
5 eggs, separated
100g / 3½oz ground almonds

To finish
butter and flour for greasing and dusting

Preheat the oven to 180°C/350°F/gas 4. Butter an 18cm/7in square cake tin and dust with flour – if you are using a round tin choose a 20cm/8in diameter. The cake will be easier to remove if you line the base with baking parchment.

Melt the chocolate with the rum, the butter and sugar in a bowl set over a pan of simmering water. Remove from the heat and allow to cool a little. Meanwhile, whisk the egg whites until they hold soft peaks. Beat the egg yolks into the still-runny chocolate. Mix in the ground almonds, then fold in the whisked whites, a little at first so that the mixture lightens and can accept the rest.

Spread the mixture in the prepared tin. Bake for 40–50 minutes, until the cake is well risen and firm to the finger. Leave to cool before removing from the tin. If it cracks on top, that's part of the charm – fix it with a sprinkle of icing sugar. Cut into bite-sized squares.

Good with . . . fresh strawberries – the little wild ones that arrive early in the season; sliced oranges; vanilla ice-cream. Accompany with a chilled glass of one of the delicate, flowery muscats they make in Provence.

Bizcocho valenciana

Valencian madeira cake

A madeira cake, very simple, flavoured with orange zest and cinnamon, made with olive oil rather than butter – perfect for anyone worried about cholesterol. An excellent cut-and-come-again cake which keeps fresh in a tin for weeks.

Choose a rectified olive oil – all those not designated virgin or extra-virgin will have been heat treated and therefore good for cake-making. For baking, virgin oils must be heated to rid them of the rawness and strength of flavour so desirable in savoury dishes.

Serves 6–8

175g / 6oz plain flour
2 level teaspoons baking powder
1 teaspoon ground cinnamon
½ teaspoon salt
3 eggs, forked up to blend
200ml / 7fl oz light olive oil
175g / 6oz sugar
1 small orange, juice and finely grated zest

Preheat the oven to 180°C/350°F/gas 4. Oil a 1kg/2lb loaf tin.

Sieve together the dry ingredients, then either work in the rest of the ingredients with a wooden spoon or tip everything into the food processor. Beat until smooth and free of lumps. The mixture should be soft enough to drop from the spoon.

Drop the mixture into the prepared tin, spreading it into the corners. Bake for 45–50 minutes, until well risen, firm to the finger and shrunk from the sides. Leave to rest and loosen for 10 minutes. Transfer to a wire rack to cool.

Perfect with . . . fresh strawberries dressed with orange juice, as the Valencians like them, or sliced peaches and a dessert wine. Delicious with a *crema catalana* (page 277).

Torta de almendras
Valencian almond sponge

This is an easy recipe – all the main ingredients weigh the same – and a favourite in my own household. It appears as a birthday cake, as a special dessert at dinner parties – any occasion where something delicious is required. It looks like a modest brown pancake but tastes sublime.

Serves 6–8

4 medium eggs
250g / 8oz caster sugar
250g / 8oz ground almonds
finely grated zest of 1 lemon

For the syrup
1 tablespoon honey
1 small glass sweet wine – *vin d'orange* **or Marsala**
juice of 1 lemon

Preheat the oven to 190°C/375°F/gas 5. Grease and line an 18cm/7in cake tin.

In a large bowl, whisk the eggs – yolks and whites – until frothy. Sprinkle in the sugar gradually and continue to beat until the mixture is white and stiff enough for the whisk to leave a trail. This takes twice as long as you expect and is easiest done with an electric beater. With a metal spoon gently fold in the ground almonds and lemon zest. Don't be afraid to mix it thoroughly, a process known for obvious reasons as 'tiring the mixture', albeit taking care not to beat out the air.

Spread the mixture in the prepared cake tin and bake for 45–50 minutes, until well risen and shrunk from the sides. Allow to cool a little before tipping it out onto a plate.

Meanwhile, warm the honey with the wine and lemon juice in a small pan, stirring to blend. As soon as it bubbles, pour it over the warm cake.

Good with . . . slivers of melon or pear; fresh ripe figs.

Msoureki me melo

Greek honey cake

An Easter speciality of the nuns of the sister convent to the monastery of St John on the Greek island of Patmos, where Holy Week is celebrated with unmatched pomp and deep devotion. The ladies are always the ones who make the treats and sweets.

Serves 8–10

350g / 12oz plain flour
350g / 12oz fine semolina
2 teaspoons baking powder
1 teaspoon ground cinnamon
6 eggs, separated
350ml / 12fl oz almond oil
175g / 6oz honey
3 oranges, juice and grated zest
50g / 2oz slivered almonds

For the syrup
175g / 6oz honey
1 glass water
optional: 1 tablespoon orange-flower water, 1–2 curls finely pared orange zest, 1 small stick cinnamon

Preheat the oven to 180°C/350°F/gas 4. Grease and line a baking tin about 18cm/7in square.

Sift the flour with the semolina, the baking powder and the cinnamon. Beat the egg yolks in a mixing bowl with the oil and honey until light and fluffy, and fold into this the flour mixture alternately with the orange juice until you have a soft mixture that drops easily. Stir in the orange zest.

Whisk the egg whites until stiff and fold them in gently. Spread the mixture into the prepared cake tin, smooth the top and sprinkle with the slivered almonds. Bake for about 1 hour, until the cake has shrunk from the sides and is prettily browned and firm to the finger. Check after 45 minutes and cover with foil if the top looks like burning. Allow to rest for 10 minutes before turning out onto a wire rack.

Meanwhile, make the syrup. In a small pan, bring the honey to the boil with a glass of water, optional orange-flower water, orange zest and cinnamon. Turn down the heat and simmer for 3–4 minutes, until the honey has melted and the scent of cinnamon fills the air. Remove from the heat and leave to infuse. Strain over the cake before it cools. Cut into squares.

> **Good with . . .** a salad of sliced oranges; thick sheep's milk yoghurt.

Tortell de limon

Catalan lemon tart

The Catalans love creamy desserts. This is a lemon tart to die for.

Serves 6–8

For the pastry
250g / 8oz softened butter
100g / 4oz caster sugar
1 egg
350g / 12oz plain flour

For the filling
9 eggs
400g / 13oz caster sugar
300ml / ½ pint lemon juice (about 6 lemons)
1 teaspoon finely grated lemon zest
300ml / ½ pint double cream
icing sugar to finish

First make the pastry: in a warm bowl beat the butter and sugar with a wooden spoon until light and fluffy. Beat in the egg. Sieve in the flour and knead until well combined, but don't overwork or the pastry will become too elastic. Wrap in clingfilm and refrigerate for an hour.

Preheat the oven to 180°C/350°F/gas 4 and butter a 25cm/10in tart tin (preferably one with a removable base). Roll the pastry to fit the tin, trimming with a sharp knife – the scraps can be used to patch up any cracks or holes, using a damp finger. Line with foil, shiny side down, and scatter with a few dried beans or grains of rice to weight it down – not too many. Leave to rest in the fridge for another 15 minutes. Bake the tart case for about 20 minutes, until the pastry looks sandy, removing the foil and beans for the final 5 minutes. Take the tart case out of the oven and allow it to cool a little. Reduce the oven temperature to 150°C/300°F/gas 2.

Meanwhile, prepare the filling. Fork all the ingredients together to mix thoroughly, taking care not to whip in any air. Pour the filling into the pastry case. Don't let it overflow – if there's too much either you've whisked in air or the eggs were unusually large. Bake the tart for 1 hour, until just set but still a little soft and jelly-like. To check, tap the tin and if the centre is still runny return it to the oven for another 5–10 minutes. Allow to cool, then set it in the fridge for an hour. Remove the base and slip the tart gently out onto a plate. Dust with a thick layer of icing sugar and slip it under a very hot grill for a few moments, or use a sugar-iron, until the surface browns and caramelizes.

Tarte d'abricots à la crème
Provençal apricot tart

The pâtisseries of the Midi produce a succession of fruit tarts in their right season — a self-imposed discipline that suits the customers as well as the cooks. As the year turns, the autumn delivers apples and pears, winter brings dried fruits and nuts, summer berries are followed by peaches and apricots, all cooked in a creamy custard set in a crisp case of buttery pastry.

Serves 6–8

For the pastry
250g / 8oz flour
a pinch of salt
175g / 6oz cold unsalted butter
50g / 2oz caster sugar
2 egg yolks

For the custard
150ml / ¼ pint double cream
2 eggs
2 tablespoons caster sugar

To finish
500g / 1lb apricots, stoned and halved
about 4 tablespoons apricot jam

First make the pastry. Sieve the flour with the salt. Cut in the butter with a knife until it looks like fine breadcrumbs — or you can freeze the butter and grate it directly into the flour. Mix in the sugar and work in the egg yolks with the tips of your fingers until the pastry forms a soft ball — you may need extra flour or a little cold water. Leave to rest in a cool place for 30 minutes.

Preheat the oven to 180°C/350°F/gas 4.

Roll out the pastry and line a 20cm/8in tart tin. Line this with foil weighted with a spoonful of beans or dry rice (don't overload or the pastry won't take the heat). Bake 'blind' for 20 minutes or so, until the pastry looks sandy and white. Remove the foil gently and leave the case to cool.

Whisk the cream with the eggs and sugar. Lay the apricots on the tart base, cut side down, in concentric rings. Trickle the custard into the gaps. Return the tart to the oven and bake for another 30–40 minutes, until the custard is set and the pastry is crisp and golden. Let the tart cool a little before you glaze it with melted jam — diluted if thick, sieved if lumpy. Serve warm — always the best temperature for a tart.

Baklava
Turkish nut pastry

Crisp, buttery layers of filo pastry sandwiched together with a rough paste of crushed nuts then drenched in syrup – what could be more delicious? The dish appears on the menu at the Ottoman Emperor's court no earlier than the end of the fifteenth century, and has been making up for lost time ever since.

Makes at least a couple of dozen slices

1 packet (about 300g / 10oz) filo pastry
350g / 12oz shelled nuts (almonds, pistachios, walnuts), roughly chopped
250g / 8oz clarified butter (see page 16), melted

To finish
250g / 8oz sugar
1 tablespoon rosewater
200ml / 7fl oz water

Preheat the oven to 200°C/400°F/gas 6.

Unroll the filo and cover with clingfilm – when working with filo keep the sheets you are not working with covered, or they quickly become brittle and unusable.

Brush a 30cm x 20cm/12in x 8in baking tray with butter. Line with two sheets of filo, lightly dropping one on the other – air between the layers is very important. Using a pastry brush or the tips of your fingers sprinkle with melted butter. Lay on another two sheets and sprinkle on more butter. Continue until you have eight sheets in place. Scatter with all of the nuts in a thick layer. Continue with more filo sheets, sprinkling with butter between each two layers, until you have added another eight sheets. Using a sharp knife, mark into bite-sized diamonds or squares, then brush with the last of the butter. Sprinkle with water from the tips of your fingers – this helps the sheets to lie flat.

Bake for 40–45 minutes, until the pastry is brown and crisp.

Meanwhile, make the syrup: melt the sugar with the rosewater and water. Drench the hot pastry with the syrup, paying particular attention to the cuts. Return the tray to the oven for 5 minutes to dry and crisp the top layers.

Good with . . . little cups of strong black Turkish coffee flavoured with cardamom. Always accompany with a glass of iced water: sweet things – none sweeter than Middle Eastern sweetmeats – make people thirsty.

Bozîç kolaç
Serbian poppyseed strudels

Nut or seed-stuffed strudels made with yeast-raised pastry are a Christmas treat throughout the Balkans. The dough is a little tricky, but fun – especially if you have children to lend a hand with the rolling.

Makes 4 strudels to serve at least a dozen

For the filling
100g / 4oz sugar
150ml / ¼ pint water
2 tablespoons honey
50g / 2oz butter
250g / 8oz poppyseeds, pounded
   (use a grinder or pestle and mortar)
1 teaspoon ground cinnamon
½ teaspoon ground cloves

For the dough
500g / 1 lb strong bread flour
125g / 4oz caster sugar
25g / 1oz fresh yeast, crumbled
   (or 12g / ½oz dried)
250g / 8oz butter, softened
about 150ml / ¼ pint warm milk
1 egg, separated
flour for dusting

First make the filling: put the sugar in a pan with the water and bring gently to the boil, stirring until the sugar dissolves. Add the honey and all the remaining ingredients. Stir over the heat until well blended, then leave to infuse on the side of the stove.

To make the dough, either put all the ingredients except the egg white in the food processor and knead everything with the dough-hook into a softish dough, or sieve the flour, add the sugar, yeast (fresh or dried) and rub in the butter with the tips of your fingers until the mixture looks like fine bread-crumbs, then work in the milk and egg yolk until you have a soft, elastic dough. Cut into four, knead each piece into a ball on a flour-dusted surface, pat flat and roll out into a rectangular sheet as thin as a pound coin.

Spread the warm filling over each sheet and roll up like a swiss roll, tucking in the ends. Lay on a greased baking sheet, leaving plenty of space between. Set them in a cool place – the bottom of the fridge – for an hour or longer, even overnight if convenient.

Preheat the oven to 190°C/375°F/gas 5.

Prick the tops and paint with the reserved egg white. Bake for 35–45 minutes, until the strudels are well risen and prettily browned. Transfer to a rack to cool. Store in an airtight tin – they are best after a few days. Serve cut into thin slices, with strong, sweet Turkish coffee.

Biskota me arra
Albanian walnut biscuits

The walnut tree, for those who wish to pin it down geographically, is a native of south-east Europe, which makes the nuts a storecupboard staple in much of Mediterranean Europe and throughout the Balkans. In areas too high or too cold for the olive tree – such as the mountains of Albania – walnut oil was the poor-man's substitute for olive oil, used for frying and pastry-making as well as for dressing salads. The residual paste went into tart-fillings, biscuits and cakes, and the shells were used for fuel. All very frugal – but that's the way of the walnut.

Serves 6–8

250g / 8oz plain flour
1 teaspoon ground cinnamon
100g / 4oz freshly ground walnuts
100g / 4oz caster sugar
4 tablespoons walnut oil
1 large egg, lightly forked
halved walnuts for decoration

In a roomy bowl, sieve the flour and the cinnamon into the ground nuts and sugar. Mix well. Work in the walnut oil and enough egg to make a ball of softish dough – you may need a little water. Cover with a clean cloth and leave to rest for an hour in the fridge to firm up.

Preheat the oven to 220°C/425°F/gas 7.

Roll out the dough to the thickness of a pound coin. Cut out neat little rounds with a biscuit cutter and transfer to a well greased baking sheet. Press a half walnut into each biscuit.

Bake for 15–20 minutes, until the biscuits are just changing colour. As with shortbread, the colour shouldn't be too dark. Transfer gently to a wire tray. The biscuits crisp as they cool; if they remain soft, bake them a little longer. Store in an airtight tin.

> Good with ... Turkish orange sherbet (page 299); Turkish coffee; rosewater parfait (page 298); any of the ice-creams or sorbets; oranges with honey (page 275); stuffed figs (page 271); Catalan pears in red wine (page 274).

Craqueti
Provençal almond biscuits

Crisp little biscuits, much like the Italian dipping biscuits, to be taken with coffee or an infusion of lime-blossom or camomile. Most delicious with a glass of a flowery dessert wine: all the great wine-making nations produce these delicious wines, and they remain somewhat neglected except in their own home territory, where they are customarily taken as an aperitif.

Serves 6–8

250g / 8oz whole unpeeled almonds
250g / 8oz plain flour
250g / 8oz caster sugar
½ teaspoon grated nutmeg
½ teaspoon salt
3 medium eggs
flour for dusting
egg and milk for gilding

Preheat the oven to 180°C/350°F/gas 4.

Pick over and rinse the almonds, but don't skin them. Sieve the flour into a bowl and mix in the sugar, nutmeg and salt. Whisk the eggs lightly.

Work all the ingredients together thoroughly, adding just enough egg to make a soft dough – add a little milk if necessary. Divide the dough into two pieces. On a well floured table form each piece into a thin roll about 20cm/8in long.

Transfer the rolls to a well greased baking tray. Brush the tops with a little egg and milk and bake for 10–12 minutes, until golden. Remove from the oven and quickly cut each roll into slices as thick as your little finger. Arrange the slices on a baking rack and leave to cool. If they don't crisp perfectly, slip them back into the oven for another 5 minutes or so. Allow to cool completely before storing in an airtight tin.

> **Good with** . . . lavender ice-cream (page 302) – what could be more exquisite?

Biscotti della Befana
Italian Epiphany marzipan biscuits

The housewives of the Garfagna valley above Lucca bake these crisp little cookies for 6 January, the Feast of the Epiphany, the day when Italian children traditionally receive their presents from la befana, the Epiphany witch. On the eve of the feast, children go around disguised and masked, dressed as witches, wolves, devils and other popular monsters, and knock on doors to ask for a treat – these little biscuits or some other sweet thing. The biscuits are not of any particular design, although stars, hearts and fishes are the most usual. My instructress, the priest's elderly housekeeper – herself a grandmother – used the special cutters her mother gave her to press out the shapes, and a small pair of spiked tongs for roughing up the surface before baking.

Makes 30–40 biscuits

For the dough
500g / 1lb self-raising flour
350g / 12oz caster sugar
3 eggs, lightly forked
75g / 3oz softened unsalted butter

For the marzipan topping
100g / 4oz ground almonds
1 egg white, lightly beaten
100g / 4oz sugar
2–3 drops pink or red food colouring

Preheat the oven to 180°C/350°F/gas 4.

Tip the flour and sugar onto the table, make a well in the middle and drop in the eggs and softened butter. Work together until you have a firm dough. Roll out or pat the dough to the thickness of a pound coin and cut into festive shapes with biscuit cutters. Transfer to a baking tray lined with baking parchment. Pat the trimmings together lightly and re-roll so that you can cut out as many biscuits as possible.

Make the marzipan: in a bowl work all the ingredients together to form a softish pink paste (red is the colour of celebration all round the Mediterranean). Top each biscuit with a small disk of marzipan. Snip the surface of the paste with scissors to form little sharp peaks.

Bake for 15–20 minutes, until golden. Transfer carefully to a baking rack. At this point they're still soft – they crisp as they cool.

Polvorones
Spanish almond biscuits

Literally translated, 'dusty biscuits'. Very soft and delicate, wrapped up in scraps of tissue paper for storage, these are the treat all good Spanish children hope to find in their shoes when the Three Kings bring them their presents on Twelfth night. The fat used is pure white lard, mild and sweet and made by melting pork fat very slowly in the lowest possible oven with a little water to keep it from any possibility of browning; commercially prepared stuff won't do. This is a beaten dough – rather easier and quicker than the more familiar rubbing-in method.

Makes about 30 biscuits

250g / 8oz plain flour
100g / 4oz blanched almonds, roughly ground
1 teaspoon ground cinnamon
1 teaspoon ground cardamom
250g / 8oz fresh white lard, softened (or unsalted butter)
100g / 4oz icing sugar
1–2 tablespoons cold water

Sieve the flour into the ground almonds in a mixing bowl and stir in the spices. In a separate bowl, beat the lard with the icing sugar until they are light and fluffy – this is easiest in a food processor. Work this mixture into the flour and ground almonds until you have a soft ball of dough. Cover with a clean cloth and leave to rest for an hour in a cool place to firm up.

Preheat the oven to 180°C/350°F/gas 4.

Roll the dough out to twice the thickness of a pound coin. Cut out neat little rounds with a biscuit cutter and transfer to a well greased baking sheet. Press together the scraps with the tips of your fingers and cut out as many more rounds as you can.

Bake for 15–20 minutes, until pale gold. Transfer gently to a wire rack and leave to cool. The end result is like very soft, crumbly shortbread. Wrap in scraps of tissue paper before storing in an airtight tin.

Frittelle di carnevale

Italian carnival biscuits

Every pasticceria *throughout Italy sets out great trays of these airy little fritters in the run-up to Lent. The shapes change from town to town, but the basic biscuit-paste – an enriched pasta-dough – changes little. The simplest shape looks like rags, as if the trimmings from a batch of fresh pasta had been dropped in hot oil. Other popular shapes are knots, slashed squares, folded four-cornered stars. The only rule is that the dough must be very thinly rolled and the shape must not interfere with the lightness of the finished fritter.*

Serves 4–6

250g / 8oz strong bread flour (Italian double-zero, for preference)
½ teaspoon baking powder
½ teaspoon salt
2 egg yolks
1 tablespoon soft butter or mascarpone
small glass grappa or any white spirit
semolina for dusting
oil for deep-frying
icing sugar and ground cinnamon to finish

Sieve the flour, baking powder and salt into a roomy bowl. Make a well in the centre and drop in the egg yolks. Work together in a circular movement with your hand, adding the butter or mascarpone and enough grappa to make a softish dough. Knead thoroughly for 10 minutes to develop and stretch the flour. Form into a ball, skim lightly with oil, cover and leave to rest for an hour.

Roll out the dough on a floured surface (rural housewives use a new broomhandle), until the sheet is transparent. Sprinkle lightly with semolina and set to rest again for another 15 minutes. Cut into any shape you fancy.

Heat a pan of oil until a faint blue haze rises (test with a cube of bread – it should gild and crisp in less than a minute). Slip in the fritters, a few at a time, and fry until they are puffed and golden. Drain on kitchen paper and dust with icing sugar and cinnamon while still warm.

Good with . . . lightly sweetened mascarpone for dipping; *vin santo.*

Nonnettes aux amandes

Provençal almond macaroons

Versions of these deliciously chewy little biscuits are found throughout the Mediterranean. Nothing to them, really – hence the name. It was the Arabs who taught the Europeans the art of the sweetmeat, for which the northerners have much to thank the southerners. Anything made with almonds and sugar is almost certainly of Arab origin, including marzipan, nougat and all the other little nut-based treats that give such pleasure at weddings and other celebrations.

Makes about 24

250g / 8oz caster sugar
125g / 4oz ground almonds
2 egg whites
3–4 drops almond essence
2–4 sheets rice paper

To finish
flaked almonds

Preheat the oven to 180°C/350°F/gas 4. Grease two baking sheets and line with the rice paper.

Mix the sugar, ground almonds, egg whites and almond essence – there's no need to beat the whites first – to make a thickish paste (you may need a little water or a little less egg white).

Using a teaspoon and a wet finger, form small balls about the size of a quail's egg. Space the balls out on the rice paper and flatten slightly. Top each ball with a flaked almond.

Bake the macaroons for 10–15 minutes, until lightly browned. Cool on a wire rack and tear off excess rice paper.

Good with . . . any ice-cream or other creamy dessert, or serve as they are, with a glass of dessert wine or *vin d'orange* or any fruit-based *eau de vie* – the Provençaux love their stickies, as do I.

Sorbetto di fragoli

Neapolitan strawberry sorbet

The most exquisite of sorbets – simple but perfect, with the fragrance of the sunny berries intensified by the sharpness of the lemon. The pleasure of freezing fresh fruit juices for summer refreshment was known in China before it reached the Arab world, arriving in Sicily during the eleventh century. The first sorbetti were milky drinks sweetened with honey much like the Spanish horchata – the Moors in Spain used packed snow from the mountains of Granada to ice their summer refreshments. The Neapolitans took the whole sybaritic business a stage further, using not honey but sugar syrup to sweeten their sorbets and sugar to stir into their imported coffee. Harbourmasters' records show that in a single year, 1625 – at a time when the now-universal sweetener was still barely known in the rest of Europe – the city of Naples imported an astonishing 1,500 tons of crystallized cone-sugar from their Arab trading partners on the southern shores of the Mediterranean.

Serves 4–6

500g / 1lb strawberries, rinsed and hulled
juice of 1 lemon
1 small glass cold water
100g / 4oz caster sugar
1 egg white

Combine the berries with the lemon juice, a glass of cold water and the sugar and leave the mixture to form its own syrup for half an hour or so. Tip everything into the liquidizer and process to a purée. Freeze until just crystallized, then liquidize with the egg white and freeze again.

Serve as the Neapolitans did – still do, on special occasions – as a palate-cleanser and appetite-reviver between one savoury dish and another. A city that has endured more than its fair share of famine, Naples understands only too well the pleasure of feast.

> **Good with . . .** tiny cups of very hot, very black, very sweet espresso coffee.

Dondurma laban gül

Turkish rosewater parfait

Ices made with yoghurt are simple to prepare since they do not need to be beaten during the freezing process: the crystals that form are tiny and the texture remains naturally smooth. Orange-flower water or any fruit syrup can be used instead of the rosewater to flavour.

Serves 4–6

1 large tub (500g / 1lb) natural yoghurt
6 tablespoons caster sugar
2 tablespoons rosewater (depending on strength)
2–3 drops red food colouring

Whisk the yoghurt in a bowl until smooth, then stir in the sugar and rose-water, adding just enough food colouring to turn the mixture the palest rose pink. Transfer to a freezing container and freeze hard. Or tip into ice-cube trays, slip a cocktail stick into the centre of each cube and freeze for at least 3 hours, until perfectly firm. Pop the cubes out of the trays and freeze in bags. Exquisitely refreshing.

Good with . . . *baklava* (page 289) and any nut pastry; fresh strawberries.

Serbeti portakal

Turkish orange sherbet

The perambulating sherbet-seller, dressed to the nines to appeal to the ladies, has long been a feature of Middle Eastern street-life. These days you'll be more likely to find him in a corner of the souk, presiding over a mechanical presser. At home, the lady of the house serves a sherbet after the coffee.

Serves 4–6

600ml / 1 pint fresh orange juice
juice of 2 lemons
600g / 1lb white sugar

Mix the two juices with the sugar in a roomy pan. Bring slowly to the boil, stirring so that all the crystals dissolve. As soon as it boils whip it off the heat. Cool and pour into well scalded bottles. Seal and store in the fridge. Dilute to taste and serve poured over crushed ice.

Good with . . . Serbian jam pancakes (page 279) or any crisp, nutty biscuits.

Gelato di limone
Sicilian lemon ice-cream

Something in the combination of sea, sunshine and soil gives the lemons of Sicily an aston-ishing fragrance and intensity of flavour. In Sicily the simplest of antipasti is a dish of finely sliced lemons so sweet you can eat them just as they are.

Serves 4–6

600ml / 1 pint single cream
2 lemons, juice and zest
4 egg yolks
100g / 4oz sugar

In a small pan bring the cream to the boil with the lemon zest. As soon as it foams, pull to the side of the stove and leave to infuse for 10 minutes. Mix the egg yolks and the sugar together in a bowl and whisk in the strained, lemon-scented cream. Set the bowl over a pan of simmering water, and continue to whisk until it thickens enough to coat the back of a spoon; be patient – it can take 20 minutes or more. Leave to cool and then whisk in the lemon juice and freeze as usual in your ice-cream machine if you have one. If all you have is the ice compartment of the fridge, you will have to take the ice out when it is nearly solid and beat it thoroughly to incorporate as much air as possible.

Bring the ice-cream out of the freezer into the fridge 30 minutes before you are ready to serve.

> Good with . . . Italian polenta and orange cake (page 282); crisp sugary biscuits; meringues; any of the nut-flour or olive-oil cakes such as the Greek convent cake on page 286.

Safran ve kakule dondurmasi
Turkish saffron and cardamom ice-cream

A delicately flavoured ice-cream from eastern Anatolia, where the Persian influence is strong. Among the Ottoman Turks of Istanbul, rosewater and vanilla are the preferred flavourings for sweet things. Throughout the region, the usual thickening for a cream-ice is salep, the powdered root of an orchid, rather than the egg yolks used here.

Serves 6–8

300ml / ½ pint full-cream milk
about 8 threads of saffron
2–3 whole cardamom pods
4 egg yolks
100g / 4oz caster sugar
300ml / ½ pint single or whipping cream

In a saucepan bring the milk to the boil with the saffron and cardamom pods, remove from the heat, and leave to infuse for 10 minutes. Take out the cardamom pods and liquidize the milk and its saffron with the egg yolks and the sugar. Pour the mixture into a bowl set over a pan of simmering water and whisk until it thickens enough to coat the back of a spoon. Let the custard cool and then whisk in the cream. Freeze in an ice-cream maker or sorbetière if you have one. If all you have is the ice compartment of the fridge, you will have to take the ice out when it is nearly solid, beat it thoroughly to incorporate as much air as possible, and refreeze.

Bring the ice-cream out of the freezer into the fridge 30 minutes before you are ready to serve.

Good with . . . fresh fruit salads; stewed figs with walnuts (page 271).

Glâce au parfum de lavande

Provençal lavender ice-cream

A strange and sophisticated confection from Provence, land of lavender. Perhaps not so strange – dried lavender is used as a flavouring herb throughout the Middle East.

Serves 4–6

For the crystallized petals
75g / 3oz caster sugar
15g / ½oz fresh lavender flowers

For the ice-cream
300ml / ½ pint milk
1 sprig fresh lavender
4 egg yolks
100g / 4oz caster sugar
300ml / ½ pint double cream, lightly whipped

First, make the crystallized petals. Spread the sugar in a small frying pan over a medium heat and wait until it is brown and caramelized. Don't stir. Shake to mix. Don't take your eye off it for an instant. Stir in the petals and pour onto an oiled plate. Leave to cool and harden, and then pound to a fine powder.

To make the ice-cream, heat the milk and lavender sprig until just boiling, remove from the heat, cover and leave to infuse for 30 minutes in a warm place.

Meanwhile, whisk the egg yolks and sugar in a bowl until light and creamy. Whisk in the infused milk (remove the lavender first) and set over a pan of simmering water, stirring constantly until the custard coats the back of a wooden spoon. Cool. Fold in the whipped cream and transfer to a container for freezing. When half frozen, fold in the lavender powder. Re-freeze. Give it another stir before it freezes hard.

Transfer from the freezer to the fridge 30 minutes before serving to let it soften a little.

Good with . . . a delicate fruit tart such as the Provençal apricot tart (page 288); any crisp nutty biscuits.

Horchata
Spanish nutmilk

Visitors to Spain may have noticed this refreshing nutmilk, a legacy of the Moors, on sale in cartons in supermarkets, or sold like a milkshake in ice-cream parlours. Although the commercial variety is made with tigernuts, this version is made with the more delicately flavoured and expensive almonds. You can grind the almonds in the coffee-mill — it's important that they be freshly crushed.

Serves 4–6

250g / 8oz almonds, scalded and skinned and freshly pulverized
I litre / about 2 pints water
I tablespoon caster sugar (more if you like)
I small stick cinnamon

Stir the ground almonds into the water, cover and leave to infuse overnight. Next day, strain the milky liquid into a saucepan, stir in the sugar and add the cinnamon stick. Bring to the boil and leave to cool. Refrigerate, removing the cinnamon stick just before serving.

Serve iced in a tall glass.

Good with ... Valencian almond sponge (page 285); oranges with honey and almonds (page 275).

Chocolate con canela

Hot chocolate with cinnamon

A cup of steaming hot chocolate fragrant with cinnamon is the best pick-me-up after a feria-time night on the tiles in Andalusia. The egg yolk thickens and enriches – very comforting – although a teaspoonful of cornflour slaked in a little water will perform the same function. Use single cream if you prefer, but in Spain the country people much prefer condensed milk. Normally accompanied by dough fritters – churros – for dunking.

Serves 4

50g / 2oz best-quality dark chocolate (look for 70% cocoa solids)
600ml / 1 pint hot water (not boiling)
1 teaspoon ground cinnamon
1 egg yolk
4 tablespoons condensed milk (or single cream)
sugar to taste

Break the chocolate into small pieces and melt it very gently over a low heat in a small pan with 150ml/¼ pint of the water. As soon as it liquefies, whisk in the rest of the hot water. Add the cinnamon and whisk until perfectly smooth. Remove from the heat. Fork together the egg yolk and condensed milk or cream and mix into the hot chocolate liquid. Whisk over the heat until it is silky and smooth – don't let it boil. Add sugar to taste – about 1 teaspoon per serving.

> Good with . . . doughnuts or any buttery pastries for dunking.

Chay
Moroccan mint tea

The visitor to a Moroccan home is always welcomed with something sweet – and mint tea is sweetened to within an inch of its life. The senior lady of the house performs the ritual of the tea-making, allowing the household as well as the hostess an opportunity to get the measure of a stranger. You will need a roomy teapot made of silver or any other metal – china cools the liquid too quickly. Mint tea is always sweetened in the pot and served in little decorated glass tumblers. You can find these in any Middle Eastern kitchenware shop. The mint used is Mentha viridis, particularly that from Meknes, which has firm dark stalks and highly perfumed leaves with a dark red blush to the underside, while the mint of Fez is considered less fragrant. In spring orange-blossom can be included in the infusion. In winter, when mint is less abundant, the tea can be made with sage or wormwood, a bitter herb used in the brewing of absinthe, both soothing and calmative to the stomach. Other possible inclusions are lemon verbena, sweet marjoram, sweet basil and peppermint.

Serves 4–6

about 1 litre / 1½ pints freshly boiled water
2 level tablespoons green tea (this is not essential – country people often use mint alone)
a generous handful of fresh mint
150g / 5oz lump sugar

Heat the teapot with boiling water. Swill it out and put in the tea. Pour in a little more water – just enough to soak the leaves. Swirl it round and pour out the water without losing the leaves. Cram in the mint in a bunch. Pour in enough boiling water to fill the pot – it must completely cover the leaves or the tea will be bitter. Let it infuse for at least 5 minutes. Add the sugar, stir thoroughly, pour out a single glassful and return this to the pot.

Serve your guests carefully, pouring from a great height to make sure the liquid is well aerated. Take care that the tea is perfectly free of any leaves.

Good with . . . any Middle Eastern syrup-soaked pastries, halvas and the biscuits with romantic names – gazelles' horns, ladies' navels – of which Morocco has a large repertoire.

Principal Sources Consulted

Andrews, Colman: *Catalan Cuisine* (Grub Street, 1997)

Bas'an, Ghillie: *Classic Turkish Cookery* (Taurus Parke, 1997)

Boisvert, Clotilde: *La Cuisine de Plantes Sauvages* (Paris, 1984)

Calera, Ana Maria: *Cocina Valenciana* (Madrid, 1983)

Carter, Elizabeth: *Majorcan Food and Cookery* (Prospect Books, 1989)

Chantiles, Vilma Liacouras: *The Food of Greece* (New York, 1979)

David, Elizabeth: *Mediterranean Food* (John Lehmann, 1950)

Del Conte, Anna: *Gastronomy of Italy* (Bantam, 1987)

Davidson, Alan: *Mediterranean Seafood* (Penguin, 1981)

Guinaudeau, Zette: *Traditional Moroccan Cooking* (Reprint, Serif, 1994)

Hobhouse, Henry: *Forces of Change* (Sidgwick & Jackson, 1989)

Gray, Patience: *Honey from a Weed* (Prospect Books, 1986)

de Haroutunian, Arto: *Middle Eastern Cookery* (Century, 1982)

Helou, Anissa: *Lebanese Cuisine* (Grub Street, 1994)

Jenkins, Nancy Harmon: *The Mediterranean Diet Cookbook* (Bantam, 1994)

Kremezi, Aglaia: *The Foods of Greece* (Stewart Tabori Chang, 1993)

Kaneva-Johnson, Maria: *The Melting Pot: Balkan Food and Cookery* (Prospect Books, 1995)

Lladonos i Giro', Josep: *Cocina Catalana* (Barcelona, 1992)

Mallos, Tess: *The Complete Middle Eastern Cookbook* (Grub Street, 1995)

Mouzannar, Ibrahim: *La Cuisine Libanaise* (Beyrouth, 1983)

Reboul, J.-B: *La Cuisinière Provençale* (Marseilles, 1895)

Roden, Claudia: *A Book of Middle Eastern Food* (Penguin, 1970); *The Book of Jewish Food* (Viking, 1997)

Salaman, Rena: *Greek Island Cookery* (Ebury, 1987)

Santich, Barbara: *The Original Mediterranean Cuisine* (Prospect Books, 1960)

Simeti, Mary Taylor: *Sicilian Food* (Grub Street, 1999)

Spoerri, Daniel: *Mythology and Meatballs* (US, 1982)

Vence, Celine (ed): *Cuisine du Terroir* (Blenheim House, 1987)

Wells, Patricia: *At Home in Provence* (Kyle Cathie, 1997)

Wolfert, Paula: *Good Food from Morocco* (John Murray, 1989), *The Cooking of the Eastern Mediterranean* (HarperCollins, 1994)

Zubaida, Sami and Richard Tapper (eds): *Culinary Cultures of the Middle East* (I.B.Tauris, 1994)

Index